WALKS IN CENTRAL LONDON

Brown Eyed Sheep

Brown Eyed Sheep
P.O.Box 13456
London
W14 0XE

Published by Brown Eyed Sheep

Copyright © David Backhouse 1997

David Backhouse asserts the moral right to be identified as the author of this work.

ISBN 0 9530424 0 5

Printed in Great Britain by Cox & Wyman Reading

CONTENTS

Thanks are expressed to: Mark Addis, Paula Augar, Phillip Augar, Kathleen Backhouse, Oliver Billker, Julie Corfield, Nick Edwards, John Glynn, Sarah Glynn, Lawrence Hobbis, Nickie Jacobs, Rob Jacobs, Helen Marra, and Andrew Spriggs.

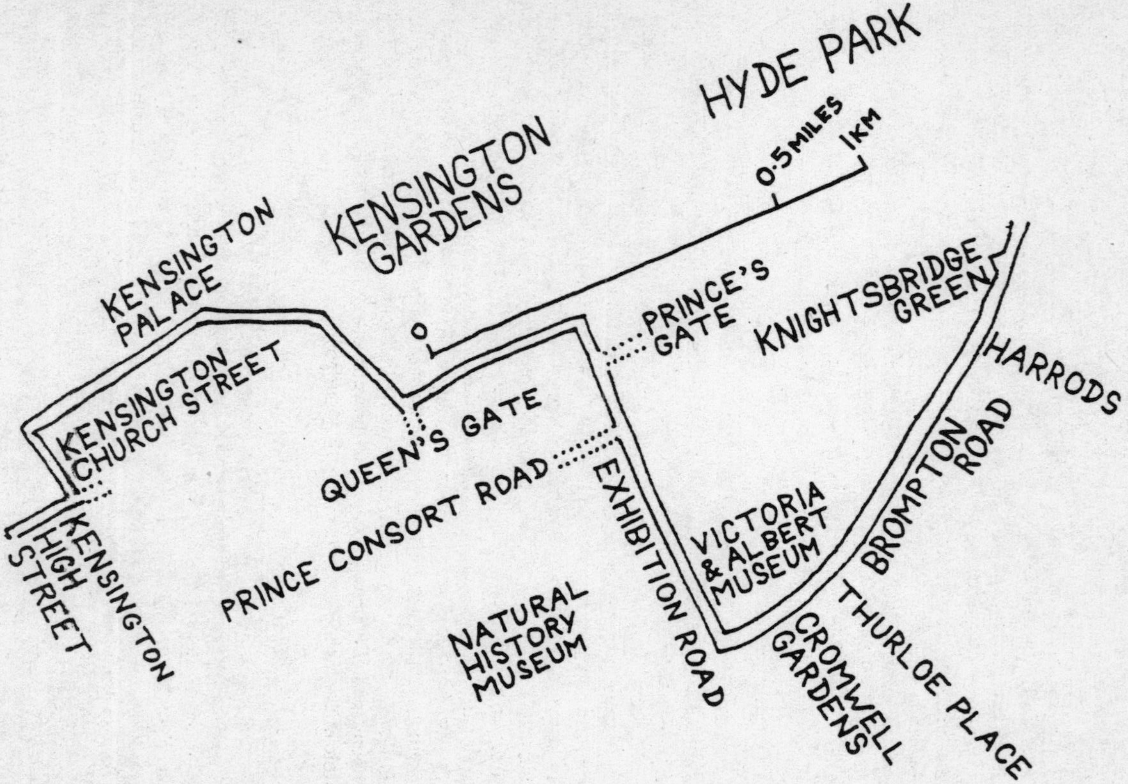
HYDE PARK
0·5 MILES
1KM
KENSINGTON GARDENS
KENSINGTON PALACE
KENSINGTON CHURCH STREET
QUEEN'S GATE
PRINCE'S GATE
KNIGHTSBRIDGE GREEN
HARRODS
BROMPTON ROAD
THURLOE PLACE
CROMWELL GARDENS
VICTORIA & ALBERT MUSEUM
EXHIBITION ROAD
PRINCE CONSORT ROAD
NATURAL HISTORY MUSEUM
KENSINGTON HIGH STREET

1.Kensington Gardens and Knightsbridge

To Start

Go to High Street Kensington underground station, which is on the District and Circle Lines. Leave the station and turn right into Kensington High Street.

Biba

On the right are branches of BhS and Marks & Spencer. The shops occupy what used to be the Derry & Toms department store and then at the end of the 1960s became the Biba store, the trendiest shop in London.

Barbara Hulanicki and her husband Stephen Fitz-Simon (1937-1997) opened the first Biba shop in Abingdon Road in 1963. They opened the Biba store in Kensington High Street in 1969.

Hulanicki sold control of the business to a womenswear retailer which was itself subsequently taken over by a property company. The property company closed down Biba. The Biba name faded in the mid-1970s. The brand is now owned by Ellen Shek, a figure in the Hong Kong fashion industry.

Northcliffe House

On the right is Derry Street. On the left (east) side of Derry Street is Northcliffe House the home of both the national newspaper The Daily Mail and London's Evening Standard.

Harold Harmsworth 1st Viscount Rothermere (1868-1940) would probably have spent his working life as a civil servant had not his elder brother been Alfred Harmsworth Lord Northcliffe (1865-1922), the most original newspaper proprietor in early C20th Britain. Rothermere supplied his brother with the solid managerial support which allowed Northcliffe the freedom to play to his own strengths. Eventually, the brothers divided their newspaper empire. Rothermere built his own business around the middle market Daily Mail newspaper.

The Daily Mail's interventions in politics during the 1920s and 1930s earned it a notoriety. In 1924 the Daily Mail published a forged letter allegedly written by Grigory Zinoviev, a member of the Soviet Politiburo. The Zinoviev Letter called upon British Communists to conduct subversive activities. Its publication played a role in the downfall of Britain's first Labour government.

Barkers

On the right is Barkers the department store.

John Barker (1840-1914) worked as a manager for the innovative retailer William Whiteley (1831-1907) in Whiteley's Bayswater department store. When, in 1870, Whiteley refused him a partnership, Barker, with the help of a backer, opened a drapery shop in Kensington High Street.

Barkers is now owned by the House of Fraser department store group.

Direction

Cross over Kensington High Street to the bottom of the eastern side of Kensington Church Street (the side with the Pizza Hut and The Prince of Wales pub).

Kensington High Street

To your right is the easternmost section of Kensington High Street which contains the fashion emporiums Kensington Market on the southern (right) side and Hype Designer Forum on the northern (left).

Direction

Walk up Kensington Church Street. Turn right into York House Place. Go along the alley with the series of black lampposts set along its centre.

Cross over Kensington Palace Gardens into Kensington Gardens.

Kensington Palace Gardens

Kensington Palace Gardens is a private road.

In 1841 the Commissioners of Woods & Forests decided to raise some money to improve Kensington Gardens by granting building licences on the Palace's kitchen gardens. The road was laid out by the architect Sir James Pennethorne (1801-1871) in 1843. The first developer went bankrupt because Kensington was not regarded as being a socially proper address for the aristocracy and haute bourgeoisie.

It took the holding of the Great Exhibition of 1851 in Hyde Park to place Kensington within the social Pale for high society. The development of Kensington Palace Gardens was continued successfully by Samuel Morton Peto and Thomas Grissell (the builders responsible for the Reform Club and Nelson's Column).

During the C20th a number of the road's mansions became embassies.

Kensington Palace

In 1689 King William III (1650-1702) and Queen Mary II (1662-1694) bought Kensington House from the 2nd Earl of Nottingham. William III used Kensington Palace, as it became known, in order to be close to London. For the king, Kensington's principal attraction was its location to the west of London which gave him some relief from his asthma with which he was afflicted.

The Palace also had the additional advantage of being handy for Hampton Court Palace, several miles to the west, which was his favourite English residence.

Extensions and alterations of the Palace were carried out by the architects Sir Christopher Wren (1632-1723) and Nicholas Hawksmoor (1661-1736).

The Palace was the principal royal residence until 1760. Since then it has been used as a place to park assorted royal relatives. The young Queen Victoria (1819-1901) lived here prior to her 1837 accession to the throne.

State Apartments

In 1889, upon the occasion of Queen Victoria's 70th birthday, the State Apartments of Kensington Palace were opened to the public. In 1912 the State Apartments were used to accommodate the London Museum. Two years later the Museum moved to Lancaster House and the Apartments were closed. In 1923 the State Apartments were re-opened.

Princess Margaret

Princess Margaret, the younger sister of the present Queen, is one of the royals who lives in Kensington Palace.

In the late 1940s Princess Margaret and her friends the `Margaret Set' became the object of media interest. The group largely condensed around the lively and unstuffy Sharman `Sass' Douglas (1928-1996), the daughter of Lewis W. Douglas, the United States Ambassador to Britain. When Sharman returned to the United States in 1950, the Princess became the focus of the group.

On aggregate Princess Margaret is the royal who has probably received the most unfavourable press. Since the 1980s she has largely been left alone.

Group Captain Townsend

Group Captain Peter Townsend (1914-1995) was a decorated war hero who in 1944 became an equerry to King George VI (1895-1952), and who went on to become Deputy Master of the Household in 1950. On King George VI's death in 1952, the Queen Mother moved out of Buckingham Palace and appointed Townsend as the Comptroller of her new Household. Princess Margaret lived with her mother. It was then that a relationship between the Princess and the Group Captain began to develop.

Townsend's marriage ended in divorce in 1952, he having been the `innocent' party. The British press broke the story of his and Princess Margaret's relationship in July 1953. In the social climate of the early 1950s, it was unthinkable that a member of the royal family should marry a divorced person; at the time divorcees were barred from the Royal Enclosure at Ascot. Princess Margaret was under the age of 25 and therefore unable to legally marry without the approval of the Sovereign and Parliament.

Sir Allan Lascelles (1887-1981), the Queen's Private Secretary, was particularly opposed to the couple's relationship. (Lascelles had played a prominent part in the Abdication Crisis of 1936, when he had opposed King Edward VIII's (1894-1972) wish to marry the American divorcee Wallis Simpson (1896-1986).) In 1953 it seemed as though the couple were intending to marry. Without consulting the Queen, Lascelles raised the matter with the Conservative Prime Minister Winston Churchill (1874-1965). After Lascelles brought pressure to bear on Townsend, the Group Captain accepted a form of exile by becoming the air attache at the British embassy in Belgium.

In August 1955 the Princess had her 25th birthday. In autumn 1955 Townsend returned to Britain. Within the Cabinet the influential Conservative peer the 5th Marquis of Salisbury (1893-1972), who was then the Lord President of the Council, made it clear that he would oppose any attempt by the government to pass legislation through Parliament to sanction the match.

In October 1955 the Princess, with Townsend's assistance, made a public statement that they no longer intended to marry.

Princess Margaret and Lord Snowdon married in 1960. The couple divorced in 1978.

Princess Diana and the Royal Divorce

Princess Diana also lives in Kensington Palace.

In December 1992 the Conservative Prime Minister John Major announced that Prince Charles and Princess Diana had parted.

In June 1994 Prince Charles appeared in an I.T.V. television documentary in which he admitted to the journalist Jonathan Dimbleby that he had committed adultery.

In November 1995 Princess Diana was interviewed by Martin Bashir for the B.B.C. Television current affairs programme `Panorama'. This was the first time that she had been interviewed directly on television since before her marriage. News of her action became public knowledge on the same day that she informed Buckingham Palace of what she had done.

The programme attracted an audience of 21m in the United Kingdom. (In February 1994 23.9m people watched the iceskaters Torvill & Dean failing to win an Olympic gold medal for their ice dance routine. In December 1996 24.3m watched an episode of `Only Fools and Horses', a comedy show.)

In February 1996 Princess Diana agreed to a divorce.

Princess Diana is believed to have received c£17m as her divorce settlement. She was allowed to stay in her apartments in Kensington Palace and an annual sum of £350 000 is given to her to run her private office.

Direction

Cross Kensington Palace Gardens and continue along the path which runs along the southern edge of the Palace's grounds.

The Statue of King William III

In front of Kensington Palace's principal south front is a statue of King William III (1650-1702).

The Heinrich Baucke statue of King William (1907) was given to King Edward VII (1841-1910) by his nephew Kaiser Wilhelm II of Germany. The gift has a very precise reading. The German emperor was appealing to his uncle for Germany and Britain to unite against Britain's old enemy France. (The whole of King William's adult life had been geared to the restriction of French influence in western Europe.) In 1914 Britain and France went to war against Germany.

Coneys

To the left are Kensington Palace's grounds. In the early evening it is often possible to view the `royal' rabbits.

Rabbits were introduced to Britain from the Mediterranean in the C12th.

The myxomatosis virus was first recorded as breaking out at Edenbridge in Kent in October 1953. In 1954 the myxomatosis virus ravaged the British rabbit population

Rabbits are viewed by many farmers as being a far worse pest than foxes have ever proved.

Kensington Gardens

During the C16th Hyde Park and Kensington Gardens became a private royal park.

After the opening of Hyde Park in the 1630s, Kensingon Gardens remained the Sovereign's private garden. Its current character was in large part determined by Queen Caroline (1683-1737), King George II's (1683-1760) consort. The Queen's ambitions extended to incorporating Hyde Park within Kensington Gardens and thus closing it to the public. She asked the then Prime Minister, Sir Robert Walpole (1676-1745), whether the scheme would prove expensive. He replied that it could be achieved for "The price of two Crowns". (A Crown was a coin worth 25p in contemporary money.)

When the court was at Richmond, King George II permitted Kensington Gardens to be opened to `respectably dressed' people on Saturdays. The Gardens' Broad Walk became a fashionable place where Society could parade itself to itself.

King William IV (1765-1837) opened the park to the public throughout the year.

Direction
Cross the large north-south walk and then take the right path which forks to the south-east. Follow the path as it curves southwards and passes across another very straight path which has bushes and small trees planted along it.

Squirrels
The red squirrel is native to Britain, the grey squirrel is a recent arrival from North America.

The Introduction of Grey Squirrels
During the late C19th and early C20th there were a number of separate releases of greys squirrels. The squirrels were seen as ornamental and it was thought that they would live in small pockets close to where they had been released.

In 1939 the importation of grey squirrels was made illegal. In the late 1940s and the early 1950s grey-squirrel shooting clubs were issued with free cartridges and a small bounty was paid out by the carcass.

Squirrels' Habitat and Diet
Other than at a few sites, it is very rare to see a red squirrel in England. Reds are more agile than grey squirrels. Reds are able to thrive in pure coniferous forests because their superior agility means that they can reach cones that greys can not.

Reds do not do well in deciduous woodland, especially when they are competing with greys; broadleafed woods are capable of supporting six times as many greys as reds. This is because the red is a fussier eater than the grey. There are some berries and seeds (ash, hawthorn, rowan, and yew) which reds will eat but which greys will not. Greys are able to eat acorns safely whereas reds, if they eat too many, are killed by the tannin which the acorns contain.

Squirrels As Diet
According to the writer Jonathan Raban (`Old Glory' Picador (1986) pp.163-4), the taste of squirrel is akin to that of over-hung pheasant. The natives of Wisconsin, with whom he was partaking of this delicacy, regard the back legs as the best bit of the creature.

Direction
Continue along the path until you are looking southwards through Queen's Gate, a gate, down Queen's Gate, a street with wedding cake houses along it.

Queen's Gate
On the right of Queen's Gate the road at No. 182 (the first east facing house) was the flat where the comedian Benny Hill (1924-1996) lived from 1960 to 1986.

Direction

Turn left and walk eastwards along Albert Memorial Road, the broad path which runs along the inside of the park's southern edge.

Royal College of Art

The modern building on the right is the Royal College of Art (1961), a postgraduate art and design university.

The idea for a national school of design came to the painter Benjamin Haydon (1786-1846) in 1823; at the time Haydon had time for speculation since he was then languishing in the King's Bench Prison for Debtors. In 1837 the Government School of Design was set up following a formal recommendation made by a Select Committee of the House of Commons in 1835. The School was opened in Somerset House in rooms which had been vacated by the Royal Academy.

The architect John Papworth (a.k.a. John Buonarroti) (1775-1847) was the first principal of the School of Design. In 1841 the government founded schools of industrial design in the provinces. The best of the provincial students came to London to the School for further training.

In 1852 the Museum of Ornamental Art opened in Marlborough House. In 1853 the School became the National Art Training School. The School moved to Marlborough House.

In 1857 both the School and the Museum of Ornamental Art moved to the `Brompton Boilers' (later the Victoria & Albert Museum) in South Kensington.

Christopher Dresser (1834-1904) was a lecturer at the School. Dresser's designs foreshadowed the Arts & Crafts Movement.

In 1967 the Royal College received its royal charter, which conferred university status upon it.

Princess Louise

The Royal College of Art acquired its `Royal' in 1896 as a result of educating Princess Louise (1848-1931), a daughter of Queen Victoria

After so many sculptures being made of its members, the royal family produced a sculptor. For many years a statue of Queen Victoria, the work of the Princess, could be admired on the east side of the Round Pond in Kensington Gardens.

Albertpolis

On the right is the Royal Albert Hall (1871), the best known feature of Albertpolis the cultural and educational district.

After the Great Exhibition of 1851, the event's Commissioners bought 86 acres of land bounded on the north by Kensington Gardens and on the south side by the Cromwell Road. This site became Albertpolis, a cultural and educational centre, the occupants of which include the Royal Albert Hall, Imperial College, the Royal College of Art, and the Royal College of Music.

The Royal Albert Hall

In 1851 Prince Albert (1819-1861) included a great central hall as part of his vision of Albertpolis. After several false starts, the scheme was started when Sir Henry Cole (1808-1882) came up with the idea for raising the money for building the Hall by selling 1300 seats at £130 apiece - each of these seats carrying the right to attend every performance at the Hall (subsequently lowered to c80 a year). The building was designed by Captain Francis Fowke (1823-1865) of the Royal Engineers.

Eric Clapton

The rock guitarist Eric Clapton gives the Hall a sense of purpose. Most Decembers he plays a dozen or so concerts in it. It is reputed that after a while he tires of seeing the same faces in the front rows. His response to this is to buy up the seats himself and give the tickets for them to other people.

Kensington Gore

The road to the left (east) of the Hall is called Kensington Gore.

(Kensington Gore is the fake blood which is used in theatrical, television and cinematic work.)

Gore House

During the 1840s the Hall's site was occupied by Gore House, where the popular author the Countess of Blessinton (1789-1849) and her step-daughter's husband the dandy Count d'Orsay (1801-1852) conducted a celebrated salon. Their financial extravagance forced them to leave England for Europe.

The Albert Memorial

On the left is the Albert Memorial (1876), which commemorates Prince Albert (1819-1861), Queen Victoria's consort, who died in 1861. The Prince's statue within the monument holds a copy of the catalogue of the Great Exhibition.

Since 1988 the Memorial has been enshrouded by scaffolding. The present restoration of the Memorial was started in 1990.

Albert Hall Mansions

On the right, eastwards of the Albert Hall, are Albert Hall Mansions (1879). The Norman Shaw (1831-1912) designed Mansions were London's first purpose-built block of flats.

In the 1840s South Kensington had been regarded as a socially undesirable area in which to reside; the Great Exhibition brought the area favourably into the affluent classes' consideration. The development of flats in the 1870s was a response to the scarcity of building land in Kensington and the more socially desirable districts (flats already existed but were in the form of tenements for the working classes). The flats were spread over a number of floors so that masters would not have to sleep on the same floor as their servants.

Pressure on land has led to many of the original flats being divided.

The Royal Geographical Society

On the right, eastwards of Albert Hall Mansions, is the home of the Royal Geographical Society.

Sir Richard Burton

The explorer Sir Richard Burton (1821-1890) is commemorated by a bust in the Society's headquarters.

In 1857 Burton and John Hanning Speke (1827-1864) sought to discover the source of the River Nile. Together, they discovered Lake Tanganyika. At that point, Burton made the mistake of deciding to rest, while Speke opted to press on. Speke discovered that Lake Victoria was the river's source and then returned to

London, where he promptly lauded his achievement. On his return Burton took distinct umbrage at Speke's conduct and sought to rubbish the man's claim. To reaffirm his discovery, Speke embarked on a second journey to Lake Victoria, this time taking with him the explorer James Grant to act as a witness.

Speke is commemorated by a rather large (especially so when compared to Burton's bust) obelisk in Kensington Gardens.

Hyde Park

The southern section of Hyde Park contains Rotten Row and hosted the Great Exhibition of 1851.

Rotten Row

Rotten Row is a sand riding track which runs parallel with the southern side of Hyde Park. Its name is a corruption of Route du Roi, a reference to its leading westwards towards Kensington Palace. It was built c1690 and was kept well lit at night in order to provide a relatively safe route between Kensington Palace and the West End. The original Knightsbridge Barracks were built in order that help might be at hand in the event of a robbery taking place.

In the C18th Rotten Row was a place where the aristocracy would parade to one another in their finery.

The Great Exhibition

The idea for the Great Exhibition of 1851 came to Henry Cole (1808-1882) while he was working in the Public Record Office as an assistant keeper. The Exhibition's purpose was to showcase the technical and material advances which had been made in the preceding years. In 1850 a Royal Commission was instituted to raise funds for the project. (Subsequently, Cole became the founding director of the South Kensington Museum (now the Victoria & Albert Museum), which was founded with part of the proceeds from the Exhibition.)

The Exhibition was held in Hyde Park in the Sir Joseph Paxton (1801-1865) designed Crystal Palace. The Palace was erected on a twenty acre site near the Prince of Wales's gate between Carriage Road and Rotten Row.

(Not everyone liked what they saw. The designer William Morris (1834-1896) was moved to found Morris & Company as a reaction to the furniture he saw displayed at the Great Exhibition.)

At the Exhibition's closure the Crystal Palace was bought by the Brighton Railway Company which re-erected it in 1854 in an extended form at Sydenham in south London, as an exhibition and leisure centre (which people could travel to and from via the company's railway line). The Palace played a role in allowing Norwood and Sydenham to become fashionable middle-class districts during the later C19th (a character they have since lost).

The Crystal Palace was destroyed by fire in 1936.

Direction

When Albert Memorial Road runs into the road which crosses the park, walk through the Coalbrookdale Gate and walk out of the park through the Alexandra Gate.

The Kennedys

To the left are two closely parallel roads - the busy Kensington Road to the north and Princes Gate to the south.

No. 14 Princes Gate, the last of the wedding cakes at the far end, was the residence of Joe Kennedy, the father of President John F. Kennedy, when he served as the United States Ambassador to the Court of St.James during the years 1937-40.

The Iranian Embassy

The next door but one wedding cake to the right (No. 16) is the Iranian Embassy. The Iranian flag is green, white and red with a red emblem within the white.

In May 1980 the Special Air Service (S.A.S.), the specialist Army regiment, achieved public prominence when some of its members conducted a successful raid on the embassy. The raid broke a siege which had started after terrorists had stormed the building and taken a number of people siege.

Subsequently, there was a long running dispute about whether or not the Iranian government should pay for the building's restoration.

Salman Rushdie

Salman Rushdie is an Indian-born British novelist who was educated at Rugby the public school and Oxford University and who then worked as an advertising copywriter.

His literary breakthrough as a writer came with the publication of his novel `Midnight's Children' (1981) which won the Booker Prize. His public image in Britain was mixed.

The book `Satanic Verses' was published in 1988. The book treated Islam in a controversial manner. In February 1989 a fatwa against Rushdie was issued in Iran. In April 1989 he went into hiding.

The novelist has made considerable contributions to the cost of his own protection. He is meant to have become something of a dab joystick at computer games. He rebuilt a public profile by appearing on electronic media and by going unannounced to literary conferences and events.

In March 1993 the Labour Party made the gesture of having Rushdie meet the then party leader John Smith (1938-1994) in the House of Commons and having the event publicly reported. In May 1993 Rushdie met the Conservative Prime Minister John Major for half an hour.

In September 1993 `Midnight's Children' was named the best winner in the twenty-five years of the Book Prize. In October 1993 Rushdie's Norwegian publisher was shot outside his own home.

In September 1995 Rushdie attended the Writers Against The State debate in Westminster Central Hall. This was the first time since his going into hiding that his attendance at an event had been pre-announced.

In February 1997 the 15 Khordad Foundation of Qom announced that the bounty on Rushdie's head stood at US$2.5m.

Article 19 is an anti-censorship group which has supported Rushdie.

Direction

Cross Kensington Road and walk southwards down Exhibition Road.

The National Sound Archive

On the right, at No. 29 Exhibition Road, is the British Library's National Sound Archive.

Among its many activities, the National Sound Archive maintains the National Life Story Collection. The Collection, which was founded in 1988, is intended to preserve a cross-section of personal histories as a means of illuminating the present age to a future one.

The Royal College of Music

On the right Prince Consort Road runs eastwards into Exhibition Road. The grey buildings along the left (south) side of Prince Consort Road belong to Imperial College. The brick building is the Royal College of Music, which was founded in 1883.

Sir George Grove

Sir George Grove (1820-1900) served as its first director from 1882 to 1894. Grove's great work was his `Dictionary of Music & Musicians' (1879-89). Grove was by training a civil engineer. In 1850 he was appointed the Secretary to the Society of Arts and in 1852 of the Crystal Palace. He became a reviewer of concerts which were held in the Palace.

Imperial College

On the right, on the western side of Exhibition Road, are the main buildings of Imperial College.

The City & Guilds College (founded in 1878), the Royal College of Science (1845), and the Royal School of Mines (1851) were set up on land in South Kensington which was bought with surplus funds from the Great Exhibition of 1851. The three colleges federated with one another and received a royal charter which established Imperial College in 1907. The following year Imperial became a School of the University of London. In 1988 St.Mary's Hospital Medical School (1854) became the fourth constituent college of the now Imperial College of Science, Technology & Medicine.

T.H.Huxley

T.H.Huxley (1825-1895) was the great propagandiser of Darwinianism. In 1854 he was appointed a lecturer on natural history at the Royal School of Mines.

There were distinct parallels between the careers of Charles Darwin (1809-1882) and Huxley. Both men circumnavigated the globe on scientific expeditions and thus witnessed personally both its similarities and its diversities. Both were experts on crustaceans. In trying to classify his finds, Huxley was drawn down many of the conceptual paths which Darwin had himself followed while on `The Beagle'.

It was Huxley who had the great public debate on evolution in Oxford with Bishop Wilberforce (1805-1873) in 1860. (During the debate, the bishop inquired whether Huxley was descended from the apes on his father's side or his mother's).

In 1863 Huxley's `Man's Place in Nature' was published. The book was an anthropological reworking of Darwinism. The tome contains the famous procession of skeletons which proceed from small, stooped ape to upright man; it is an image which is now so deeply embedded in the modern world's visual culture that it seems to be almost without origin.

Huxley's belief in the theory did not extend to endorsing all of its implications. He refused to support social Darwinianism as the handmaiden of racism, and he was aware of how bleak Darwin's materialism ultimately was.

The Imperial Institute

The Imperial Institute (1893) was founded after the Imperial Exhibition of 1886 as part of the celebrations of Queen Victoria's Golden Jubilee. The Institute's heir is the Commonwealth Institute which resides in a building (1960) at the western end of Kensington High Street. All that is left of the original Imperial Institute building is a large white tower (which is topped by a green dome of oxidised copper, which stands in the campus of Imperial College. (Quite why there should be a large, unutilised tower on the campus has perplexed numerous students and lecturers at Imperial.)

The Church of The Latter-Day Saints

On the left on the corner of Exhibition Road and Princes Gate Mews is the Kensington branch of the Church of Jesus Christ of Latter-Day Saints (the Mormons).

The first Mormon mission arrived in Britain in 1837.

Preston in Lancashire is home to the oldest, continuous Mormon congregation in the world.

Family History

The Exhibition Road building contains the Hyde Park Family History Centre. The Mormon Church in Utah's Family History Library has the world's largest collection of genealogical records.

The Mormons have a particular belief about how people should be married if they are to enter heaven. Therefore, they are of the habit of remarrying the dead to one another.

Joyce McKinney

Many Britons' primary mental association with Mormonism is the memory of Joyce McKinney. In September 1977 McKinney, an American former Mormon, reputedly abducted Kirk Anderson, an American Mormon, who was then working in England. She was arrested, and charged. While out on bail, she fled back to the United States. The tabloid newspapers feasted on the episode's more lurid aspects.

The Science Museum

On the right is the Science Museum.

In 1852 the Museum of Ornamental Art opened in Marlborough House. The Museum included the museum of the Central School of Practical Art, which was made up of a number of exhibits bought by the government at the end of the Great Exhibition. In 1857 the Museum moved to Brompton and became the South Kensington Museum.

In 1898 a Parliamentary Select Committee recommended that the Museum should be divided into scientific and artistic sections - the Science Museum and what became the Victoria & Albert Museum.

In 1913 the Science Museum moved from the Brompton Boilers across the road to its present site.

Robinson Heath

`Heath Robinson' is the term used by Britons to refer to any contraption or procedure that seems overcomplex in relation to the task it is meant to deal with.

William Heath Robinson (1872-1944) was born in Hornsey Rise and trained first at the Islington School of Art and then at the Royal Academy Schools. Robinson's initial ambition was to be a landscape artist but instead he became C20th Britain's best-loved comic artist. He produced a number of books as well as commercial work, the latter notably for Guinness the beer company. Many of his illustrations were of fantastically complex machines that were intended to execute the simplest of tasks. The world he created was comforting for his contemporary audience because it implied that the rapid changes that they were experiencing were largely absurd.

The Victoria & Albert Museum

On the left is the start of the side of the Victoria & Albert Museum, which is a museum of the Applied Arts, applied that is to just about anything and everything.

Sir Henry Cole (1808-1882) and Prince Albert (1819-1861) were responsible for setting up the Museum of Manufactures, which opened in Marlborough House in 1852. In 1853 it became known as the Museum of Ornamental Art. In 1857 it was merged with the School of Design (founded in 1837) to form the South Kensington Museum.

In 1884 the National Art Library opened within the Museum.

In 1899 the Museum, after a heavy hint from Queen Victoria (1819-1901), renamed itself in honour of her and her late husband.

The Museum contains some paintings and sculptures. It has good collections of drawings by Raphael and paintings by John Constable (1776-1837).

The Museum has a number of satellites: the Museum of Childhood in Bethnal Green, the Theatre Museum in Covent Garden, the Wellington Museum at Hyde Park Corner, and the country houses (now firmly city-locked by suburbia) Ham House and Osterley Park.

The Natural History Museum Earth Galleries

On the right are the Natural History Museum Earth Galleries.

The first Director of the Geological Survey prompted the establishment of the Museum of Economic Geology. Originally, the Museum resided in Craig's Court, Whitehall.

The Geological Museum in Exhibition Road opened in 1935. In 1985 the Museum became part of the Natural History Museum.

Earthquakes

Britain experiences about 400 tremors a year, however, only about one in twenty is noticed by members of the public.

There is a nearby geological fault which runs from Kent to Belgium. In 1580 two people were killed by an earthquake in London.

The Natural History Museum

The nucleus of the British Museum's natural history collection amassed by Sir Hans Sloane (1743-1820). In 1781 the Museum received the Royal Society's repository, and, in 1820, the botanical collection of Sir Joseph Banks (1743-1829).

In 1856 the zoologist Sir Richard Owen (1804-1892) was appointed the first superintendent of the Museum's natural history department. Owen established five sections - Botany, Entomology, Mineralogy, Palaeontology, and Zoology. In 1860 the trustees of the British Museum voted to hive off the department. The Natural History Museum opened in South Kensington in 1881.

Mick the Miller

Mick the Miller was a greyhound. His stuffed body is preserved in the Natural History Museum. Mick won the 1929 and 1930 Greyhound Derbies. He had a part in the movie `Wild Boy' (1934). He is one of its best known exhibits and yet on the railings in front of the Museum there are signs which state that dogs are not admitted into it.

Piltdown Man

In 1912 a skull was unearthed by Charles Dawson, a country solicitor and amateur archaeologist, in a gravel pit at Piltdown in Sussex. The skull seemed to provide evidence of the `missing link' between apes and men. In the 1950s it was established that the cranium was from a modern man and that the jaw came from an orang-utan. The hoax's effect was to muddy the waters of evolutionary anthropology.

Martin Hinton (1883-1961), a curator of zoology at the Natural History Museum, is the generally favoured candidate for the creation of Piltdown Man. Hinton was known to have carried out a number of hoaxes and to have developed a grudge against Arthur Smith Woodward (1864-1944), the Museum's keeper of palaeontology.

Another candidate for the hoaxer is Sir Arthur Conan Doyle (1859-1930), the creator of Sherlock Holmes. Conan Doyle had a house nearby.

Direction

Turn left into Cromwell Gardens. (Cromwell Gardens becomes Thurloe Place and then Brompton Road.)

The Ismaeli Centre

On the right is the Ismaeli Centre, a Muslim cultural and religious centre. The Centre houses the Aga Khan Foundation (United Kingdom).

The Aga Khans

In Britain the Aga Khans have been well-known as racehorse owners for most of the C20th. Aly Khan (1911-1996), the father of the present Aga Khan, acquired additional fame through his marriage to the cinema actress Rita Hayworth.

The Yalta Memorial

On the right, to the east of the Ismaeli Centre, is the Yalta Memorial (1981). The Memorial commemorates those people who were forcibly repatriated by the Allies to Eastern Europe and the Soviet Union after the Second World War.

Nikolai Tolstoy

During the Second World War, at the Yalta Conference (February 1945), Churchill and Roosevelt gave into Stalin's desire that all Russian nationals should be returned to the U.S.S.R. at the end of the conflict. After the war's end among those who were forcibly repatriated were Cossacks, who had collaborated with the

Nazis, and Croats, who had done likewise, to the Soviet Union and Yugoslavia respectively.

In the 1970s the writer Nikolai Tolstoy and Lord Bethell drew attention to the matter. In 1986 Nikolai published a book `The Minister & The Massacre'. The book criticised the former soldier Lord Aldington and others for their part in the affair.

In 1986 the journalist Christopher Booker, the former diplomat Lord Brimelow (1915-1995) (who had been involved in the matter as a junior civil servant), and Brigadier Anthony Cowgill started investigating what had happened. In 1990 the triumvirate produced a report which stated that many of the Cossacks had undergone only a short period imprisonment upon their return to the U.S.S.R. before being released.

In 1987 Nigel Watts published a pamphlet which alleged that Lord Aldington had committed war crimes. A court determined that Watts had repeated a libel and sentenced him to 18 months in jail. In 1989, at the conclusion of a trial, £1.5m in damages were awarded to Lord Aldington against Nikolai Tolstoy. Aldington has not received any of the 1989 award, both Tolstoy and Watts having been declared bankrupt.

The European Human Rights Commission referred the case to the Court of Human Rights in Strasbourg. The grounds for the referral were that the size of the award violates Tolstoy's freedom of expression as guaranteed by the European Convention on Human Rights. In July 1995 the European Court of Human Rights refused to overturn the libel judgement against Tolstoy.

Sir Henry Cole

On the right, the house by the red pillar box at the junction of Thurloe Place and Thurloe Square (No. 33 Thurloe Square) was the home of Sir Henry Cole (1808-1882), the first director of the South Kensington Museum (now the Victoria & Albert Museum).

Christmas Cards

The 1840 introduction of the penny post gave a large boost to the Christmas-time custom of exchanging letters. The first Christmas cards were made in 1843. They were devised by Cole, then a young civil servant, who found that he did not have enough time to be able to write his Christmas letters. Therefore, he commissioned a printer to produce some cards for him to send instead. When the cards were retailed commercially - by Felix Summerly Home Treasury - they cost a shilling each (being individually hand-coloured), as a result only the well off could afford them. Therefore, they were not an immediate popular success.

With the advent of cheaper processes for colour printing Christmas cards began to become an established feature of the Yuletide season.

Robins

The use of the common-or-garden British bird the robin on Christmas cards stems from a form of pun. Victorian postmen having had a red uniform (to mark the fact that they were in royal service, red being the colour of royalty) had the nickname of `robins'.

Cabmen's Shelter

In the middle of Thurloe Place, almost opposite the eastern end of the Victoria & Albert Museum, is a green hut. The hut is a Cabmen's Shelter.

Scattered across London are the last thirteen Landed Gentry's Cabmen's Shelter Fund shelters. The shelters look like overgrown garden huts and are painted a rather mournful green. Their purpose was to provide somewhere, other than pubs, for cabmen to shelter in from the cold and the wet. The shelters came into being at the instigation of the social reformer the 7th Earl of Shaftesbury (1801-1885). The thirteen are still in operation and are run under the auspices of the Heritage of London Trust.

Brompton Oratory

On the left, to the east of the Victoria & Albert Museum, is the London Oratory (1897), which is generally known as the Brompton Oratory.

An oratory is a congregation of secular priests, or fathers (not monks), who are bound by the three religious vows - poverty, chastity and obedience. The Institute of the Oratory of St.Philip Neri & The Immaculate Heart of Mary was founded in Rome in 1575.

In 1848 the Institute was introduced into England by Cardinal Newman (1801-1890) and Father Faber (1814-1863). The Institute moved to Brompton in 1854. The present church was opened in 1884, and was completed in 1897. The Oratory served as London's most important Catholic place of worship until Westminster Cathedral opened in 1903.

Harrods

On the right is Harrods the department store.

In 1849 Henry Charles Harrod took over a small grocer's shop in the then village of Knightsbridge. In 1861 his son Charles Digby Harrod purchased the business from him. The store tapped the westward growth of London from Belgravia. By the 1880s, Harrods was employing 100 shop assistants.

In 1883 the building was destroyed by fire; it was soon rebuilt.

In 1889 Charles Digby Harrod sold Harrods to a limited liability company. In 1891 the company appointed the retailer (later Sir) Richard Burbridge (1847-1917) as the store's general manager. Burbridge took the store upmarket.

In 1898 Harrods installed the first escalator in London; at its top an attendant dispensed brandy to those overcome by the ride.

In 1913 Harrods Buenos Aires branch was set up. In 1914 the company acquired Dickins & Jones.

For many years the Lonrho conglomerate tycoon `Tiny' Rowland had a running conflict with Fayed brothers, over the Egyptians' 1985 purchase of Harrods and the House of Fraser department store business. The Rowland-Fayed dispute was `officially' ended in October 1993 when the Fayeds and Mr. Rowland joined together in lowering a pair of sharks that had been hung in the Harrods food hall - the larger shark was symbolically eating the tail of the smaller one.

Knighstbridge Green

On the northern side of Brompton Road the kerb goes north for about 15 metres and then slowly rejoins the main line of Brompton Road. This space and the alley which runs north of it are known as Knightsbridge Green. They are all that is left of what was once a village green.

Tattersall's

In the north-western corner of Knightsbridge Green is a pub called Tattersall's. The pub takes its name from a horse auctioneer.

In 1766 Richard Tattersall (1724-1795) set himself up as an auctioneer. He acquired premises near Hyde Park Turnpike. While at Hyde Park Corner, Tattersall's established a close association with the Jockey Club, the body which used to run British horseracing. The Club maintained subscription rooms on Tattersall's premises for its members.

In 1865 Tattersall's lease expired (and its site promptly disappeared beneath an extension of St.George's Hospital). The business was moved to the south-west side of Knightsbridge Green. In 1939 it left London and went to Newmarket, where it still operates.

Scotch House

At the end of Brompton Road on the junction with Knightsbridge is Scotch House the clothes retailer.

Tartans and Kilts

The original kilt (the fealeadh mor in Gaelic) was an untailored plaid wrapped around the body. The short kilt (the fealeadh beg) is supposed to have been devised in the 1730s by Thomas Rawlinson, an English ironmaster who was working in Scotland. Rawlinson wished to provide his workforce with something less cumbersome than the fealeadh mor to work in.

Following the Battle of Culloden (1746) tartans were banned. In 1782 the ban on them was lifted by the government following a sustained campaign by the Highland Society of London.

Variegated clan tartans were a product of the early C19th rehabilitation of Scottishness; an appeal to the old as opposed to the new of the French Revolution (better a Jacobite than a Jacobin). In 1815 the Highland Society invited clan chiefs to send them copies of their tartans to act as the basis for a collection.

The writer Sir Walter Scott (1771-1832) had a talent for instant tradition, as was instanced by the Prince Regent's (later King George IV) (1762-1830) 1822 visit to Scotland. Scott was responsible for generating much of what has come to be viewed as Scottish kitsch. At the same time, he revealed to the world the beauty of the Highlands.

To Finish

Descend into Knightsbridge underground station, which is on the Piccadilly Line, entrances to which are to be found on both sides of Sloane Street's juncture with Knightsbridge.

To Continue

Cross Sloane Street and walk eastwards along the south side of Knightsbridge.

SWALLOW STREET

ALBEMARLE STREET

SWALLOW STREET

FORTNUM & MASON

STRATTON STREET

GREEN PARK GATES

1KM

0·5 MILES

0

PICCADILLY

HYDE PARK CORNER

GROSVENOR CRESCENT

BELGRAVE SQUARE

KNIGHTSBRIDGE

WILTON PLACE

0

2. Hyde Park Corner and Piccadilly

To Start
Go to Knightsbridge underground station. Ascend the stairs which are on the east side of Sloane Street's juncture with Knightsbridge.

Knightsbridge Barracks
The western end of Knightsbridge the road runs south of Hyde Park. Between the road and the park is Knightsbridge Barracks.

At the end of the C18th buildings were erected for the Horse Guards on the site of Knightsbridge Barracks. The flamboyant T.H.Wyatt (1807-1880) buildings (1880) were demolished in 1966. The present-day barracks were designed by Sir Basil Spence (1907-1976).

Direction
Walk eastwards along Knightsbridge.

Harvey Nichols
On the right is Harvey Nichols the department store.

Benjamin Harvey (d.1850) opened a linen shop in Knightsbridge, which grew into Harvey Nichols. The store has been on its present site since 1880.

Harvey Nichols was bought by Debenhams in 1919. In October 1991 the store was bought by Dickson Concepts, a company owned by Dickson Poon, a Hong Kong-based businessman.

In June 1995 the company announced that it was opening a store in Leeds what was formerly the Empire Arcade. It is also considering opening other stores in Manchester and Glasgow.

In April 1996 Harvey Nichols floated on the London Stock Exchange. Dickson Concepts retained a 50.1% holding.

In September 1996 Harvey Nichols opened a roof-top restaurant below the art deco Oxo Tower on London's South Bank.

The Royal Thames Yacht Club
On the left is the Royal Thames Yacht Club. A mast stands in front of the Club. In 1775 the Duke of Cumberland (1745-1790) presented a silver cup to be awarded to the winner of a race between sailing vessels `never let out for hire' over a course from Westminster Bridge to Putney and back. This led to the formation of the Cumberland Fleet, a sailing club. After a process of evolution the Fleet became the present-day Royal Thames Yacht Club.

Direction
Turn right into Wilton Place.

The Berkeley
On the left is The Berkeley (1972), part of the Savoy Group of hotels.

The original Berkeley hotel was built off Piccadilly on what had been the gardens of Devonshire House. The Berkeley in Wilton Place is its successor.

There is a swimming pool on top of the hotel.

St.Paul Knightsbridge

St.Paul Knightsbridge is a fashionable church, many of the incumbents of which have gone on to become bishops. One who did not was the Rev. Donald Harris (1906-1994), who was its vicar from 1955 to 1978. Harris was given to referring to his wealthier parishioners as `trout', and when being visited by one of them in the late afternoon he was given to pronouncing `trout for tea'.

Direction

When Wilton Place joins Wilton Crescent turn left into the Crescent and follow the Crescent as it curves to the right. The Crescent runs into the northern corner of Belgrave Square.

Belgrave Square

The wedding cake mansions of Belgrave Square were largely built with bricks made from clay which was excavated from the square itself. (The central garden is at a lower level than the road which surrounds it.)

Direction

Leave the square via Grosvenor Crescent. Grosvenor Crescent also enters Belgrave Square at its northern corner.

Grosvenor Crescent's eastern end comes out onto Hyde Park Corner roundabout. Turn left.

Constitution Arch

The Decimus Burton (1800-1881) designed Constitution Arch (1828) at Hyde Park Corner was originally called the Wellington Arch, and then Green Arch and is now known as Constitution Arch. It was originally erected nearby, opposite the main entrance to Hyde Park. Until 1883 the arch was topped by a statue of the 1st Duke of Wellington (1769-1852), the victor of the Battle of Waterloo (1815). Wellington's London town house, Apsley House, is on the north side of the roundabout. In 1883 the arch was moved to its present site and the duke's statue was removed to the army town of Aldershot in Hampshire. His presence was continued by the erection of an equestrian statue in 1888.

In 1912 the statue of `Peace in Her Chariot', cast in some sinister-looking metal, was placed on top of the arch. (Ms. Peace's bearing is such that she could almost certainly give deportment lessons to the four horsemen of apocalypse.)

The gated central passage is reserved for the use of royalty.

The Lanesborough

To the left (west) is The Lanesborough, a luxurious hotel, which is located in the former St.George's Hospital building.

St.George's Hospital

St.George's Hospital was founded in 1733 by a group of former governors of the Westminster Hospital, who had been of the opinion that the Westminster's buildings were not up to its needs. For their new foundation they acquired the then `suburban' residence of Lord Lanesborough at Hyde Park Corner.

The hospital moved to Tooting in south London in 1980.

Direction
Turn left and use the Hyde Park Corner tube station subway to cross Knightsbridge. Ascend at Exit 3 on the northern side of Knightsbridge. Upon emerging, turn around and start to walk eastwards towards Piccadilly.

Hyde Park Corner Screen
To the left is Decimus Burton's (1800-1881) Hyde Park Corner Screen (1825). Through the screen it is possible to see to the right the Queen Elizabeth Gate. The Gate was unveiled by Queen Elizabeth the Queen Mother in July 1993. It appears as one might expect the illustration on a razor wire manufacturer's corporate Christmas card to look.

Apsley House
Apsley House (1778) was built for Lord Apsley (later 2nd Earl Bathurst) (1714-1794). In 1804 it was bought by the Marquis of Wellesley (1760-1842) who in 1817 sold it to his younger brother the 1st Duke of Wellington. Until his 1852 death, the House was Wellington's London home.

House Numbers
The Duke, as part of a campaign to encourage householders to adopt house numbers, agreed for Apsley House to take the address Apsley House, No. 1 London, Hyde Park Corner. (A sign to the left of the main door gives the building's address as being not No. 1 London but rather No. 149 Piccadilly.)

The Wellington Museum
In 1947 Apsley House was presented to the nation by the 7th Duke of Wellington (1885-1972) under the Wellington Museums Act of 1947; the family retained apartments within the building. In 1952 the house was opened as The Wellington Museum. It is administered by the Victoria & Albert Museum.

The Royal Spanish Art Collection
Much of the Museum's collection originally hung in the royal palaces of Spain. During the Napoleonic Wars, the French emperor placed his own brother Joseph Bonaparte upon the Spanish throne as a puppet king. This caused the peoples of Spain to rise up against their French overlords. This popular rebellion has given the world the term `guerilla' warfare, guerilla coming from the Spanish word for war `guerra'.

Quite apart from the strategic value of tying down some of Napoleon's forces in the Iberian Peninsula, the rising struck a note of sympathy amongst the British - of a nation rising against its oppressors. Using Portugal as a base, the British pursued active military operations in Spain.

From April 1809 these operations were conducted under the leadership of the Duke of Wellington. In June 1813 the Duke defeated Joseph Bonaparte at the Battle of Vittoria. In the French army's baggage train was a large proportion of the Spanish royal art collection. Wellington offered to return the collection but King Ferdinand VII declined and gave the collection to the Duke as a gesture of thanks.

The Goya Portrait of the Duke of Wellington
In 1812 the Spanish painter Goya was commissioned to paint the Duke of Wellington. Most of the portrait was done in a series of sittings and the artist took

it away for finishing. However, the Duke's military career progressed from glory to glory and as he was awarded a long series of medals and honours so he felt they should be incorporated into the portrait. Goya acted as he was instructed. However, he found some of the medals hard to paint, notably the Order of the Golden Fleece. On seeing the finished painting, the Duke chose to give the work to a distant relative.

The Canova Statue of Napoleon
Apsley House contains the Napoleon statue (1810) by the Italian sculptor Canova. There is a story that Napoleon had the statue removed from The Louvre because its accompanying gilt figure of Victory is poised as though about to depart. In 1816 the statue was bought by the British government and given by the Prince Regent (the future King George IV) (1762-1830) to Wellington.

Harriette Wilson
Harriette Wilson (1789-1846) was a highly successful courtesan who sought to exploit her exploits by writing her memoirs. She and her publisher John Joseph Stockdale (1770-1847) showed the proofs to her numerous ex-lovers, intending to induce them to pay her hush money to have her leave them out of the book.

Wilson is famed for having induced Wellington, her supposed former lover, to exclaim "Publish and be damned!", a now stock phrase in the English language.

When Walters and Stockdale did publish the book in 1826, they made a lot of money but promptly lost it in a series of libel suits, ruining themselves into the bargain.

Direction
Use the pedestrian subway to the east of the Wellington Museum to cross Park Lane. Emerge at the Piccadilly steps of the Hotel Inter-Continental Exit.

Walk along Piccadilly.

The Hard Rock Cafe
On the left, at No. 137 Piccadilly, is the first The Hard Rock Cafe, which was opened in 1971 by Peter Morton and Isaac Tigrett.

In 1988 Mr. Tigrett sold his share of the business, consisting of the Hard Rock operations in Europe and the eastern United States to Pleasurama. Mr. Morton was left with the business in the western United States. In 1989 Pleasurama was taken over by Mecca which was itself taken over by the Rank Organisation.

In June 1996 Rank bought in Mr. Morton's share of the business. Morton retained licensing rights for Hard Rock hotels casinos. At the time of the deal he had recently opened a Hard Rock casino hotel in Las Vegas.

No. 133 Piccadilly
On the left, at No. 133 Piccadilly, is The Royal Air Force Club.

The Porters' Rest
On the right, opposite No. 127 Piccadilly, is the porters' rest (1861). The rest was constructed to temporarily take the weight of loads that foot porters were carrying on their backs.

The Japanese Embassy

On the left, at Nos. 101-104 Piccadilly, is the Japanese Embassy.

The In & Out

On the left, at No. 94 Piccadilly, is The Naval & Military Club, which was founded in 1862 by a group of officers. The Naval & Military is known as the `In & Out' after its gateposts. The Club is due to move to new premises in 1999.

Lord Palmerston

When the building was a private residence, one of its occupants was the Prime Minister Lord Palmerston (1784-1865).

In 1863 the Irish journalist Timothy O'Kane cited Palmerston as the co-respondent in his divorce case. At the time the premier was 79. The opposition leader Benjamin Disraeli (1804-1881) was against seeking to try to make political capital from the matter, as he felt that there was no way in which Palmerston would come out of such without his standing being enhanced - either through the purity of his conduct or through testimony to his vigour in old age.

Two years later Palmerston was found dead on the billiards table of Brocket Hall in Hertfordshire after an entanglement with a maid.

The Green Park Gates

On the right, opposite No. 92 Piccadilly, are a set of wrought iron gates, which stand at the northern end of Green Park's Broad Walk.

The gates were made c1735 for what became the 1st Lord Heathfield's (1717-1790) house at Turnham Green (Lord Heathfield was an Army officer who was very fond of cats). In 1837 the gates were re-erected at Chiswick House, the Dukes of Devonshire's country house near London. In 1898 they were moved to stand in front of the Dukes' London town house - Devonshire House in Piccadilly. In 1921 the gates were re-erected where they now stand.

Through the Gates it is possible to view a vista at the end of which is the Queen Victoria Memorial (1911). The Memorial stands in front of Buckingham Palace.

Green Park

King Charles II (1630-1685) added Green Park to the other royal parks. It is the smallest of the royal parks in central London.

Baroness Burdett-Coutts

On the left, between Bolton Street and Stratton Street, is No. 80 Piccadilly, the birthplace and home of the Victorian philanthropist Baroness Burdett-Coutts (1814-1906).

Burdett-Coutt's family money was derived from the Coutts & Company bank. The baroness tried to do something to counter the depredations of the East End's poverty. She underwrote the building of a set of dwellings (1862) in Columbia Square, Bethnal Green, and provided a means by which the East End's population might buy affordable nutritious food - the Columbia Market (1869), also in Bethnal Green. Although the market failed within the space of a few years, her efforts did do something to improve conditions for ordinary people in the area.

Burdett-Coutts and the novelist Charles Dickens (1812-1870) had a great friendship which was in part based on their shared desire to improve the lot of the urban poor.

Langan's

On the left is Stratton Street. On the left (western) side of Stratton Street is Langan's the restaurant, one of the high shrines of London celebrityhood.

The restaurant was founded by Peter Langan (d.1988) in 1976. Mr. Langan was bibulously inclined, his drunken exploits and lack of good manners were renowned. The actor Michael Caine, who owns a number of upmarket restaurants in London, was his partner in the business.

The Ritz

On the right, the first building on the southern side of Piccadilly is The Ritz hotel.

The Paris Ritz opened in 1898. Cesar Ritz was able to finance its creation through the profits he had skimmed off from The Savoy in London while he was managing it. He was found out by The Savoy's owners and sacked in 1898, as was its great chef Auguste Escoffier. The pair moved on to Ritz's new London enterprise the Carlton Hotel (New Zealand now occupies the site).

The London Ritz was designed to the specifications of Ritz. He had retired from the business by the time it opened in 1906. His professional nerve having been broken reputedly by the strains imposed first by arranging accommodation for dignitaries attending the coronation of King Edward VII (1841-1910), and then by the coronation being put off for a year because the king suffered a near fatal case of perityphlitis.

The hotels and the great private houses co-existed for a while. The Ritz management inquired of the 2nd Viscount Wimborne (1903-1967) whether he would be prepared to sell them a section of his garden as they were thinking of enlarging the hotel. The Viscount replied that he was contemplating extending his garden and would the company like to sell him their hotel. The family sold their property to an insurance company in the late 1940s.

In 1976 the Trafalgar House conglomerate bought the hotel from the Bracewell-Smith family; at the time, the business was suffering from a downturn in its market as a result of the rise in oil prices after the Seven Days' War. In 1978 Trafalgar House converted the hotel's ballroom into a casino.

In the early 1990s the hotel was perceived as being slightly awkward in that it was neither a big hotel (allowing for economies of scale) nor a small one (allowing intimacy to compensate for the lack of amenities such as phalanxes of underemployed doormen).

David and Frederick Barclay, the publicity shy west London twins, have amassed much of their fortune through their involvement in the hotel and property businesses. In October 1995 they bought The Ritz from Trafalgar House for £75m.

The Great Piccadilly Town Houses

On the left is Berkeley Street.

Following the Restoration of the monarchy in 1660 a row of great town houses was built on the north side of Piccadilly to the west of Swallow Street - Berkeley

House, Burlington House, and Clarendon House. The only one to survive is Burlington House.

Devonshire House
Devonshire House (1737) was built on what had been the site of Berkeley House. In 1918 the 9th Duke of Devonshire (1868-1938) sold the property. Devonshire House was pulled down in 1924. (Bricks from it were used to resurface Trent Park in Enfield. The House's gates were re-erected on the north side of Green Park at the end of the Broad Walk.)

Albemarle Street
On the left is Albemarle Street.

Clarendon House was sold to the 1st Duke of Albemarle (1608-1670) c1664 and was renamed Albemarle House. Twenty years later it was pulled down and Albemarle Street was built upon the site.

John Murray
On the left, at No. 50 Albemarle Street, is the publishing company John Murray.

In 1762 the original John Murray (1745-1793) retired from the marines on half-pay. In 1768 he bought William Sandby's bookselling business at No. 32 Fleet Street. Murray was followed in the business by his son also John Murray (1778-1843). In 1812 the firm moved to No. 50 Albemarle Street.

The second John Murray was the poet Byron's (1788-1824) friend and publisher. However, their friendship was by no means always harmonious. Murray turned down `The Vision of Judgement' (1822) which was published by the brothers Leigh and John Hunt.

Brown's Hotel
On the left, at No. 31 Albemarle Street, is Brown's Hotel. A Union Jack flag is usually flown above the hotel's entrance. The building's exterior is painted brown.

Brown's traces its origins back to 1666. However, it has been operating on its Dover Street premises only since 1837, when it was run by James Brown, Byron's former butler.

In 1876 London's first long-distance telephone call was made by Alexander Graham Bell from Brown's Hotel to Ravenscourt Park, which lies several miles to the west.

The hotel is renowned for its discretion.

The Royal Institution
On the right, at No. 31 Albemarle Street, is The Royal Institution, a body for the diffusion of scientific knowledge, which was founded in 1799 by Sir Benjamin Thompson Count Rumford (1753-1814), an American, who was a noble of the Holy Roman Empire.

The Davy-Faraday Research Laboratory commemorates two individuals closely associated with the Institution. In 1801 Humphry Davy (1778-1829) was hired as a lecturer in its laboratory; the following year he was made its Professor of Chemistry. In 1813 Michael Faraday (1791-1867) was hired as Davy's assistant; in 1833 Faraday was made the Institution's Professor of Chemistry.

In 1801 the Institution appointed Thomas Young (1773-1829) as its Professor of Natural Philosophy. Young both propounded the wave theory of light and deciphered the British Museum's Rosetta Stone.

Lectures given were not purely scientific, they included a series given in 1840 by Thomas Carlyle (1795-1881) on Heroes.

Nowadays, the Royal Institution is best known for its annual lectures for children in the Christmas holidays. These are televised.

Isetan

On the left, at No. 59 Piccadilly, is the Isetan shop. In large part, the shop's trade is derived from catering to Japanese visitors to the United Kingdom.

Old Bond Street

On the left is Old Bond Street.

Thomas Agnew & Son

On the left, at No. 43 Old Bond Street, are the premises of Thomas Agnew & Son the art auctioneers. A green flag hangs above the premises's entrance.

In 1817 Thomas Agnew was made a partner in a Manchester general dealing business, the activities of which included buying and selling paintings. Through Agnew's influence the firm became increasingly focussed on paintings. In 1860 Thomas Agnew & Son opened premises in London in Waterloo Place.

William Agnew M.P. (1825-1910), through the professional advice he proferred, was responsible for shaping many of the great private collections that were amassed in the late C19th.

In 1876 Agnew's commissioned its Old Bond Street premises, the first purpose-built dealers' galleries in London.

In February and March each year Agnew's holds its Annual Exhibition of English Watercolours and Drawings.

Members of the Agnew family are still involved in the business.

Charbonnel et Walker

On the left, at No. 28 Old Bond Street (on the southern side of the east entrance to The Royal Arcade), are the premises of the confectioners Charbonnel et Walker.

The Old Bond Street company was founded in 1875. There was a rumour that King Edward VII (then Prince of Wales) (1841-1910) was responsible for establishing Mme. Charbonnel in the business, she supposedly having been one of his mistresses.

Benson & Hedges

On the right, at No. 13 Old Bond Street, is the original Benson & Hedges tobacconists shop. The shop has a green awning.

Richard Benson and William Hedges set up their business in 1873.

In 1955 the British rights of the Benson & Hedges cigarette brand were sold to Gallaher the cigarette company.

Cigarette Manufacturers

The popularisation of cigarettes in Britain was in part the result of overseas military ventures.

Until the Crimean War of 1854-6 smoking cigarettes had been something that only poor people did. The habit was picked up from the Turks, with whom the British and French were allied.

Prior to the First World War of 1914-8 many ordinary Britons were pipe smokers. However, troops in the conflict appreciated the convenience of cigarettes and thereby led a change in British social patterns.

<u>Direction</u>
Continue east along Piccadilly.

<u>The Burlington Arcade</u>
On the left, at No. 51 Piccadilly, is the Burlington Arcade (1819).

In 1819 the 1st Earl of Burlington (1754-1834), the owner of Burlington House (now the home of the Royal Academy of Arts), commissioned the architect Samuel Ware (1781-1860) to design the Burlington Arcade. Reputedly, one of the reasons why his lordship did such was his wish to find a means of stopping passers-by from throwing their empty oyster shells into his garden. Oysters were a fast food of early C19th London.

In the mid-1950s the present Duke of Devonshire sold it to the Prudential life assurance company.

Some of the arcade's present-day businesses are descended from its first occupants.

<u>Oysters</u>
Oysters changed from being a commonplace item to being an expensive delicacy because the oyster population was severely undermined by disease and by a number of hard winters.

In Britain oysters should only be eaten during a month with an `r' in it.

<u>Burlington House</u>
On the left, to the east of the Burlington Arcade, is Burlington House, the only surviving great Piccadilly town house. However, the building has been much altered and now has a front which was remodelled in the 1870s.

<u>The Royal Academy of Arts</u>
The Royal Academy of Arts was founded in 1768, its first president was the painter Sir Joshua Reynolds (1723-1792). The Academy started life in Pall Mall, from 1780 it resided in Somerset House, from 1838 in a wing of the National Gallery, and since 1869 it has been in Burlington House.

Burlington House was fairly palatial to start with, its extension and rebuilding having been one of the many amusements of the architect-earl the 3rd Earl of Burlington (1694-1753). In the late C19th Old Burlington House was extended by an additional floor being added and a number of galleries built on to its northern face.

<u>The Royal College of Art Gang Revolution</u>
By the early 1960s the Royal Academy had acquired a reputation among artists for being hidebound and reactionary. It was then subjected to a palace revolution by the `Royal College of Art Gang'. The Gang's members included Hugh Casson, Roger de Grey (1918-1995), Frederick Gore, Colin Hayes, and Carel Weight. The Gang went on to become the new Royal Academy establishment: Casson was its President from 1976 to 1984 and De Grey from 1984 to 1993. Under their influence the Academy was careful to draw in Britain's leading artists and architects as A.R.A.s and R.A.s;

the likes of the painters Peter Blake and David Hockney, and the architects Sir Norman Foster and Sir James Stirling (1926-1992) would have been unlikely to have been interested in becoming members of the Academy had it continued in the state it was in at the start of 1960s.

A.R.A.s and R.A.s

Recruits to the Academy are chosen by election in which the existing membership vote. New members first hold an Associateship; there are thirty A.R.A.s. A.R.A.s can be elected to full Royal Academician status; there are forty R.A.s. Once an Academician reaches the age of seventy-five s/he becomes a Senior Academician.

The length of time which an artist has had as an A.R.A. has limited bearing on the speed with which s/he becomes a R.A., although when the competition is less keen there may be something of a sympathy vote. When elected an artist submits a diploma work which then becomes a permanent part of the Academy's collection.

The Royal Academy Summer Exhibition

Each year, during June, July and August, the Academy holds its Summer Exhibition. Amateurs and professionals alike submit works for consideration by the Hanging Committee. The Committee, which is drawn from the Academy's membership, has the task of whittling down the submissions to a number which can and should be hung. The works exhibited can be purchased.

The first annual show was held in 1769.

Loan Exhibitions

The Royal Academy started holding loan exhibitions in 1870.

The Sackler Galleries

The Royal Academy's Sackler Galleries were made possible through the generosity of the American philanthropists Jill and Arthur Sackler (d.1987). The Norman Foster-designed Galleries were opened in 1991.

The Learned Societies

There are a number of learned societies which are housed in Burlington House.

The Society of Antiquaries

The roots of the Society of Antiquaries date back to the late C16th. The Society's charter dates from 1751.

The Linnean Society

The Linnean Society was founded in 1788. The Society owns the collection of Linnaeus (1707-1778), the Swedish naturalist.

The stimulus for the Society's formation was (later Sir) James Edward Smith's (1759-1828) ownership of the collection, which he had purchased in 1783 after Sir Joseph Banks (1743-1829) had declined to do so. The Society's membership assumed that Smith would at his death leave the collection to the Society. He did not. The Society was obliged to purchase the collection from Smith's heirs.

In 1858 it was to the Linnean Society that Charles Darwin (1809-1882) and Alfred Russel Wallace (1823-1913) read their first joint paper on evolution by natural selection.

The Geological Society

The Geological Society was founded in 1807 and incorporated in 1825.

The Royal Astronomical Society

The Royal Astronomical Society was founded in 1820.

Red Telephone Boxes

Just inside of Burlington House's front entrance are two red telephone kiosks.

The architect Sir Giles Gilbert Scott (1880-1960) won a competition held by the General Post Office (the G.P.O.) to design a kiosk with his Kiosk No. 2 design. The Burlington House kiosks are Scott's original models. His design went into production in 1927. In 1935 he produced a simplified version of the design, the K6, which became ubiquitous.

(The National Telephone Kiosk Collection is at The Avoncroft Museum of Buildings, Bromsgrove, Hereford & Worcester.)

Fortnum & Mason

On the right, at No. 181 Piccadilly, is Fortnum & Mason.

Hugh Mason had a shop in St.James's market. His lodger was William Fortnum, a servant in the royal household. The perks of Fortnum's position included the disposal of any candles which had not been finished; these Mason sold on their store. In 1707 the pair set up a stall in Piccadilly on the site of the present-day shop. (Members of the Fortnum family continued to serve in the royal household.)

Fortnum & Mason's reputation was aided by the Great Exhibition of 1851. The store's food displays were one of the sights which many of the Exhibition's visitors included in their itinerary of London.

The company's hampers became standard fare for Britain's ruling classes in the C19th, whether it was fighting wars in distant lands or having a day at the races.

In 1896 Fortnum & Mason was an obvious first British customer for Mr. Heinz's canned food. The store's hampers contained food that was meant to be preserved while it travelled great distances across the globe or up the Thames Valley.

Fortnum's Fountain Restaurant & Soda Bar is a place for afternoon tea.

The Albany

On the left Albany Court Yard leads to The Albany.

In 1792 Frederick Duke of York & Albany (1763-1827) exchanged his Whitehall house (Dover House) for the 1st Viscount Melbourne's (1748-1819) house on the north side of Piccadilly.

In 1802 the builder Alexander Copland bought The Albany, as it had become known. Copland commissioned the architect Henry Holland (c1746-1806) to draw up plans for the building's conversion into a series of private residential chambers; it consists of two rows of chambers which were built in the house's garden and linked by a covered passage.

Flats in The Albany are known as `sets'. Originally the 69 sets were rented out to either bachelors or widowers. No women were admitted unless close relatives.

Hatchard's

On the right, at No. 187 Piccadilly, is Hatchard's the bookshop.

John Hatchard (1769-1849) opened a bookshop at No. 173 Piccadilly in 1797. In 1801 he moved to No. 187. In Hatchard's time the shop was as much a social meeting place for the literary-minded as it was a bookshop.

Hatchard's is now owned by EMI the music company.

Warrants

Above the shop's entrance can be seen a number of warrants, which testify to its commercial patronage by senior members of the royal family.

Warrants are issued by four members of the royal household: the Sovereign, the Sovereign's heir-apparent, and the consorts of past and present Sovereigns. Warrants are issued for a number of years - ten years in the first instance - and end automatically with the death of the issuer.

Warrants are periodically reviewed and if the business is no longer used then the warrant will often be removed.

Some businesses, such as Hatchard's, accommodate more than one warrant.

The warrant is attached to a specific individual within the company and if that person leaves the business (be it through death, retirement, or change of employer) then the warrant is reconsidered.

Swallow Street

On the left Swallow Street runs into Piccadilly.

Before Regent Street was cut, Swallow Street was the West End's principal north-south road.

St.James Piccadilly

On the right, opposite the bottom of Swallow Street, is the Church of St.James Piccadilly (1684).

St.James Piccadilly was built to serve the neighbourhood which the Earl of St.Albans (c1604-1684) had developed on the St.James's Fields estate. Despite the fact that Sir Christopher Wren (1632-1723) designed and built dozens of churches, St.James Piccadilly was the only parish church that he ever built on a new site.

In the early C18th St.James Piccadilly was the most fashionable church in London; three of its vicars went on to become Archbishops of Canterbury.

Simpson

On the right, at No. 203 Piccadilly, is Simpson the clothes retailer.

Simeon Simpson (d.1932) founded his Stoke Newington tailoring business in 1894. The business was taken over by his son Alexander Simpson (d.1937) who in 1934 invented a self-supporting trouser waist-band. The waist-band was utilised in DAKS clothing, DAKS being a contraction of `Dad's Slacks'.

In 1936 the company opened its store in Piccadilly.

The outbreak of the Second World War meant that the company's high quality products were purchased by the military. With the conflict's end there came the opportunity to build good-will towards the DAKS brand through producing quality suits.

To Finish

Walk to Piccadilly underground station, which is on the Bakerloo and Piccadilly Lines.

To Continue

Walk to eastern end of Piccadilly Circus and turn right into Haymarket.

3. St.James's

To Start

Go to Piccadilly underground station which is on the Bakerloo and Piccadilly Lines. Leave the station and walk to the east end of Piccadilly Circus. Turn right into Haymarket.

Haymarket

The first evidence of the Haymarket hay market dates from the 1650s. The market was probably stimulated into being by the nearby presence of the Royal Mews to its east. The Mews was a large stables complex, which occupied most of what is now Trafalgar Square.

In 1830 the market moved to the then newly built Cumberland Market (in what is now NW1).

Sogo

On the right is Sogo the Japanese department store, which caters in large part to the Japanese community in London and Britain as a whole.

Fribourg & Treyer

On the left, at No. 34 Haymarket, is a gift shop. One of the panes in the shop's righthand set of windows reads `Fribourg & Treyer, Tobacconists To His Majesty and Purveyors of Foreign Snuffs to the Royal Family'. The business was established in 1720. The shop was constructed c1770.

The business of Fribourg & Treyer closed in 1981.

Football, Football

On the right is Football, Football the soccer themed restaurant, which opened in Haymarket in March 1996. The restaurant was the idea of Terry McQuade and Bobby Keetch (1941-1996), both of whom played the game professionally.

Theatre Royal Haymarket

On the left is the Theatre Royal Haymarket, the history of which goes back to 1720.

Henry Fielding

In 1736 the playwright Henry Fielding (1707-1754) produced his `Historical Register, For the Year 1736' at the Theatre Royal. The production lampooned the then Prime Minister Sir Robert Walpole (1676-1745). In 1737 Parliament passed the Licensing Act which firmly put the London stage under the official control of the Lord Chamberlain, one of the senior members of the royal household. (This was a control from which it was not released until 1968.)

Her Majesty's Theatre

On the right is Her Majesty's Theatre, which opened in Haymarket in 1705. It was designed by Sir John Vanbrugh (1664-1726), who was not only a playwright but also an architect. Its name was resonant with the need for theatres to operate within the protection of the royal court.

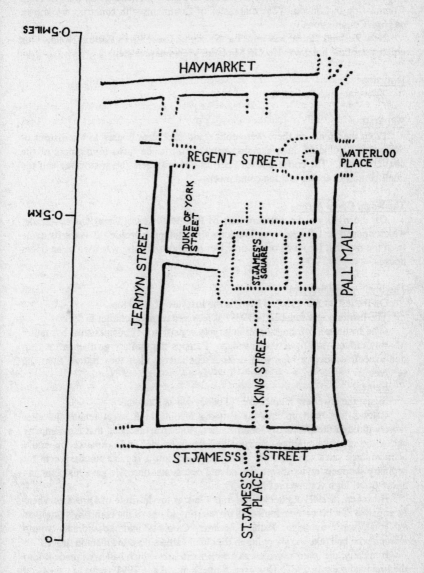

New Zealand House

On the right is New Zealand House, the New Zealand government's High Commission in London. (The embassies of Commonwealth countries are known as High Commissions.)

New Zealand House was built on the site of Cesar Ritz's Carlton Hotel. One employee of the hotel was Ho Chi Minh the Vietnamese leader.

Direction

Turn right into Pall Mall.

Pall Mall

From the 1690s on there were coffee and chocolate houses in the district of St.James's. Some of these establishments were the de facto forerunners of the district's clubs. The coffee houses acted as venues where the aristocracy and the intelligentsia of C18th London could meet.

The Royal Opera Arcade

On the right, on the northern side of Pall Mall, is the Royal Opera Arcade, which opened in 1816 and was London's first shopping arcade. It takes its name from the fact that for much of the time Her Majesty's Theatre was used as an opera house.

The Institute of Directors

On the left, at No. 116 Pall Mall, is the Institute of Directors.

The Institute was founded in 1903. It received its royal charter in 1906.

(The Institute's paintings seem to largely consist not of businessmen but rather of army officers and naval commanders. Perhaps the military gentlemen took up non-executive directorships with defence contractors after they retired from the services.)

Ratners

Signet the jewellery retailer used to be known as Ratners.

Ratners was built up into the Britain's leading high street retailer jeweller largely through the efforts of Gerald Ratner. Ratner appreciated that the company should be strictly a retailing operation and that if he took it downmarket he would achieve large sales volumes. He turned jewellery into a regular purchase item for ordinary shoppers rather than a special and occasional one. He gave his company a low-price, high volume profile.

However, in 1991 Ratner was giving a talk at the Institute of Directors where he engaged in a bit of over-frankness by referring to one of the company's products as "total crap"; overnight Ratners became `Crapners' and the ordinary young women who had taken to shopping in the chain's stores deserted them in droves.

Ironically, the `crap' remark was a well-worn joke which had even made it into the financial press in 1987. However, Ratner's mistake in 1991 seems to have been to place it late in the day in an otherwise rather dull speech, he did this after having been told that the audience at the Institute expected some humour, when he himself had assumed that they would want some rather more conventional fare. As a result, it seemed not so much an instance of realism and humour being blended, as a case of a retailer having disdain for his customers.

The remark, combined with a drop in retail volume, as a result of the then recession, and the fact the company had incurred a high level of debt to finance its growth, almost caused the business to fold.

Mr. Ratner left the company, which in turn discarded its Ratner retail brand.

Regent Street Memorials

To the right, at the bottom of Regent Street, are three memorials. The large one at the back is to those who fought and died in the Crimean War of 1854-6.

The small memorial, at the front on the right, is to Sidney Herbert (1820-1903), a writer and social theorist of whom most Britons have never heard but whose grave in Highgate is of more interest to many visiting Americans than is that of Karl Marx.

Florence Nightingale

The small memorial at the front to the left is to Florence Nightingale (1820-1910), the founder of modern nursing.

The memorial was first major monument to Florence Nightingale. It was unveiled in February 1915, a time when the wholesale slaughter of soldiers on the battlefields of Mons and Ypres was still fresh in the public mind. As a result, the government of the day felt the event was untimely and chose not to have a formal unveiling ceremony. Therefore, it had workmen remove the statue's covering sheets at seven o'clock in the morning.

The Athaneum

On the left, across Waterloo Place from the Institute of Directors, is The Athaneum, a club which was founded in 1824 by the scientist Humphry Davy (1778-1829), the painter Sir Thomas Lawrence (1769-1830), the politician the 4th Earl of Aberdeen (1784-1860), and the writer and politician John Wilson Croker (1780-1857). (It was Wilson who devised `conservatism' as a political term.) The club was intended to provide to the wants of `scientific and literary men and artists'. William Makepeace Thackeray (1811-1863) wrote some of his novels in the club's library.

In the C20th the club has had a clerical and cerebral reputation.

The Travellers

On the left, at No. 106 Pall Mall, is The Travellers Club, which was founded in 1819. It has long drawn many of its members from the Foreign & Commonwealth Office.

The Reform Club

On the left, at No. 104 Pall Mall, is The Reform Club.

The Great Reform Act of 1832 reformed the electoral system, thereby opening the way for modern Parliamentary democracy to develop in Britain. The Act was the creation of members of the Whig Party. The Reform Club was founded by Whigs in 1836.

The Club is no longer politically aligned.

The Star & Garter

On the left, at No. 100 Pall Mall, is on what was the site of The Star & Garter Tavern, which in the C18th was one of the London inns where gentlemen and aristocrats from the same region or county as one another could, if they so chose, associate on a given day of the week while they were in London.

The Birth of Cricket

It was through one of its regional/county groups that The Star & Garter became the midwife of modern cricket. Originally, cricket was a game which was particularly played in the counties to the south of London - Surrey, Sussex, and Kent.

In 1550 a form of cricket was played at Guildford School. In 1700 the first organised match of which there is a record took place on Clapham Common (now part of the south London inner city).

Cricket was codified in the C18th because gamblers were waging large sums on the outcome of individual matches. In 1755 a committee met at The Star & Garter to draw up the rules of cricket. In 1774 another committee met at the tavern to revise the 1755 regulations.

The first great cricket match in England was contested between Kent and All England in 1774 on the artillery ground outside the Honourable Artillery Company's headquarters in the City of London.

The game's rules were essentially set by 1787, a hundred years ahead of most other sports.

In 1787 Thomas Lord, with the financial backing of Charles Lennox and the 9th Earl of Winchilsea (1752-1826), opened a cricket ground on what is now Dorset Square. Lennox was a Sussex landowner and Winchilsea a Kent one (Lord came from Yorkshire). (In 1811 Lord moved the ground's turf to St.John's Wood.)

(During the mid-C19th the British showed a marked talent for `inventing' sports. The invention consisted not so much of devising the activities as of writing down formal rules and regulations for what were already well-established past-times. This tendency to regulate was born out of the leisure which many upper-middle class Britons enjoyed as the fruits of the Industrial Revolution.)

The Wicked Lord Byron

The Nottinghamshire Club was another of the regional/county groups which used to meet at The Star & Garter. It was while attending the Club in 1765 that the 5th Lord Byron (1722-1798) (the poet Byron's greatuncle) fell into an argument with his cousin William Chaworth (d.1765) over game on their estates. The argument escalated into a duel in which Lord Byron mortally wounded Chaworth.

His Lordship was tried by his peers in the House of Lords and found guilty of manslaughter but was discharged under the statute of privilege as a peer.

The R.A.C.

On the left, at No. 89 Pall Mall, is The R.A.C. or Royal Automobile Club. The Club was founded in 1897 and has a larger membership than most of the club's in the district.

The Army & Navy

On the right, on the western corner of Pall Mall and St.James's Square, is The Army & Navy Club, which was founded in 1837 by a group of officers who had served in the East India Company's army in India and who, upon returning to Britain, were dismayed at the length of the waiting lists to join clubs such as the United Services Club. The membership was opened to naval officers at the suggestion of the Duke of Wellington (1769-1852), the club's patron.

Schomberg House
On the left, at Nos. 80-82 Pall Mall, is Schomberg House (1698).

The 1st Duke of Schomberg (1615-1690) was King William III's (1650-1702) second-in-command at the Battle of the Boyne (July 1690). Schomberg House was built for the 3rd Duke (1641-1719).

Nell Gwynne
On the left, at No. 79 Pall Mall, is where Nell Gwynne (1650-1687) lived from 1671 to 1687. Gwynne is the best remembered of King Charles II's (1630-1685) mistresses. She is supposed to have first attracted the king's attention while selling oranges in a theatre.

United Oxford & Cambridge Club
On the left, at No. 71 Pall Mall, is The United Oxford & Cambridge Club, which was formed in 1971. The oldest of its antecedents, The Oxford & Cambridge University Club, was founded in 1830.

In February 1996 the club voted to admit women on equal terms to men.

Boydell's Shakespeare Gallery
On the right, at No. 52 Pall Mall, was Boydell's Shakespeare Gallery.

Alderman John Boydell (1719-1804) was a printseller who became wealthy through exporting British-made prints to Europe. In 1787 Boydell commissioned 35 of the day's leading painters to produce works which illustrated scenes from the plays of Shakespeare. His plan was to make money both by charging people to view the original paintings in his Shakespeare Gallery and to have engravings made of them which could be sold on to the public. The scheme proved unsuccessful. Most of the painters produced undistinguished examples of their work, Henry Fuseli (1741-1825) seeming to be the only artist whose imagination was truly fired by the project. The Gallery opened in 1789.

Boydell's commercial eminence was acknowledged in his 1790 election as Lord Mayor of the City of London. However, the outbreak of the French Revolution the previous year had an adverse effect on his printselling business which in turn affected his ability to finance the Gallery. As a result, he was driven to petition Parliament to allow him to run a lottery to dispose of his paintings and prints.

Rothman's of Pall Mall
On the right, at No. 65 Pall Mall on the corner with St.James's Street, is Rothman's of Pall Mall.

Louis Rothman (d.1926) opened a kiosk in Fleet Street in 1890. Rothman was an innovative retailer, both creating the Pall Mall brand of cigarettes and inventing menthol cigarettes.

Direction

Turn right into St.James's Street.

Mark Masons Hall

On the left, at No. 86 St.James's Street, is Mark Masons Hall, a freemasons' building.

Berry Brothers & Rudd

On the right are the bow-fronted premises of the wine merchants Berry Brothers & Rudd, which was founded in 1698.

The Berry and Rudd families still run the business. The firm owns Cutty Sark, one of the world's principal whisky brands.

Pickering Place

On the right, immediately to the north of Berry Brothers & Rudd's premises is an archway which stands at one end of a passageway. At the far end of the passageway is Pickering Place, which was built in the 1730s. It is a type of court which has almost disappeared from London but which was once a commonplace feature of the city.

The Texan Legation

To the right, just within the passageway, is a plaque which commemorates the Legation of the Republic of Texas to the Court of St.James. The Legation occupied a building on the site during the years 1842-5.

Lock & Company

On the right, at No. 6 St.James's Street, is Lock & Company the hatseller. The business was founded on the west side of St.James's Street in 1676. It crossed the road to its present premises in 1763.

The Bowler Hat

In 1850 the original `bowler' hat was designed to be worn by the (pheasant) beaters of William Coke (the Coke family were Norfolk landowners). Coke stipulated that the hat should be hard and also close-fitting so that it would not be blown off easily. The contract was sub-contracted by Lock to Thomas Bowler & Company. The prototype was tested by being jumped upon. In a modified form, the hat became ubiquitous fashionable headware in the late C19th and early C20th. Lock's staff are reputed to refer to the hat as a `coke'.

Lobb

On the right, at No. 9 St.James's Street, is Lobb the shoemakers, which was founded in 1866. It is still run by the Lobb family.

No. 74 St.James Street

On the left is No. 74 St.James's Street.

In November 1995 the property came on to the market as a private residence. The asking price was £60m.

Truefitt & Hill

On the left is the barbers Truefitt & Hill, which was founded in 1805.

The Carlton Club
On the left, at No. 71 St.James's Street, is The Carlton Club, which was founded by members of Tory Party after their defeat at the 1831 general election, when only 179 tories were elected to the House of Commons. The club's members did not have to be members of the Conservative Party until 1912.

King Street
On the right is King Street, which in the mid-C18th was a centre of the fine art trade. The street is now known for its auction houses. Occasionally, the auction houses resell some of their predecessors' wares.

Christies
On the left (north), at No. 8 King Street, are the premises of the fine art auctioneer Christie's.

In 1766 James Christie (1730-1803), a former midshipman, founded his general auction house. By the early 1800s the business had become fashionable for its art sales.

Spink & Son
Just beyond Christie's, at Nos. 5-7 King Street, is Spink & Son, London's principal specialist in numismatic items (coins and medals). John Spink established himself as a goldsmith in Lombard Street in 1666. In April 1994 Christie's bought the business.

Almack House
On the right, at No. 28 King Street, is Almack House.

William Almack (d.1781) kept a tavern at No. 49 Pall Mall. Mr. Almack's success in providing facilities for gentlemen's clubs led him to try a more ambitious venture. In 1765 he established Almack's Assembly Rooms in King Street, on the site which is now occupied by Almack House.

The Rooms' tenor was established by Almack setting up a committee of titled ladies who determined who might and might not be admitted to the Rooms' weekly balls. For nearly a century after its opening Almack's Assembly Rooms was one of the principal venues for aristocratic social life in London. In the 1830s the Rooms began to go into decline as a fashionable venue.

St.James's Place
On the left (west) side of St.James's Street is St.James's Place.

Spencer House
Hidden away at the far end of St.James's Place on the left (south) is Spencer House (No. 27), the former town house of the Spencer family. Spencer House overlooks Green Park.

The 1st Baron Montfort (1705-1755) commissioned the architect John Vardy (1718-1765) to design him a town house. Montfort was an inveterate and ultimately unselective gambler, who had received his peerage through paying money for it. Having ruined his estate he committed suicide in 1755. The house's lease was then bought by the 1st Earl Spencer (1734-1783).

The Spencer family stopped living in the house during the 1920s. In 1985 8th Earl Spencer granted a 125-year lease on the building to J. Rothschild Holdings.

Justerini & Brooks

On the left, at No. 61 St.James's Street, is Justerini & Brooks the wine merchants, which was founded in 1749 by George Johnson and Giacomo Justerini. Justerini's cordial proved highly popular and he retired to Italy a wealthy man.

In 1831 Alfred Brooks bought the business from the Johnson family.

The Economist Building

On the right, at Nos. 25-27 St.James's Street, is The Economist Building (1964).

The financial magazine `The Economist' was founded in 1843 by James Wilson (1805-1860) and stayed with his descendants until it was sold in 1928. Its first glory days were under Walter Bagehot (1826-1877), Wilson's son-in-law.

The present-day `The Economist' is essentially the creation of Geoffrey Crowther (later Lord Crowther) (1907-1972). In 1938 Crowther was appointed the magazine's editor. He turned it from being a City of London periodical into one of the world's most influential weeklies.

Brooks's

On the left, at No. 60 St.James's Street, is Brooks's, a club which was founded in 1764 by William Almack (d.1781) in his tavern at No. 49 Pall Mall. In 1778 the club moved to St.James's Street where it came under the management of William Brooks (d.1782). In the late C18th many of the club's members entertained themselves by gambling for very high stakes.

In the late C18th Brooks's was the great Whig club (while White's was the great Tory one).

Boodle's

On the right, at No. 28 St.James's Street, is Boodle's, the club which Edward Boodle founded in William Almack's Pall Mall tavern. In 1783 the club moved to No. 28 St.James's Street, where it has been ever since.

White's

On the right, at No. 37 St.James Street, is White's, a club.

In 1693, an Italian using the name Francis White (d.1711), opened White's Chocolate House in St.James's Street. White's became a bete noire of the satirist the Rev. Jonathan Swift (1667-1745). Within the chocolate house an inner club emerged, its members became famed for their willingness to lay a wager on the outcome of almost anything.

The Arthur family succeeded the Whites as the club's managers. In 1755 Robert Arthur bought Nos. 37-38 St.James's Street. The chocolate house business ceased trading and the club moved into the new premises.

With the advent the French Revolution in 1789 the club became politicised. The Whig politician Charles James Fox (1749-1806) and his supporters withdrew from White's to Brooks's, while White's members supported Pitt the Younger (1759-1806) and his Tory government.

Following the tories' electoral defeat at the 1831 general election, the Carlton Club was founded. This had the effect of depoliticising White's.

Beau Brummell

In 1811 the club's bow window was installed. The dandy `Beau' Brummell (1778-1840) and his friends disported themselves in the window, thereby turning it into the `shrine' of fashion.

Direction

Turn around, go down St.James's Street slightly and turn left into Jermyn Street.

Wiltons Restaurant

On the left, at No. 56 Jermyn Street, is Wiltons Restaurant, which is owned by the merchant banking Hambro family, who acquired it in 1942 rather than see it closed down as a result of the Second World War.

Bury Street

To the right is Bury Street. On the left (east) side of Bury Street is Quaglino's, part of the Conran restaurant empire.

Alfred Dunhill

On the left, on the north-western corner of Jermyn Street with Duke Street, is Alfred Dunhill.

In 1907 Alfred Dunhill opened his first upmarket tobacconists shop.

Over the years the company extended itself into retailing smokers' requisites and from there moved into similar pocket sized items such as pens and watches.

Rothmans, the tobacco and luxury goods company, now controls the business.

The Cavendish Hotel

On the right, on the south-eastern corner of Jermyn Street with Duke Street, is The Cavendish Hotel.

Mrs. Lewis (d.1952) was a gifted cook whose culinary skills were appreciated by King Edward VII (1841-1910). She was able to use her reputation to help set herself up as the proprietress of The Cavendish. Her reign over her somewhat Bohemian establishment lasted through the first half of the C20th.

Tramp

On the left, at No. 40 Jermyn Street, is Tramp the nightclub.

Johnny Gold, a bookmaker, opened his first nightclub in 1963. Mr. Gold opened Tramp in 1969.

J.Floris

On the right, at No. 89 Jermyn Street, is the perfumer J.Floris Ltd., which is descended from a barbershop opened by Juan Famenia Floris, a Majorcan, in 1730. (At the time, Majorca was a British possession. Spain recaptured it during the American War of Independence of 1775-83.)

Paxton & Whitfield

On the right, at No. 93 Jermyn Street, is the cheese shop Paxton & Whitfield, which can trace its antecedents back to a business which was established in Clare

Market, near the Aldwych, in the early 1700s. The business's founder was one Sam Cullum, the son of a Suffolk swordmaker (the Cullum disappeared from the business's name in 1797). The company has been in its present premises since the late 1860s.

Direction

Turn right into Duke of York Street. Enter St.James's Square from the north side.

St.James's Square

In 1661 King Charles II (1630-1685) granted Henry Jermyn Earl of St.Albans (c1604-1684) a lease on the crown-owned land between St.James's Street and Haymarket. (St.Albans may have been secretly married Charles's widowed mother Queen Henrietta Maria (1609-1669).)

The district's street pattern was lain down by the Earl in the 1670s.

The Equestrian Statue of King William III

The William III Monument (1807) in the garden of St.James's Square was sculpted by John Bacon the Younger (1777-1859).

The equestrian statue has rather a mixed message. It shows King William III (1650-1702), dressed as a Roman general. In contrast, the reigning king King George III (1738-1820) was very much a stay-at-home king; his periodic 'insanity' came on top of his disinclination to lead the nation's military forces in the war which was then being waged against Napoleonic France. However, the horse which William is riding is about to step on the molehill which caused the animal to fall. The fall, which threw the Dutch king, was popularly believed to have caused his death (he died from pneumonia contracted while recovering from it). Therefore, the mortality of the soldier-king is blatantly portrayed.

Chatham House

The nearest house on the western side of the square's northern side to Duke of York Street, at No. 10 St.James's Square, is Chatham House.

Among some of the British experts on international affairs who attended the Peace Conference held at Versailles after the First World War, there emerged the view that there was a need for the better exchange of ideas and information about international affairs. Thus, in 1920 the British Institute of International Affairs was founded. The Institute moved into Chatham House in 1923.

The Royal Institute of International Affairs maintains a policy of its being free from both political and governmental influence.

Chatham House Rules

Chatham House Rules are a practice by which it is agreed that what is being said is not to be reported. The Rules can be in operation in places other than Chatham House itself.

Ada Countess of Lovelace

No. 12 St.James's Square was the home of Ada Countess of Lovelace (1815-1852). The Countess was both the daughter of the poet Lord Byron (1788-1824) and, through her mathematical ability and her association with Charles Babbage (1792-1871), an important figure in the early history of computing.

The London Library

At No. 14 St.James's Square, on the north end of the square's western side, is the London Library which was founded in 1841 by the historian and man of letters Thomas Carlyle (1795-1881). Carlyle desired that the Library should stock the sort of books which commercial circulating libraries did not hold and which the British Museum library refused to lend out. In 1845 the Library moved to its present-day premises.

East India, Devonshire, Sports & Public Schools Club

At No. 16 St.James's Square is the East India, Devonshire, Sports & Public Schools Club.

The East India United Services Club was established in 1849 to provide a London club for retired officers of the East India Company and for those current officers who were on leave in Britain. In 1862 the club bought the freehold of No. 16 St.James's Square. During the C20th a number of clubs have amalgamated with it, thus giving it is present name - the East India, Devonshire, Sports & Public Schools Club.

Hervey House

On the eastern section of the square's north side is No. 6, the site of what was from 1677 to 1955 Hervey House was the town house of the Hervey family.

Frederick Hervey (1730-1803) was a younger son of the noted fop Lord Hervey, a son of the 1st Earl of Bristol. In order to assist his material well-being Frederick Hervey was set upon a career in the Church of Ireland. He rose to become Bishop of Derry in 1768. However, in 1779 he inherited the family Earldom and set himself to properly indulging his tastes both for building country houses in the latest fashion and for travelling about the continent in great luxury. The numerous Hotels Bristol across Europe commemorate the bishop and his extravagance, e.g. the Hotel Bristol in the Rue du Faubourg St.Honore, Paris, and the Hotel Bristol in the Karntner Ring, Vienna.

Norfolk House

At the southern end of the square's eastern side, at No. 31 St.James's Square, is Norfolk House, the town house of the Howard Dukes of Norfolk (their previous residence having been on the Strand).

In 1737 King George II (1683-1760) turned Frederick Prince of Wales (1707-1751) out of St.James's Palace. The Prince rented Norfolk House before moving into Leicester House.

Direction

Turn around and walk back up Duke of York Street. Turn right into Jermyn Street.

Trumper

On the left, at No. 20 Jermyn Street, is Geo. F. Trumper, Gentlemen's Perfumer.

Direction

Turn left into Regent Street.

To Finish

Walk northwards to Piccadilly Circus and descend into Piccadilly underground station, which is on the Bakerloo and Piccadilly Lines.

To Continue

Walk northwards to Piccadilly Circus and turn right.

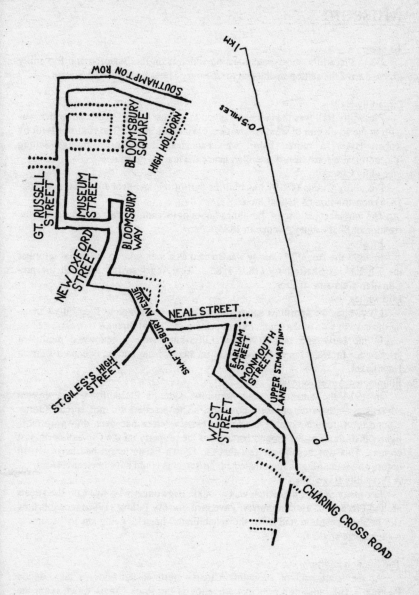

4. Leicester Square and The British Museum

To Start

Go to Piccadilly underground station which is on the Bakerloo and Piccadilly Lines. Leave the station by the exit to Coventry Street and Leicester Square.

Piccadilly Hall

Piccadilly Hall was the nickname given to a house, long since gone, which was built at the south end of what is now Great Windmill Street. The Hall was built by Robert Baker, a retired tailor, who had made his fortune through selling `piccadillies', a form of ruff or collar, hence the house's nickname.

Piccadilly Circus

Piccadilly Circus (1819) was built as part of the architect John Nash's (1752-1835) construction of Regent Street.

The circular pattern of buildings around Piccadilly was destroyed by the creation of Shaftesbury Avenue in 1886.

Eros

In 1893 the Angel of Charity was erected as a memorial to the social reformer the 7th Earl of Shaftesbury (1801-1885). The Angel swiftly acquired the pre-Christian nickname of Eros.

Lillywhites

Lillywhites the sportings goods store is on the south side of Piccadilly Circus, on the eastern side of the southernmost section of Regent Street.

In the early and mid-C19th the Lillywhites were a renowned family of cricketers. In 1863 James Lillywhite, a member of the family, opened a shop in Haymarket.

Illuminated Advertisements

In 1910 the tenants on the north-east side of Piccadilly Circus erected advertising billboards on their premises. The practice did not spread further around the Circus is because the Crown Estate's leases had been drawn up more tightly than those of the ground landlord of the property on the Circus's north-east corner. This was despite the fact that the Crown Estate leases had been written before any such thing as illuminated advertisements could have been envisaged.

A Piccadilly Bagwoman

For many years Chris Kitch was a junkie bagwoman who lived on the streets around Piccadilly. Her biography `Pavement For My Pillow' (1996) recounts how she became destitute and how she rehabilitated herself, going on to become a postgraduate student.

The London Pavilion

At the south end of Piccadilly Circus's north-eastern side is the London Pavilion. The building's principal attraction is the Rock Circus which is on the corner of Great Windmill Street.

Rock Circus

The Rock Circus is a Madame Tussaud's venture. It consists of wax figures depicting the history of rock and pop music since the 1950s.

The Trocadero

To the east of the southern end of Great Windmill Street is Coventry Street, the northern side of which is taken up by The Trocadero.

The Trocadero began its life in the 1740s as a tennis court and has been associated with leisure ever since.

In 1849 Robert Bignell (d.1888), a wine merchant, opened The Argyll Rooms, a nightclub and casino. They acquired a bad reputation and in 1878 he closed them after he was refused a new licence. In 1882 he opened The Trocadero Palace music hall.

During the 1970s and 1980s the Trocadero was kept closed by planning wrangles.

Joe Lyons

The Trocadero Corner House was the most luxurious of the Lyons Corner House tea-shops.

J.Lyons & Company was founded by Isidore and Montague Gluckstein. The company's senior staff were largely drawn from the Gluckstein family and their relatives the Salmons. Joseph Lyons (1847-1917) was also a relative of the Glucksteins. Lyons's outgoing, amiable personality made him an ideal frontman for the business. The Salmons and the Glucksteins did not wish the business to become confused in the public's mind with the tobacco business which already bore their surnames.

Lyons the business was established in the late 1880s. It opened its first tea shop in Piccadilly in 1894. The chain spread rapidly. In 1904 the Glucksteins and the Salmons sold off their tobacco interests to Imperial Tobacco, thereby leaving them free to concentrate on Lyons. The same year the company entered the food wholesaling business, selling Lyons-branded packet tea to retailers. The company then expanded into a range of goods that could be associated with its tea-shops, e.g. cakes, ice cream and coffee.

In January 1925 the uniform of the Lyons waitresses was changed from an Edwardian style to one influenced by the contemporary flapper fashion. In their new uniform the Lyons waitresses became popularly known as `Nippies'.

J.Lyons was swallowed up by Allied Breweries in 1978 to form Allied Lyons (now Allied Domecq). The last of the tea-shops were closed in 1981.

Planet Hollywood

On the western corner of Coventry Street and Rupert Street is Planet Hollywood the movie-themed restaurant, which was founded in 1991 by Robert Earl and Keith Barish. (Earl has run The Hard Rock Cafe business for the Rank Organisation.)

The Comedy Store

Opposite Rupert Street is Oxendon Street. On the western side of Oxendon Street is The Comedy Store, which was opened in 1979 by Don Ward in Gossips nightclub in Dean Street, Soho.

In 1985 the club moved to Leicester Square and in December 1994 it moved to Haymarket House, Oxendon Street, a venue which can seat 400.

The mid-1990s comedy boom's roots lie in the Comedy Store.

The Fashion Cafe

On the eastern corner of Coventry Street and Rupert Street is The Fashion Cafe, which opened in 1996.

The Cafe de Paris

To the east of the Fashion Cafe is The Cafe de Paris, which in the inter-war years was a nightclub of international renown.

The Cafe is responsible for the presence of Coventry Street on the British version of the board game Monopoly. The game's streets were selected in the mid-1930s.

In 1996 The Cafe de Paris re-opened.

The Swiss Centre

Coventry Street crosses Wardour Street and turns into New Coventry Street. On the north (left) side of New Coventry Street is The Swiss Centre.

People often meet under its clock, which does little to help the site's pedestrian congestion (the same can be said of reading guide-books).

Leicester Square

New Coventry Street leads into Leicester Square.

Albert Grant

Albert Grant M.P. (ne Abraham Gottheimer) (1831-1899) was a company promoter who engaged in flamboyant gestures to help generate publicity for himself and his ventures. In 1874 Grant bought the garden which fills the square's centre. He paid for it to be beautified and then presented it to the Metropolitan Board of Works (the forerunner of the London County Council).

Some of Grant's business practices were questionable. He ruined himself through the expense of his luxurious lifestyle and by engaging in litigation to try to defend his reputation which had been called into question by the financial press.

Grant is commemorated on the monument in the garden's centre.

Entertainment

In the 1840s New Coventry Street was cut. This increased the amount of traffic which flowed through Leicester Square. The character of the square began to shift from being predominantly residential to being predominantly commercial. Entertainment became the square's principal trade.

The Alhambra opened in 1858. The Empire opened in Cranbourn Street in 1884, and was followed by Daly's in 1893, and The Hippodrome in 1900.

In the 1920s revues were a feature of London theatre life - Charles Cochran (1872-1951) dominated the form, while at times Andre Charlot (1892-1956) mounted four revues simultaneously. With advent of the Great Depression, the revues faltered - they were capital intensive and their audience was no longer so affluent.

The great Variety Palaces of Leicester Square were all converted into cinemas - The Alahambra became the Odeon Leicester Square, the Royal London Panorama became the Empire Cinema, and Daly's in Cranbourn Street became the Warner Cinema.

The Odeon

On the eastern side of Leicester Square is The Odeon Leicester Square. (There is a second Odeon on the western end of the square's southern side.)

In 1920 Oscar Deutsch (1893-1941) entered the film business by acting as the Midlands agent for a film distribution company.

In 1930 Deutsch opened his first Odeon cinema in Birmingham's Perry Barr; Odeon was an acronym for `Otto Deutsch entertains our nation'. During the early 1930s Deutsch was careful to build his cinemas in relatively prosperous areas which had growing populations. As a result, his chain was weighted towards the south-east. He did not seek to challenge established cinemas or to buy existing chains. By the mid-1930s he had developed his business into one of the principal circuits.

Deutsch benefitted from an alliance with the American studio United Artists, which took a stake in Odeon. In May 1937 Odeon merged with County, another circuit in which United Artists had a holding. Thereafter, Odeon started to acquire established cinemas and became a national chain.

The Moon Under Water

To the south of the Odeon is The Moon Under Water, a J.D.Wetherspoon pub.

J.D.Wetherspoon

The J.D.Wetherspoon pub company was founded by Tim Martin, a New Zealander barrister, who was unable to find anywhere that he wanted to go to for a drink and so set about doing something about his predicament.

Martin named the Wetherspoon business after a particularly straight-laced school teacher who had taught him and whom he regarded as being about the last person ever likely to run a pub. The chain's use of `Moon' comes from a 1946 essay in which George Orwell (1903-1950) described his ideal pub `The Moon Under Water' which had every characteristic that he desired in a pub other than the fact that it did not exist.

Martin opened the first Wetherspoon pub in 1983. He has specialised in converting previously unlicenced premises into Wetherspoon outlets rather than buying those pubs which the big breweries wished to sell off. The company has had a close relationship with the brewer Scottish & Newcastle.

J.D.Wetherspoon has refined its formula over the years to its current character. It is currently seeking to develop beyond its London base.

Savile House

Savile House occupied a site just to the west of the centre of the north side of the Leicester Square. The Empire cinema now occupies the site.

Following the 1751 death of his father, Prince George (the future King George III) (1738-1820) moved into Savile House. He moved out of the house upon inheriting the throne in 1760.

The Gordon Riots of 1780

In the 1670s a series of laws were passed which excluded Catholics and those Protestants who were not members of the Church of England from the political mainstream of English life. (Individual Catholics and non-Anglican Protestants continued to exercise political influence, but they could not sit in Parliament.)

The first Catholic Relief Act of 1778 started the long process by which Catholics were brought back into the mainstream of British political life. The measure was intended to create greater domestic harmony, the American War of Independence then being in progress on the other side of the Atlantic. However, the law proved deeply unpopular with many of London's middle-class Anglican citizens. In 1780 a protest was organised by the M.P. Lord George Gordon (1751-1793). The protest got out of hand and degenerated into several days of rioting which had to be suppressed by the military.

During the Gordon Riots, Savile House was attacked because Sir George Savile M.P. (1726-1780), a proponent of religious toleration, had introduced the Catholic Relief Act into Parliament.

The Catholic Emancipation Act of 1829 permitted Catholics to sit in Parliament. (There still remained a number of measures which affected Catholics and non-Anglican Protestants.)

Leicster Place
Leicester House

From the eastern end of the north side of Leicester Square rises Leicester Place, which occupies what was once the site of Leicester House (1635), the town house of the Sydney Earls of Leicester.

The House is best remembered as the home of various members of the Hanoverian dynasty, a particularly dysfunctional royal family.

In 1717 the Prince of Wales (the future King George II) (1683-1760) quarrelled with his father King George I (1660-1727), moved out of his apartments in St.James's Palace and took up residence in Leicester House.

In 1742 the now King George II's son Frederick Prince of Wales (1707-1751) moved into the house.

The Equestrian Statue of King George I

In a fine piece of point scoring Prince Frederick went to the trouble of erecting in Leicester Fields (now Leicester Square) an equestrian statue of his grandfather, King George I. The nub of this gesture being that, in Frederick's view, George I was a king who it was worth raising a statue to whereas King George II was not.

The statue went on to have a somewhat chequered history. It was taken down for the last time 1871, thereafter it disappeared.

Church of Notre Dame de France

On the right (east) side of Leicester Place is the Church of Notre Dame de France.

Barker's Panorama

In 1793 the painter Robert Barker (1739-1806) opened a panorama show in Leicester Place. The Panorama, which consisted of paintings and optical illusions, enabled people to see spectacular images of faraway places and events. The shows were carried on until 1864.

In 1868 the building was acquired by French Catholics. The circular wall of the Church of Notre Dame de France, is a relic from the C18th `panorama'.

The Prince Charles Cinema

The Prince Charles Cinema is at the northern end of Leicester Place, on the eastern corner of the junction with Lisle Street. The price of the Prince Charles's tickets tends to be cheap by London standards.

The Rocky Horror Show

The Prince Charles has for years laid on late-night screenings of the movie `The Rocky Horror Picture Show'.

Richard O'Brien conceived of The Rocky Horror Show in 1965. The Show was largely the fruit of his having grown up in a time-warp (provincial New Zealand), watching old horror films on television. The Show was launched as a musical in The Royal Court's Theatre Upstairs and became something of a minor hit. It was turned into a movie which failed to make much of an impact at the box-office. However, in the United States a cinema started to run late night screenings of it and thus the cult was born.

Old Slaughter's

Cranbourn Street is an eastward continuation of the northern side of Leicester Square. One of the buildings which was demolished in order to enable the street to be built in 1843 was Old Slaughter's, which stood on the western side of the Charing Cross Road.

In 1692 Thomas Slaughter (d.1740) founded what became Old Slaughter's Coffee House in a building on the west side of St.Martin's Lane. The coffee house's customers included the writer and magistrate Henry Fielding (1707-1754), the novelist, playwright and poet Oliver Goldsmith (1728-1774), and the painter and engraver William Hogarth (1697-1764).

The Royal Society for the Prevention of Cruelty to Animals

The Treatment of Cattle Act of 1822 was the first instance of animal welfare legislation. The measure was sponsored by Richard Martin M.P. (1754-1834) and the 2nd Lord Erskine (1776-1855). Its passage stimulated the Rev. Arthur Broome, the vicar of Bromley-by-Bow, to call for a public meeting held at Old Slaughter's Coffee House to found what became the Society for the Prevention of Cruelty to Animals.

In 1840 Queen Victoria (1819-1901) granted the Society the right to term itself `Royal'. (Europeans sometimes draw attention to the fact that the Society for the Prevention of Cruelty to Children is not Royal. Indeed, it was not founded until 1884.)

In March 1996 the Charity Commission told the R.S.P.C.A. to tone down its protests about animal experiments and not to campaign against experiments which are regarded as benefitting mankind.

Direction

Cross over Charing Cross Road. Continue along Cranbourn Street. Turn left into Upper St.Martin's Lane.

Stringfellows

On the right, at No. 16 Upper St.Martin's Lane, is Stringfellows the nightclub. Peter Stringfellow started in the nightclub business with the Black Cat Club in his native Sheffield in 1962. He moved his activities to London in 1980 and opened

Stringfellows on Upper St.Martin's Lane. In the late 1980s he moved to America but is once again active in Britain.

Direction
Turn left into West Street.

The Ivy
On the left, at the junction of West Street and Litchfield Street, is The Ivy restaurant, which has long been intimately associated with London's theatrical life. It was opened in 1911.

St.Martin's Theatre
On the right is St.Martin's Theatre, which houses the West End production of `The Mousetrap', which was written by the detective fiction author Agatha Christie (1890-1976). The play started its run at The Amdassadors Theatre in November 1952 and transferred to St.Martin's Theatre in 1974.

Direction
Turn around. Walk back to Upper St.Martin's Lane and turn left.
Go northwards along Monmouth Street.

Seven Dials
Monmouth Street runs into Seven Dials Dials. The district's development was started by Thomas Neale the Master of Mint (d.c1699) during the 1690s. The area acquired a bad reputation as a slum and thieves' den.

In 1773 the original Seven Dials monument which stood in the centre of where the roads converge was dismantled. For a long time, this was held to have happened because a rumour somehow started that treasure had been buried beneath it. If so, the gold hungry mob were remarkably considerate in their dismantling of the monument. Its taking down was actually a piece of social engineering; it was thought that the monument provided a gathering place for anti-social elements. (It does not seem to have been considered that by dismantling it more space was being created for more anti-social elements to assemble in.)

The monument went on to lead a somewhat peripatetic life until it was finally re-erected on Weybridge Green.

The current Seven Dials monument (1989) is a replica of the original.

Direction
Turn right into Earlham Street (the second road to the right).

The Donmar Warehouse
On the left, at No. 41 Earlham Street, is The Donmar Warehouse.

One of the former uses of The Donmar's building was as a banana ripening warehouse. The theatre owner Donald Albery (1914-1988) bought the building in 1960 and converted it into a small theatre, naming it after himself and the ballerina Margot Fonteyn.

In 1976 the Royal Shakespeare Company took over The Donmar Warehouse and used it as a showcase for new writing. The theatre is no longer run by the Company but has retained an innovative reputation.

EuroBananas

The early and mid-1990s saw a banana war between the EuroBanana and the DollarBanana. EuroBananas come predominantly from Anglophone and Francophone parts of the Caribbean (Martinique and Guadeloupe are legally integral parts of France) although some are grown in Crete, Madeira and the Canary Islands. DollarBananas come from Spanish-speaking Latin America. The conflict was in large between American fruit companies and the British and French governments, which regarded themselves as being obliged not to undermine the island economies which were underpinned by banana exports.

Direction

At the end of Earlham Street, turn left into Neal Street. At the north end of Neal Street, turn left and cross over first Monmouth Street and then Shaftesbury Avenue. Once over the road, turn right and walk up the Avenue until you reach St.Giles High Street. Turn left into St.Giles High Street.

St.Giles-in-the-Fields

On the left is the Church of St.Giles-in-the-Fields.

The Leper Hospital of St.Giles

A hospital for lepers (named after their patron saint St.Giles) was founded on the site of St.Giles's in 1101 by Queen Matilda (1080-1118), the consort of King Henry I (1069-1135).

The church started out as the chapel of this monastic hospital but soon started serving the local people. The hospital was closed by King Henry VIII (1491-1547) in 1539.

The Great Plague of 1665

The Great Plague of 1665 is reputed to have first broken out in the parish of St.Giles-in-the-Fields. The church's rebuilding in 1733 was in part caused by structural damaged caused by the necessity in 1665 of burying numerous corpses in a very short period of time, thereby unsettling the soil in a way which the normal burial rate did not.

(From 1910 to 1918 an outbreak of plague occurred in south-east Suffolk, the first case being reported in Freston, a village to the south of Ipswich. The outbreak was probably connected with the plague which broke out in China in the 1850s.)

The Journey To Tyburn

St.Giles-in-the-Fields had a tradition of concern for outcasts continued for many centuries. The church extended a `cup of charity' (the cup usually being full of beer) to Newgate prisoners who were on their way to to be hanged at Tyburn.

(Reputedly, the expression `gone west' (for someone having died) refers to the westward journey from Newgate to Tyburn. (However, it may also have a root in Celtic mythology.))

Centre Point

The white skyscraper is Centre Point (1965), which was designed by Seifert & Company. In November 1995 the National Heritage Secretary bestowed listed building status upon the structure.

Harry Hyams

The developer Harry Hyams built up the property company Oldham Estates. Hyams developed the company as a business which only acquired properties that it could let out to blue chip clients. He was the person behind the 15-year controversy of Centre Point. Planning permission was applied for in 1959 and the building was finished by 1965. Hyams then left it vacant. He had the perception to realise that, in view of the level of inflation in the British economy during the 1960s and 1970s, Oldham's long-term profits from the building would be damaged if it entered into an unfavourable covenant. Therefore, he utilised the company's cash flow to wait until the market had reached a favourable state from Oldham's viewpoint. All the time, Centre Point's value was rocketing.

In September 1987 MEPC, a rival property company, purchased Oldham Estates by buying the Co-operative Insurance Society's 67% stake in the company. Hyams contested the takeover. He now has a minority holding in MEPC. In the mid-1990s MEPC's profits were in large part derived from its Oldham Estates properties.

Government Net Curtains

The brick edifice on the north side of the east end of St.Giles High Street is a government building. Net curtains are a feature of many government buildings in central London. The curtains' purpose is to mitigate the effect of flying glass in the event of a bomb exploding nearby.

Direction

Cross over to the north side of St.Giles High Street. Turn right and walk eastwards back down to Shaftesbury Avenue. At Shaftesbury Avenue turn left into the Avenue section which leads northwards towards Bloomsbury Street.

James Smith & Sons

On the right, on the south-east corner of the junction of Bloomsbury Street and New Oxford Street, at No. 53 New Oxford Street, is the umbrella shop of James Smith & Sons, which was founded in 1830. The business has been here since 1867.

Direction

Cross to the north side of the eastern section of New Oxford Street. Walk east along New Oxford Street. When New Oxford Street joins Bloomsbury Way, go along Bloomsbury Way.

St.George Bloomsbury Way

On the left is the Church of St.George Bloomsbury Way (1731), which was built under the Fifty New Churches Act of 1711. The church was designed by the architect Nicholas Hawksmoor (1661-1736). It was built in large part because the respectable parishioners, who inhabited the newer, northern part of the parish of St.Giles-in-the-Fields, disliked having to pass through the notorious, thief-infested Rookery, on their way to and from St.Giles-in-the-Fields. (The Rookery was the setting for William Hogarth's (1697-1764) print `Gin Lane' (1751.)
The construction of New Oxford Street (1849) destroyed the Rookery.

St.George

St.George was a Christian martyr who died at Lydda (in modern Turkey) in the early C3rd. In the C6th stories of his supposed exploits began to be attached to him. In the C12th he became associated with the slaying of a dragon; this association may have derived from the myth of Perseus, who is supposed to have slain a sea monster near Lydda.

St.George became known to the English as a result of the Crusades to the Holy Lands. King Edward III (1312-1377) turned him into the national saint.

Direction

Retrace your way to New Oxford Street. Turn right into Museum Street.

Mudie's

On the western corner of New Oxford Street and Museum Street was Mudie's the commercial lending library.

Charles Mudie's (1818-1890) father was a stationer and newspaper seller who ran a small circulating library from his shop. In 1840 Mudie opened his own shop on what is now Southampton Row, and in 1842 he established his own lending collection. His literary tastes ran towards the theological and the philosophical.

His library was much used by students of the newly established University of London. Mudie established the practice whereby, for the price of a guinea (£1.05p), an individual could borrow a book from the collection for up to a year or exchange it for another book; at the time, many books cost more than a guinea. Mudie's business grew rapidly. Part of its appeal lay in his policy of stocking `worthwhile' novels, so that subscribers could be sure that they were not going to be shocked or dismayed by a volume they took out.

In 1852 the firm moved into its New Oxford Street premises. Branches were established in provincial cities, such as Manchester and Birmingham, as well as in other parts of London. By the 1860s Mudie was a major force in English publishing, one whose tastes could influence the size of print runs and the pricing of a book. In the 1880s his influence went into decline, undermined in part by the growth in literacy which led publishers to develop popularly-priced reprints.

Museum Tavern

At the end of Museum on the right is The Museum Tavern, a fine Victorian-style pub.

Direction

Turn right into Great Russell Street.

British Museum

On the left (north) side of Great Russell Street is the British Museum.
Montagu House and The Empress of China

The first building on the site which is now occupied by the British Museum occupied was a town house (1686) built by Ralph Montagu 1st Duke of Montagu (1638-1709). The duke had grand ideas about the style in which he should be accommodated and rather stretched his fortune in executing them. In 1692 he recouped his fortune through marrying, as his second wife, the widowed Duchess of Albemarle (1654-1734). The duchess was extremely wealthy, she was also extremely insane. She refused to consider any proposal that was not from a crowned head. Faced with such a situation, Montagu told her that he was the Emperor of China.

Montagu's son, the 2nd Duke (1690-1749), found the house too large and chose instead to reside in a house in Richmond Terrace, Whitehall.

In 1755 Montagu House was bought as the home for the British Museum.

Sir Hans Sloane

Sir Hans Sloane (1660-1753) was an Irish-born physician who, during the first half of the C18th, had an immense annual income derived from the fees he was able to charge his patients. It rose to be higher than that of many of his aristocratic clients. He used his wealth to purchase property (notably the manor of Chelsea) and to collect a broad range of antiquarian and natural history artefacts.

The British Museum

In 1753 Sir Hans died. He left his collections to the nation on condition that a sum of £20 000 - far less than the current value - was paid to his heirs. Parliament voted money for the purchase of the collection which was duly acquired.

Montagu House was bought in 1755 with the proceeds from a state lottery and in 1759 the British Museum was opened as a secular, national institution.

From the early C19th through to the early C20th the Museum was continually physically altering itself, extending and rebuilding. Finally, it began to eject parts of itself. In 1881 the Museum's Natural History collection was moved to South Kensington where it became the Natural History Museum.

Egyptology

India made Egypt of interest to the British. In 1798 Napoleon Bonaparte sought to overthrow British dominance in India. The quickest way for him to get there was via Egypt. His attempt was thwarted by Lord Nelson (1758-1805) at the Battle of the Nile.

At the end of the C18th there was a contemporary fascination with the ancient world. That Egypt had a long and ancient history was appreciated but little could be known about it because the hieroglyphs were indecipherable. However, one of Napoleon's officers uncovered the Rosetta Stone which subsequently passed into British hands. The Stone was deciphered by Thomas Young (1773-1829).

(Egyptian items began to appear in London's sales rooms. The architect Sir John Soane (1753-1837) was able to purchase the sarcophagus of Seti I, which can be viewed in Sir John Soane's Museum in Lincoln's Inn Fields.)

Tutenkhamun

The 5th Earl of Carnarvon (1866-1923) provided the financial wherewithal for the adventurer-archaeologist Howard Carter (1874-1939) to excavate the tomb of Tutenkhamun. Thereby, Carnarvon is supposed to have brought upon himself the `curse of Tutenkhamun'. When he died in Cairo in 1923 the lights of his apartment are supposed to have blacked out and his dog back home in England to have died.

(Howard Carter's grave is in Putney Vale Cemetry.)

Dame Barbara Cartland

The reputed reason as to why the romantic novelist Dame Barbara Cartland is particularly inclined to wear pink clothes is because in 1927 Howard Carter took her into Tutenkhamun's tomb. The tomb was decorated with a lot of bright pink.

The Elgin Marbles

The Elgin Marbles are a collection of sculptures and architectural details removed from the Parthenon at Athens. The 7th Earl of Elgin (1766-1841) was the British government's envoy extraordinary at Constantinople from 1799 to 1803. In a private capacity, he bought the Marbles from the Turkish authorities. In 1816 the British Museum purchased the Marbles from the earl.

The Elgin Marbles have been the cause of a long running dispute between the Museum and the Greek government. The latter believes that the Marbles belong in Greece while the former states that it has full legal ownership of them in international law.

Tyndale's Bible

William Tyndale (c1492-1536) translated the New Testament into English, thereby making it accessible to non-Latin speakers for the first time. The book had the effect of promoting the Reformation in England. In 1526 3000 copies of Tyndale's translation were printed in Germany. Cuthbert Tunstall the Bishop of London (1474-1559) ordered the destruction of all the copies of the book which came into the possession of his diocesan authorities. In 1535 Tyndale became a prisoner of the Catholic authorities and the following year was strangled publicly, his body then being burnt. The only surviving complete copy of Tyndale's Bible is in the possession of the British Library.

Treasure Trove

The original treasure trove law dated from 1195, a time when King Richard I the Lionheart (1157-1199) wanted cash so that he could afford to conduct wars overseas.

If gold and/or silver appears to have been deliberately hidden, in order to avoid it being assessed as part of an individual's wealth, then it is regarded as treasure trove and becomes the property of the crown. However, if it appears that the item has been mislain accidentally then the item is not treasure trove. If the item is made of a non-precious material or is part of a grave then the item is not treasure trove - in both cases the item may still be of high monetary worth because of its archaeological value. When an item is not treasure trove it is usual for the finder and the owner of the land (who are usually not the same person) to come to some agreement about how the item should be disposed of.

Treasure trove hearings of coroners' courts determine whether or not an item is treasure trove.

Since the reign of King George III (1738-1820), treasure trove has not passed into the personal possession of the reigning Sovereign but rather it has gone to the Treasury. When an item is declared to be treasure trove the Treasury takes possession of it but must pay the finder/landowner the item's full value. When an item becomes treasure trove then the British Museum has the first right to buy it from the Treasury. The Museum makes purchases either out of its own (extremely modest) purchasing budget or it sets up an appeal to try to raise funds for the purchase. If the Museum does not buy the item, and nor do other museums to which it is offered, then the item is returned to the finder/landowner who is free to keep the item or to dispose of it however s/he wishes to do so which is usually by sale at auction.

In the mid-1990s about 25 finds a year were ruled treasure trove.

Treasure trove was reformed by the Treasure Act of 1996.

The British Library

The British Library is one of the great libraries of the world. While it may be smaller than those of the United States and Russia it outstrips them in many areas, having an advantage over them in terms of its greater age.

The Library developed out of a number of manuscript collections - the Cotton, the Harleian, and the Sloane. The Cottonian Library was assembled by the Cotton family in the late C17th. The collection was presented to the nation at the behest of Sir John Cotton (1621-1701). In the 1710s the Cottonian Library was housed successively in Cotton House in Westminster, Essex House off the Strand, and Ashburnham House in Westminster. The Harleian Collection of Manuscripts was assembled by Robert Harley 1st Earl of Oxford (1661-1724) and his son Edward Harley the 2nd Earl (1689-1741). In 1753 the latter's daughter, the Duchess of Portland (1715-1785), sold the collection to the government for £10 000. The purchase was authorised by the British Museum Foundation Act of 1753.

The King's Library

The King's Library contains changing displays of books and documents. Its walls are lined with cases of tomes.

Lord Lumley (c1533-1609) was the great book collector of Elizabethan England. His library was bought by Henry Prince of Wales (1594-1612), King James I's (1566-1625) eldest son, and thus became the foundation of the first Royal Library.

For an author to establish copyright of a book a copy of it had to be registered at Stationers' Hall in the City. The Royal Library had the right to receive a copy of every book registered with the Stationers' Company. In 1757 King George II (1683-1760) gave the Royal Library to the British Museum, with the gift the right of receipt was transferred to the Museum.

George's grandson and successor, King George III (1738-1820), built up a fresh and extremely splendid new Royal Library. George III's son, King George IV (1762-1830), gave this library to the British Museum in 1823. The size of George III's library necessitated extensive work building being carried out on the Museum for it to be accommodated.

The Reading Room and Library were opened in 1857.

In 1973, the British Library became a separate institution. It was formed through the merger the library departments of the British Museum and various other national libraries.

Copyright and Acquisitions

By law, a copy of every printed literary item (including dress patterns) published in Britain must be deposited with the British Library. Such is required as part of the copyrighting process. There have long been mutterings from within the British Library that large swathes of romantic fiction and vanity publishing are a positive drain on the Library in view of their initial processing and subsequent storage costs.

(The university libraries of Cambridge, Oxford, and Trinity College in Dublin, and the national libraries of Wales and Scotland are able to demand copies of books, etc., but are not statutorily obliged to preserve them as is the British Library.)

A Treasury grant assists the Library in its acquisition of other books and items. The Library also acquires items through donation.

Montague Street

Montague Street comes into Great Russell Street from the left (north).

On the right (east), at 29a Montague Street, behind a one storey brick wall is the Bedford Estate Office.

The Bedford Estate Office

In 1550 the Bloomsbury estate was granted to Lord Chancellor Thomas Wriothersley 1st Earl of Southampton (1505-1550).

In 1723 the estate was inherited by the Russell Dukes of Bedford.

The Russells sold most of the estate's freeholds in the early 1950s.

Lord Mansfield and The Gordon Riots

Great Russell Street runs into the north side of Bloomsbury Square.

The eminent judge Lord Chief Justice Lord Mansfield (1705-1793) lived in a house at the northern end of the east side of Bloomsbury Square. The site is now occupied by the London offices of the Liverpool Victoria Friendly Society.

The Gordon Riots took place over 2-8 June 1780. The riots broke out when a march organised by the M.P. Lord George Gordon (1751-1793), to protest at the repeal of anti-Catholic legislation, ran out of control. At one point the rioters tried to storm the Bank of England.

Rioters burned down the town house of Lord Mansfield. Mansfield had publicly supported the Catholic Relief Act. In addition, he was someone who had long been deeply unpopular as the result of his prominent judicial career. The fire destroyed one of the greatest legal libraries ever assembled in Britain. Many of the rioters went on to try to burn down Mansfield's country seat at Kenwood on Hampstead Heath but were diverted into drinking at The Spaniards Inn by the landlord, whereupon he sent for a detachment of soldiers who rounded them up.

21 of the riots' ringleaders were tried, found guilty, and hanged. There was a custom whereby a criminal was sometimes executed on the site of his crime. Two of the ringleaders of the riots, John Gray and Charles King, were executed in Bloomsbury Square outside what was left of Mansfield's house. (The last time a place of crime execution took place in 1816.)

Lord George was tried but acquitted. On his death he was buried in an unmarked grave in the grounds of St.James's Chapel, Hampstead Road.

Sir Hans Sloane

The north side of Bloomsbury Square runs into Bloomsbury Place.

On the left, at No. 4 Bloomsbury Place, was the home of the physician and public benefactor Sir Hans Sloane (1660-1753) from 1695 to 1742.

Direction

At the junction of Bloomsbury Place and Southampton Row turn right into Southampton Row.

Central St.Martins

On the left is the `Central' part of the Central St.Martins College of Design & Art.

The Central School of Arts & Design

The Central School of Arts & Crafts opened in Southampton Row in 1896, its first principal was the architect W.R.Lethaby (1857-1931).

The Central St.Martins College of Art & Design was formed in 1989 by the merger of the Central School with the St.Martins School of Art. Central St.Martins is a constituent part of the London Institute federation.

Sicilian Avenue

On the right is Sicilian Avenue (1905). On the left (south-west) side of Sicilian Avenue is Skoob Books, a well-known secondhand bookshop.

The Princess Louise

On the right is High Holborn. On the south (left) side of High Holborn, at No. 208 High Holborn, is the Princess Louise pub, a very fine Victorian-style pub.

To Finish

Walk to Holborn underground station which is on the south side of the junction of High Holborn and Kingsway. The station is on the Piccadilly and Central Lines.

To Continue

Cross High Holborn and walk south along the east side of Kingsway.

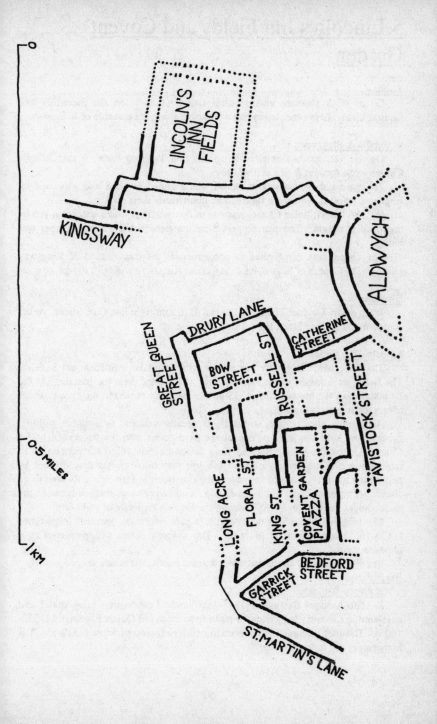

5.Lincoln's Inn Fields and Covent Garden

To Start
Go to High Holborn underground station which is on the Piccadilly and Central Lines. Leave the station and walk south along the east side of Kingsway.

St.Cecilia & St.Anselm
On the left, on the corner of Kingsway and Twyford Place, is the Catholic Church of St.Anslem & St.Cecilia (1909).

The Sardinian Ambassador's chapel was founded in 1648 and was used by English Catholics, who at the time had no churches of their own.

In 1780 the Sardinian Chapel was one of the buildings which was destroyed by the Gordon rioters. The worshippers were compensated and a new chapel was built.

The chapel was demolished to accommodate the construction of Kingsway (1905). The Church of St.Anselm & St.Cecilia Kingsway was built to replace it.

Direction
Walk down Twyford Place. At the end of it, turn right into Gate Street. At the southern end of Gate Street lies Lincoln's Inn Fields.

Lincoln's Inn Fields
The three fields originally belonged to the hospitals of St.John and St.Giles. The fields were leased to the Inns of Law which used them for pasture. At the Dissolution of the Monasteries (1535-40) the property passed to the crown, which continued leasing it to the Inns.

As London grew in size, so the fields became valuable as potential building ground. In 1613 the lease of one of the fields came into the possession of Sir Charles Cornwallis who petitioned King James I (1566-1625) for permission to build upon it. The Society of Lincoln's Inn responded to this development by petitioning the Privy Council to prevent the construction from being allowed to go ahead. After much legal toing-and-froing an agreement was reached between the leaseholders and the Inn in 1657 (during the English Republic of 1649-60).

Lincoln's Inn Fields was developed to a plan which the architect Inigo Jones (1573-1652) had drawn up in 1618. The square's centre was preserved as a pleasure ground.

In 1894 the central space was opened to the public. (It is now fenced.)

Executions
Anthony Babington
In 1586 Anthony Babington (1561-1586) and 13 others were hung, drawn and quartered in Lincoln's Inn Fields for plotting to try to kill Queen Elizabeth I (1533-1603). The plot prompted the execution of Mary Queen of Scots (1542-1587) at Fotheringay the following year.

The Rye House Plot

The Rye House Plot of 1683 was an aristocratic conspiracy which took its name from Rye House at Hoddeston in Hertfordshire. The plotters opposed King Charles II's (1630-1685) pro-Catholic policies. They planned to seize the king while he travelled back from Newmarket, having watched his horses race. The plot was discovered and the plotters were seized and tried.

The details of the plot are somewhat murky and may well have extended to Charles's murder. Some of the conspirators were pardoned by the king, others including William Lord Russell (d.1683), the heir-apparent of the Earl of Bedford, were executed in Lincoln's Inn Fields.

Sir John Soane Museum

On the left, at No. 13 Lincoln's Inn Fields (1813), is the Sir John Soane Museum. The town house was designed and built by the architect Sir John Soane (1753-1837), who lived in it until his death. Previously, he had lived at No. 12 (1792), which he had also designed.

In 1833 Sir John obtained an Act of Parliament which preserves Nos. 13-14 Lincoln's Inn Fields as a public museum. He stipulated that his collection of paintings, sculptures, books and architectural fittings should be neither disturbed nor augmented. Thus, the Museum has retained its original character. It includes a number of paintings by William Hogarth (1697-1764).

Direction

Turn around, walk back to where you entered the square, there turn left.

Farrer & Company

At the northern end of the west side of Lincoln's Inn Fields is No. 66 Lincoln's Inn Fields (Powys House), which is now occupied by Farrer & Company who are the archetypal establishment solicitors. The firm's clients include the Queen and the Prince of Wales.

William Marsden

On the right, at No. 65 Lincoln's Inn Fields, is what was once the home of the physician Dr. William Marsden (1796-1867), the founder of two London hospitals - the Royal Free (1828) and the Royal Marsden (1851).

The Royal Free

In 1827, on a winter's night, Marsden found a young woman suffering from acute exposure in the churchyard of St.Andrew Holborn but was unable to gain admission for her at any hospital. She died. The incident led him to found in 1828 the London General Institution for the Gratuitous Care of Malignant Diseases, which opened in Grenville Street, Hatton Gardens.

In 1837, at the suggestion of its new patron Queen Victoria, the hospital changed its name to the Royal Free Hospital. In 1843 the Royal Free moved into a former army barracks in the Gray's Inn Road, and, in 1974, it moved to Hampstead.

The Royal Marsden

Marsden founded the Cancer Hospital in 1851. It was London's first institution to dedicate itself solely to the treatment of patients suffering from cancer.

Sir Alfred Beatty (1875-1968) made his fortune through mining interests in Africa and gave £40 000 to help establish the Cancer Hospital Research Institute. The Institute opened in 1939 in what had been the Freemasons' Hospital (and before that the Chelsea Hospital for Women) in the Fulham Road.

In 1954 the Cancer Hospital changed its name to the Royal Marsden.

Direction

Walk down the square's western side.

Lindsey House

On the right, at Nos. 59 and 60 Lincoln's Inn Fields, is Lindsey House. The House has white columns on a terracotta background.

The Berties were Lincolnshire landowners who held the Earldom of Lindsey and the Dukedom of Ancaster. A number of the family's London town houses have survived bearing the name `Lindsey House'. The building has been attributed to the architect Inigo Jones (1573-1652).

The House has been divided.

Direction

Walk south along Lincoln Inn's Field's western side. At the square's south-west corner look along the square's southern side from west to east.

The Imperial Cancer Research Fund

The nearest large building on the south side is the Imperial Cancer Research Fund. (Along with higher education (Imperial College) and the chemicals industry (Imperial Chemical Industries a.k.a. ICI), cancer appears to be the last vestige of Empire.)

Lincoln's Inn Fields Theatre

In the centre of the square's south side once stood Lincoln's Inn Fields Theatre.

In 1660 King Charles II (1630-1685) granted a patent to Sir William D'Avenant (1606-1668) and Thomas Killigrew (1612-1683) for the `King's Company of Players'. In 1660, under the patent's protection, D'Avenant built Lincoln's Inn Fields Theatre.

John Gay

The satirist the Rev. Jonathan Swift (1667-1745) suggested to the composer John Gay (1685-1732) that he should look at London's underworld for possible subject matter. The city's criminal world was then under the dominion of Jonathan Wild (c1682-1725). Gay saw the scope for viewing Wild as an Olympian figure and thus was born `The Beggar's Opera'. `The Opera' was first performed in 1728 in a production staged by the actor-manager John Rich (c1682-1761); it was a great success and a bon mot was coined that the work `had made Rich gay and Gay rich'.

While the opera was in part a critique of the political morality of the day, none of the characters was intended to represent the then Prime Minister Sir Robert Walpole (1676-1745). However, the politician's displeasure at the `Opera' was sufficient for him to have a ban placed on `Polly' its sequel. Gay had accepted the patronage of the Duchess of Queensberry (d.1777), who hated Walpole with a passion. She was happy to disrupt the social pleasures of others if it gave her an opportunity to vent her vitriol towards the man. Walpole returned part of the custom in kind.

In 1732 Rich moved to Covent Garden.

The theatre building was demolished in 1848.

Nuffield College of Surgical Sciences

William Morris Lord Nuffield (1877-1963) created the car manufacturing company British Motor Corporation. Nuffield used his vast wealth to make public benefactions and established the Nuffield Trust to continue his good works after his death. Unfortunately, much of the Trust's wealth was tied up in shares in the company. As the British motor industry slipped into crisis during the 1960s and 1970s so the Trust's income was miniaturised. (The private Nuffield was by no means altogether a saint. He is reputed to have been of the habit of having his former mistresses marry his managers.)

The British Motor Corporation is now known as Rover and since 1994 it has been a subsidiary of BMW of Germany.

The Royal College of Surgeons

In 1540 the Guild of Surgeons was united with the Barbers' Company; both trades involved the cutting of people. In 1745 the two professions separated, the surgeons forming the Company of Surgeons. In 1797 the Company bought a house in Lincoln's Inn Fields.

In 1800 the Company of Surgeons became the Royal College of Surgeons of England.

The Hunterian Collection

The Hunterian Collection of physiological specimens was amassed by the surgeon John Hunter (1728-1793) and was originally housed in Hunter's home at No. 28 Leicester Square. Hunter had to extend the house in order to accommodate the collection.

Hunter requested in his will that his collection should be offered to the government for purchase. In 1799 £15 000 was made available to buy the collection. It was then passed on to the Company of Surgeons.

Before being bombed during the Second World War, the Royal College of Surgeon's physiological museum was the finest of its kind in the world.

Titles

Surgeons are traditionally known as `Mr.'. No doubt this is to distinguish them from plain `Drs.'.

The Land Registry

At the eastern end of Lincoln's Inn Fields southern side is the Land Registry, which was established in 1862. The Registry has records of the ownership of every property in London, freehold and leasehold, which has changed hands since 1879. Its records do not include its own Lincoln's Inn Fields building, because the building has been constantly in government ownership throughout the Registry's operation.

Lincoln's Inn

At the southern end of the square's eastern side is a gateway to Lincoln's Inn.

The Inn probably derives its name from Henry de Lacy 3rd Earl of Lincoln (c1249-1311). The earl is said to have had a particular interest in legal matters, often being called upon by King Edward I (1239-1307) to give his counsel. Lawyers are meant to have been living upon part of the site since the end of the C13th. The Society of Lincoln's Inn did not own the site's freehold until the late C16th.

The Old Hall
From 1733 to 1883 the Court of Chancery sat in Lincoln Inn's Old Hall (1492). The fictional case of Jarndyce versus Jarndyce in Charles Dickens's (1812-1870) novel `Bleak House' (1853) is meant to have been heard there. The fictional Jarndyce case was modelled on the real apparently interminable Thelusson suit.

The merchant Peter Thelusson (1737-1797) died in 1797 leaving a fortune of over £600 000, which he left tied up in a legal settlement which was intended to operate until the time of the death of his final surviving great-grandson. The size of the fortune acted as a stimulus for litigation. The matter was eventually determined by a ruling made in the House of Lords in 1857 (four years after the publication of `Bleak House').

(The settlement of the case seems to have prompted one branch of the Thelusson family to refurbish their country seat, Brodsworth near Doncaster, Yorkshire. Subsequently, the house was not redecorated. As a result, Brodsworth is one of the few surviving examples of unaltered High Victorian country house interior decoration.)

Direction
Leave the square by crossing Sardinia Street and walking into Portsmouth Street.

The Old Curiosity Shop
On the left of Portsmouth Street is The Old Curiosity Shop, which dates from 1567 and is the oldest retail shop in England. During the C19th the shop adopted the name The Old Curiosity Shop, in the hopes of being associated with the Charles Dickens's (1812-1870) 1841 novel of the same name. (The actual shop which Dickens referred to was almost certainly in Orange Street at the southern end of Charing Cross Road and no longer exists, the site being occupied by a statue of the actor Sir Henry Irving (1838-1905).

Direction
Stay with Portsmouth Street as it crosses to the left. At the junction with Portugal Street, turn right into Portugal Street.

Portugal Street
Portugal Street was named as a compliment to Queen Catherine of Braganza (1638-1705), the wife of King Charles II (1630-1685). Queen Catherine was a member of the Portugese royal family. She lived in Somerset House on the Strand.

Direction
At the junction of Portugal Street with Clare Market, turn left into Clare Market and then turn right into Houghton Street.

The London School of Economics - The L.S.E.

In 1894 Henry Hunt Hutchinson, a member of the Fabian Society, committed suicide. Hutchinson's will directed that his trustees - who included Sidney Webb (1859-1947) - should use the residue of his estate for socially progressive purposes. In 1895 the London School of Economics opened at No. 9 John Street, Adelphi, with Webb as its first chairman.

In 1900 the School became a college of the University of London. In 1902 it moved to Clare Market. The newspaper editor John Passmore Edwards (1823-1911) gave money towards the cost of the Clare Market buildings.

The London School of Economics is the world's largest higher education institute devoted to the social sciences. Its success in attracting American students has led to the quip that L.S.E. stands for `Let's See Europe'.

The Beveridge Report of 1942

The Beveridge Report of 1942 led to the birth of the welfare state. The Report was one of the most profound instances of social science shaping British society and politics.

In the 1900s William Beveridge (later Lord Beveridge) (1879-1963) worked at Toynbee Hall where he investigated the nature of employment and unemployment in London's East End. In the late 1910s he sat in the Commons briefly as a Liberal M.P.. In 1919 he became the Director of the L.S.E., moving to Oxford in 1937 to become the Master of University College.

At the outbreak of the Second World War there was a wide array of social insurance schemes. It was generally thought to be proper that something should be done to tidy up this state of affairs, especially in view of the vital role that the unions were playing in the war effort. In June 1941 a committee was appointed to study the administrative structure of the schemes; the committee's chairman was Beveridge.

The government turned the committee into an advisory body. Frank Pakenham (later Lord Longford) worked as Beveridge's right-hand man. The Beveridge Report - the Social Insurance & Allied Service Report - was published in December 1942 and was the blueprint for the modern British welfare state.

Sir Karl Popper

The philosopher Sir Karl Popper (1902-1994) moved from his native Austria to New Zealand in 1937 and in 1945 he came to Britain to take up a position at the L.S.E.. Popper's most famous work is `The Open Society and Its Enemies' (1945). For an academic philosopher, he had a very large influence outside of his own discipline. His standing was recognised by his having the rare distinction of being made both a Fellow of the British Academy and a Fellow of the Royal Society.

In 1946 Popper addressed Cambridge University's Moral Sciences Club. His fellow Austrian, Ludwig Wittgenstein (1889-1951) attended the seminar. While Popper delivered his paper, Wittgenstein paced up and down in front of the room's fireplace. He found himself unable to agree with Popper on the existence of moral views and, becoming somewhat overwrought, demanded that Popper provide him with an example of one, brandishing a handy poker to help underscore his question. Popper's example of a moral view was that "Hosts should not threaten visiting lecturers with pokers". Wittgenstein stormed out of the room.

To many Britons it was somewhat incongruous that Popper should have spent his final years living in the anonymous south London suburb of Purley.

(The international financier George Soros studied under Popper at the L.S.E. and wrote an unpublished study entitled `The Burden of Consciousness'. Soros was deeply influenced by Popper's concept of the `open society'. It is unlikely that Mr. Soros will spend his final years as a resident of Purley.)

The Phillips Machine

Among economists Bill Phillips, a New Zealander, is best known for the Phillips Curve, an economic theory on the relationship between wage inflation and the rate of unemployment, which he published in 1958. However, Phillips also has the distinction of having, in 1949, built the Phillips Machine, a device which makes economic relationships comprehensible.

The Machine is made up of a series of connected tanks, tubes and valves, through which (usually coloured) water passes. Different individual parts of the machine are held to represent different sections of the economy (e.g., tanks - balances; tubes - exports, savings, and taxation; valves - domestic expenditure, tax rates, and interest rates). If one part of the economy is affected by the opening and closing valves then it is reflected by the level of fluid in the relevant tanks. The Machine allowed economic theories to be modelled with a very small margin of error.

Edward Gellner

Edward Gellner (1925-1995) was a leading academic philosopher and social anthropologist. He studied at the L.S.E. for a Ph.D. on the Berbers of North Africa and was subsequently based there.

Gellner attracted academic attention with his book `Words & Things' (1959), an attack on the then prevailing Oxford linguistic philosophy. Gellner subjected the Oxford philosophers' concepts to an anthropological analysis based on that of Edward Evans-Pritchard (1902-1973) in `Witchcraft, Oracles and Magic Among The Azande' (1937). The Oxford philosopher Gilbert Ryle (1900-1976) refused to review the book and its publication led to a debate on the letters page of The Times newspaper.

Gellner used the same methodology on pyschoanalysis to produce `The Psychoanalytical Movement' (1985). The work was not warmly embraced by psychoanalysts.

Gellner's other work included `The Devil in Modern Philosophy' (1974) which was a study of the relationship between philosophy and contemporary life.

British Library of Political & Economic Science

Attached to the School is the British Library of Political & Economic Science, which was founded in 1896.

Direction

Continue along Houghton Street to The Aldwych. Turn right into The Aldwych.

St.Catherine's House

On the right, at the junction of The Aldwych and Kingsway, is St.Catherine's House, which now houses the Office for National Statistics.

All the births, marriages and deaths that have occured in England and Wales since 1837 have had to be registered with the office and its antecedents.

The Office was moved here from Somerset House in 1973. `Somerset House' is still used demotically by many people to refer to the Office's registry holdings.

Bush House
On the left, at the bottom of Kingsway, is Bush House.

The B.B.C. Empire shortwave service was started in 1932. This acted as the base for the Corporation's wartime services and the Overseas Division.

The Empire Service became the B.B.C. World Service.

The B.B.C. World Service is the only part of the B.B.C. to be funded by a government grant. In 1938 the Foreign Office started funding it, retaining `prescription' rights over which languages should have priority and how many hours might be broadcast in them. The Arabic Service was the first of the B.B.C. World Service services to start broadcasting.

In 1940 the B.B.C. first took office space in Bush House.

The World Service will probably pass down to history as one of the C20th's greatest international literary patrons. Its former British employees have included George Orwell (1903-1950).

Direction
Cross Kingsway. Continue along The Aldwych, which curves to the left. Turn right into Catherine Street.

The Theatre Royal Drury Lane
On the right is the Theatre Royal Drury Lane.

In 1660 King Charles II (1630-1685) granted a patent to Thomas Killigrew (1612-1683) and Sir William D'Avenant (1606-1668) for the `King's Company of Players'. In 1663, under the patent's protection, Killigrew built the first Theatre Royal Drury Lane. It was at this theatre that King Charles met Nell Gwynne (1650-1687), the best remembered of his mistresses.

The Gordon Riots
In 1780 the Theatre Royal Drury Lane was attacked by the Gordon Rioters. The rioters condemned the theatre for having allowed `papists and Frenchmen' to perform there. As a result, a guard was posted outside the theatre. The practice was discontinued in 1796. The French Revolution and the Napoleonic Wars having turned French papists into allies of England.

(A guard was also posted outside the Bank of England, it became known as the Bank Piquet and was not discontinued until 1973.)

His Majesty's Pleasure
James Hadfield was a military veteran who suffered from paranoia. He wanted to die and tried to do so in 1800 by trying to assassinate King George III (1738-1820), believing that he himself would consequently be executed. Hadfield made his assassination attempt at The Theatre Royal, however, he missed the king and was apprehended. At the subsequent trial, Hadfield's lawyer argued that Hadfield was not guilty because he had been insane at the time of the attempt. The court accepted this argument.

To prevent a repetition of such, Parliament passed the Criminal Lunatics Act of 1800, which provided for the detention of individuals who were acquitted of crimes on the grounds of insanity. Such persons were detained until `His Majesty's

Pleasure' was made known. In the early Victorian era the exercise of the Pleasure was transferred from the crown to the Secretary of State for Lunatics.

Sheridan's Fireside

In the C18th and C19th theatres burned down frequently. Richard Brinsley Sheridan (1751-1816) managed the Theatre Royal Drury Lane for many years, enjoying there his greatest successes as actor, manager and playwright. In 1809 the theatre burned down. While it was aflame, Sheridan came to watch the spectacle. As he did so he drank some port ordered from a nearby hostelry. When this sang-froid drew a comment, he remarked "Surely a man may take a glass of wine by his own fireside."

Direction

Turn right into Russell Street.

Crown Court Scottish National Church

On the left is Crown Court. The second building on the left is the Crown Court Scottish National Church, a church of the Church of Scotland.

The Church of Scotland is an Anglican sister church of the Church of England. The Church of Scotland tends to be more liberal than the Church of England on matters such as divorce.

Direction

Turn left into Drury Lane.

The Peabody Trust

The yellow brick building on the right (east) side of Drury Lane is owned by the Peabody Trust.

George Peabody (1795-1869) was an American-born financier, who chose to spend his working life in London. He built up the business from which the investment bank Morgan Grenfell is descended.

In the mid-C19th London experienced an acute housing crisis. At the time, housing was not viewed as lying among the responsibilities of local government. Peabody gave £150 000 to provide housing for London's poor and in 1864 the first Peabody buildings were erected in Whitechapel.

Direction

Turn left into Long Acre.

Freemasons' Hall

Behind you, the building on the far corner of Wild Street and Great Queen Street is Freemasons' Hall (1933).

In the early C18th freemasonry changed from being a craft activity within the building trade to being a social activity which drew together men from diverse social, political and economic backgrounds. In large part, it was symptomatic of a divided and rapidly changing society's need to overcome its own internal tensions. (English Catholics played a leading part in early freemasonry.)

In 1776 the first Freemasons' Hall was erected. The building was designed by Thomas Sandby (1721-1798). It was built further to the east of the present Hall on the site of what is now The Connaught Rooms, which incorporate some of what was the Second Freemasons' Hall.

There are about 300 000 freemasons in Britain.

There are roughly 8000 lodges in England and Wales, of which about 1500 lodges are in London alone, especially so in the City of London. Members of the more staid and hierarchical professions seem to be drawn towards freemasonry. Recruits swear on pain of death and ghastly mutilation not to reveal masonic secrets to outsiders. Morality, fraternity and charity are the brotherhood's stated aims.

The traditional pattern of recruitment was very low-key. In January 1994 the society made noises about seeking to recruit members more widely than it had done hitherto.

Freemasons and The Police

Two of the concerns about police officers being masons are that they may unduly assist the promotion of fellow masons over non-masons and that they may be members of lodges of which criminals are also members.

In April 1995 the Metropolitan Police commissioner ordered the removal of all freemasons from Scotland Yard's anti-corruption squad. This followed the abandonment of an investigation after its existence was leaked at a freemasons' dinner.

In July 1995 the Home Affairs Select Committee voted to launch an inquiry into the influence of Freemasons in the judiciary and police.

Direction

Walk west along Long Acre.

Long Acre

Long Acre developed into a centre of coach-building in the mid-C17th.

Direction

Turn left in Bow Street.

Bow Street

Bow Street Covent Garden takes its name from the road's shape - on a map it looks like a bow.

Bow Street Magistrates Court

On the left, on the corner of Bow Street and Broad Street, is Bow Street Magistrates Court, which is a stipendiary magistrates court..

The Fieldings

In medieval and early modern times law enforcement was handled primarily at the parish level. In London there was a system of parish watchhouses.

As London expanded westward a new lawlessness became evident. As the C18th progressed, it became apparent that the old parish system of law-keeping was unable to maintain order in the West End. Therefore, a system of stipendiary magistrates was set up.

In 1740 Colonel Thomas de Veil became the first Bow Street magistrate, opening his office and court at No. 4 Bow Street, Covent Garden.

Henry Fielding (1707-1754) was one of the first novelists, writing `Joseph Andrews' (1742) and `Tom Jones' (1749). He was a barrister by training. In 1748 he was appointed as the Bow Street stipendiary magistrate. Fielding secured the position because of the services he had provided as a political writer for the 4th Duke of Bedford (1710-1771), who owned much of Covent Garden.

Fielding was the first magistrate to hold the office who thought beyond his own capacity to make the position return an income. He established the Bow Street Runners, an early form of police force.

Fielding died in 1754 but his work was continued and extended by his half-brother Sir John Fielding (d.1780), a person whose achievements were all the more remarkable because he was blind. John Fielding instigated a system of foot patrols on the main roads out of London for a distance of four miles.

After The Fieldings

In 1785 the London & Police Bill failed to get through Parliament.

In 1798, to counter piracy on the river, the Thames police force was created. Initially, its costs were met by a group of West Indian merchants. However, in 1801 the government took the force over.

In 1805 the Bow Street Horse Patrol was established. The Patrol covered the roads out of London for a distance of twenty miles.

The Metropolitan Police force was legislated into existence by the Home Secretary Sir Robert Peel (1788-1850) in 1829 and it absorbed the Patrol. The Bow Street Runners were not included in the Metropolitan Police Force. Instead they remained under the magistrates until they were disbanded in 1839.

The Royal Opera House

On the opposite corner, on the corner of Bow Street and Floral Street, is the Royal Opera House (1858).

John Rich

The C18th actor-manager John Rich (c1682-1761) organised the subscription for the original building of the Covent Garden theatre (1732).

The Beef-steak Society was founded by Rich in 1735. During the winter and spring months, the Society's members would dine once a week on beef with one another. They met in the Theatre until it burnt down in 1808. Thereafter, the Society met in a variety of places before disbanding in 1867.

The Royal Opera House

Covent Garden became an opera house in 1847. It burned down in 1856.

The impressario Frederick Gye (1810-1878) raised the money to build the present Royal Opera House. Its manager Augustus Harris (1825-1873) turned it into one of Europe's foremost opera houses.

The Opera House has had quiet periods. Between 1924 and 1931 opera performances were only put on for a few weeks each summer.

During the Second World War the Opera House was used as a dance hall.

After the Second World War the Covent Garden Opera Trust was set up at the instigation of the economist Lord Keynes (1883-1946). Covent Garden became a national home for opera and ballet.

In 1959 Joan Sutherland became a star through singing the role of Lucia di Lammamor at Covent Garden. Dame Joan retired in 1990.

Direction

Turn right into Floral Street.

Bertorelli's

On the right, at No. 44 Floral Street, is Bertorelli's.

The Bertorelli restaurants were founded by the Bertorelli brothers who came from Bergazzi, a village near Bardi in northern Italy. The brothers started out running English-style cafes in Shoreditch and at Waterloo Bridge. In 1913 they opened one in Charlotte Street which was aimed at providing chauffeurs with food. The clientele became interested in what the brothers cooked for their own meals; the change from English cafes to Italian restaurants followed on. In the 1960s there were six Bertorelli-run restaurants. This is now the only family-run restaurant.

The Spaghetti Harvest Failure

There are still Britons for whom Italian food is something of a novelty.

On 1 April 1957 the B.B.C. Television current affairs programme `Panorama' broadcast a spoof documentary on the supposed failure of the spaghetti harvest due to a late frost. The `report's' `authenticity' was lent considerable weight by the fact that it was narrated by Richard Dimbleby (1913-1965), the foremost broadcast journalist of the day, the man who had provided the commentary for Queen Elizabeth II's coronation four years before.

It is still possible to find Britons who are not altogether sure that pasta does not grow on trees.

Direction

Turn left into James Street.

Paul Smith

On the right, in the western portion of Floral Street, is the showroom of the clothes designer Paul Smith.

Covent Garden

From 1536 until 1918 Covent Garden was owned by the Russell family. Their town house, Bedford House, stood between the Strand and what is now Covent Garden.

In the C17th the 4th Earl of Bedford (1593-1641) decided to take advantage of the westward growth of London by developing the property. Inigo Jones (1573-1652) acted as the earl's planner-architect. The original piazza reflected Jones's knowledge of Italian architecture. (The colonnades on the western section of the piazza's northern side used to be accompanied by others which extended along all four of the piazza's sides.)

In 1671 the 1st Duke of Bedford (1616-1700) received from King Charles II the right to have a daily vegetable-market in Covent Garden.

The 6th Duke (1766-1839) was responsible for the erection of the Central Market Building (1830). The Jubilee Hall was added in 1908.

In 1918 the 11th Duke (1858-1940) sold Covent Garden to the Covent Garden Estate Company Ltd., a private company.

The fruit and vegetable market's second market was created in 1933 to take advantage of the then low bank interest rates.

In 1962 Covent Garden was acquired by the Covent Garden Market Authority, a state body.

In 1966 a 68-acre site at Nine Elms in south London was acquired from British Rail. In November 1974 the market closed and the New Covent Garden fruit and vegetable opened in Nine Elms. Covent Garden Market was left vacant.

The Conservative controlled G.L.C. and a group of developers were eager to redevelop the district by pulling down many of the existing buildings and putting up new structures in their place. However, they were frustrated by opposition from the local community. The area was revitalised in large part through the efforts of young, independent developers who found new uses for Covent Garden's existing buildings.

The restored Covent Market Buildings were re-opened in 1981.

(There remains an indigenous population. The Seven Dials Club in Earlham Street is one of its focusses.)

Direction

Turn right into the north side of the Piazza's western side.

The Dr. Marten Department Store

On the south side of the junction of the Piazza and King Street is the Dr. Marten Department Store.

The Dr. Marten shoe sole was designed by the German entrepreneur Dr. Klaus Maertens. In 1959 Bill Griggs bought the British rights to the brand and the first Dr. Marten boot was sold in 1960.

The company's product developed over the years from being a medical and workplace brand into having a fashion image.

St.Paul Covent Garden

To the left (south) of Dr. Marten's is the Church of St.Paul Covent Garden (1633).

The 4th Earl of Bedford (1593-1641) did not like the idea of the expense of building a church for the inhabitants of the new suburb he had created. He commissioned the architect Inigo Jones (1573-1652) to design the building. Bedford hoped to keep costs down. Therefore, he instructed Jones to make sure that it was plain like a barn, to which the architect replied that the earl would have 'The handsomest barn in England'.

St.Paul's was the first new Anglican church built in London since the Reformation. It was consecrated in 1638 and given its own parish in 1645.

Punch & Judy

A plaque in front of St.Paul Covent Garden commemorates the first known performance of a Punch & Judy show in England. It was recorded by the diarist Samuel Pepys (1633-1703). Each May there is an annual Punch & Judy Festival in the churchyard.

(The Punch & Judy pub is to the east of Dr. Marten's and St.Paul's.)

Direction

Walk back along the Piazza's northern side. Turn right and walk down the Piazza's eastern side.

Russell Street

On the left is Russell Street.

Will's Coffee House

William Urwin established Will's Coffee House at No. 1 Bow Street in the early 1660s. The House was on the north-east corner of the junction with Russell Street. It became renowned as the `Wits' Coffee House', much of its reputation deriving from the poet John Dryden's (1631-1700) patronage. The diarist Samuel Pepys and the poet and translator Alexander Pope (1688-1744) were also patrons.

Will's closed in the mid-C18th.

Tips

Tea and coffee house patrons who sought good service would, before taking their sets, place some coins in the `Tip' box. `Tip' stood for `to insure promptness'.

The Theatre Museum

The fifth building on the right from the Piazza is the Theatre Museum, a museum which covers the performing arts comprehensively.

In 1955 Laurence Irving, the grandson of the actor Sir Henry Irving (1838-1905), floated the idea of a theatre museum. The Irving Collection formed the nucleus of the British Theatre Museum, which opened in 1963 in an annexe of Leighton House, Kensington.

In 1971 the British Theatre Museum was amalgamated with the Victoria & Albert Museum's theatrical collection to form the Theatre Museum, a branch of the Victoria & Albert Museum. Since 1987 it has been based in Covent Garden.

Johnson & Boswell

The fourth building on the right was once the bookshop of Thomas Davies. It was in Davies's that the lexicographer and man of letters Samuel Johnson (1709-1784) and his biographer James Boswell (1740-1795) first met one another in 1763.

Button's

Button's Coffee House was at the western end of Russell Street on the southern side.

Button's was set up by the writer and politician Joseph Addison (1672-1719) in 1713. Daniel Button was a former servant of Addison's wife the Countess of Warwick.

Button's attracted Will's clientele.

The London Transport Museum

In the Piazza's south-eastern corner is the London Transport Museum, which has been in Covent Garden since 1980.

Direction

Leave the Piazza by the alley at the eastern end of its southern side. The alley is a great rarity in London through its not having a name.

Turn right into Tavistock Street.

Country Life

On the left Hudson House (1905) occupies Nos. 2-8 Tavistock Street.

Edward Hudson (1854-1933) founded the magazine Country Life in 1897. Hudson House was designed by the architect Edwin Lutyens (1869-1944), who also, appropriately enough, designed Deanery Garden at Sonning in Berkshire as a country house for Hudson.

Country Life's readership is in large part urban. The feature of the magazine which most people who have only ever skimmed it know is the advertisements for country houses, which seem to fill the first half of the magazine.

The magazine is no longer produced in Hudson House.

Direction

Cross Southampton Street.

Maiden Street

Along Maiden Street on the right, at Nos. 34-35 Maiden Street, is Rule's, a restaurant which was established in 1798.

Direction

Turn right and walk up Southampton Street towards the Piazza. At the Piazza's southern edge turn left into Henrietta Street.

Dorling Kindersley

On the left, at No. 9 Henrietta Street, is Dorling Kindersley the publishing house.

The company was founded in 1974. It utilised the illustrator Peter Kindersley's expertise within the book trade to produce highly visual reference books.

The company is changing from its original series-oriented character and is increasingly prepared to publish individual books.

The Dorling Kindersley bookshop is at Nos. 10-11 King Street, which runs parallel to Henrietta Street to the north.

Victor Gollancz

On the left, at No. 14 Henrietta Street, are the former premises of the publishing house Victor Gollancz Ltd..

Victor Gollancz (1893-1967) set himself up as a publisher in Covent Garden in 1927. Through his previous employment at Ernest Benn Ltd., Gollancz had become a well known figure in the publishing world and was able to attract a number of well established authors to his new venture. He was an adept publicist who managed to mix left wing politics with commercial business practices, notably in the Left Book Club, which he set up in 1936. As the head of his own company he proved a great success.

The Lady

Henrietta Street runs into Bedford Street.

To the left, on the left (east) side of Bedford Street, at Nos. 38-40 Bedford Street, on the corner with Maiden Lane, are the premises of The Lady magazine.

Thomas Gibson `Tap' Bowles M.P. (1842-1922) founded The Lady in 1885. The magazine is something of a schizophrenic entity. In essence it has two readerships. The first readership are readers of it as a magazine who ignore the advertisements, while the second readership reads it for its advertisements and ignore the journalism. The magazine's advertisements are the country's national bulletin board for domestic help.

(Bowles also founded Vanity Fair, which, in its present form, is a very different magazine from The Lady.)

Crime in Store

To the right, on the western side of Bedford Street, at No. 14 Bedford Street, is the Crime in Store bookshop, a shop specialising in crime fiction.

Direction

Turn right into Bedford Street. Walk north up Bedford Street to the junction with King Street.

The Communist Party of Great Britain

On the left, at No. 16 King Street, is the former headquarters of the Communist Party of Great Britain. (No. 16 is now part of a bank.)

Party Formation

The Bolsheviks commissioned Theodore Rothstein to combine disparate elements to create a British Communist Party. The Communist Party of Great Britain was founded at the Unity Convention of July 1920. Rothenstein, having completed his work, moved to the Soviet Union.

Harry Pollitt

In 1929 the leadership of the Communist Party passed from J.R.Campbell and his associates to Harry Pollitt (1890-1960) and Palme Dutt (1896-1974). The pair successfully executed their orders from Stalin to eliminate all signs of independence within the British party's leadership.

Harry Pollitt, while following the Moscow-line, was aware of the failings of the Soviet state, he knew the charges against Trotsky were false, and he detested the Nazi-Soviet Pact of 1939. For a public figure, Pollitt had a well developed sense of humour.

Post-1945

In Britain there were no direct parallels to McCarthyism, however, its influence was felt. Left wing academics found it hard to gain promotion or change from one institution to another, while those who were not already within the hallowed halls very rarely gained admittance.

Reg Birch

Reg Birch (1914-1994) served on both the executive of the Communist Party and the general council of the Trades Union Congress. Birch was expelled from the Communist Party in 1967 for Maoism, he having taken to referring to his colleagues as "social democrats". In 1968 he formed the Communist Party of Great Britain (Marxist-Leninst). His colleagues in the Amalgamated Engineering Union were acknowledging his abilities as an officer of the union rather than endorsing his politics when they put him on the T.U.C.'s general council in 1975.

The Demise of the Communist Party

In 1984 the Communist Party split in two. The factions were effectively concentrated on two publications: the old guard grouped around the Morning Star newspaper and its editor Tony Chater, while the EuroCommunists gathered around Marxism Today magazine and its editor Martin Jacques. The Eurocommunists secured the party organisation which they dissolved in 1991.

(Jacques is now an influential figure in Demos the political think-tank.)

Moss Bros

On the north side of the junction of Bedford Street with King Street is the flagship store of Moss Bros the men's clothes retailer.

Moses Moss opened a shop in Covent Garden in 1860. In 1881 he set up two of his sons in a business on the site of the store.

The business flourished during the First World War through providing uniforms for officers and it managed to retain many of them as customers with the coming of peace.

With the advent of the Second World War the company decided to establish a provincial network of shops to help exploit the demand for tailored uniforms wherever there was a concentration of troops.

In 1958 the business adopted the name Moss Bros.

Direction

Bedford Street becomes Garrick Street.

The Lamb & Flag

On the right is Rose Street, at the north end of which is The Lamb & Flag pub, a wooden-framed building dating from 1623. The pub's exterior is Georgian.

The poet John Dryden's (1631-1700) anonymous `Essay on Satire' attacked both the Earl of Rochester (1647-1680) (who was also a poet) and the Duchess of Portsmouth (1649-1734) (who was one of King Charles II's mistresses). In December 1679 Dryden was almost assasssinated near to The Lamb & Flag by some men hired by the Duchess. His survival is commemorated in the pub annually.

Later, the pub became known as the Bucket of Blood because of its association with boxing.

The Garrick Club

On the left, at Nos. 15-17 Garrick Street, is the Garrick Club, a gentleman's club, which was founded in 1831. It takes its name from the actor David Garrick (1717-1779) and has long had associations with the theatrical profession. However, its membership is now in large part drawn from the media and the law.

The Garrick's tie is a distinctive pink and green.

Direction

Turn right and walk to the western end of Long Acre.

Dillons Arts Bookshop

On the right, at No. 6 Long Acre, is Dillons Arts Bookshop.

Stanfords
On the right, at Nos. 12-14 Long Acre, is Stanfords the mapsellers. The firm was founded in 1852.

Direction
Cross over Garrick Street and go down St.Martin's Lane.

The Chippendales
On the left, at No. 61 St.Martin's Lane, there is a plaque which commemorates that from 1753 to 1813 the site was the workshop of the furniture maker Thomas Chippendale (d.1779) and then of his son.

Sheekey's
On the right is St.Martin's Court, an alley. On the left (south) side of St.Martin's Court, at Nos. 28-32 St.Martin's Court, is Sheekey's, a renowned fish restaurant, which opened in 1896.

The Salisbury
On the southern corner of the junction of St.Martin's Lane and St.Martin's Court is The Salisbury (No. 90 St.Martin's Lane), a Victorian-style pub.

Cecil Court
On the right is Cecil Court, an alley. On both sides of Cecil Court are a number of small shops which are occupied, for the most part, by secondhand book dealers.

The Coliseum Theatre
On the left, at Nos. 33-35 St.Martin's Lane, is The Coliseum Theatre (1904), one of London's largest theatres.

Music Hall
Music hall started out in pubs which put on entertainments in the hope of drawing more customers. A music hall act which was in demand would appear in perhaps five or six separate venues a night, travelling from one to the next in a hired carriage. Each bill might well have two dozen performers on it and the major stars were often paid only a few pounds per performance.

In the 1880s musical hall was very much an entertainment for men. Customers were free to wander to the bars anytime during the performance. Music hall's conversion into variety was the achievement of theatre owners such as Oswald Stoll (1866-1942). Stoll sought to attract respectable family audiences and was relentless in his efforts to take music hall upmarket. One of the indicators by which respectability was marked was the introduction of fixed seats.

In 1904 The Coliseum Theatre opened in St.Martin's Lane as a music hall. Stoll encouraged European acts to come to Britain to perform in his theatres. In 1906 the licensing authorities gave music halls the freedom to put on short plays with small casts. In 1911 the London County Council permitted the music hall theatres to put on variety shows and full-length dramas. The owners attracted actors by paying higher wages than they were likely to receive in conventional theatres.

The English National Opera

Since 1968 the English National Opera opera company has resided at the Coliseum Theatre.

The company is largely the creation of the present and 7th Earl of Harewood (a cousin of the Queen), who was the managing director of the company from 1972 to 1985 and the president of its board from 1986 to 1995.

In January 1997 the company announced its intention of moving to a new home.

To Finish

Walk south along St.Martin's Lane and then along the east side of Trafalgar Square and then descend into Charing Cross underground station, which is on the Northern, Bakerloo and Jubilee Lines.

To Continue

Walk south along St.Martin's Lane and then along the east side of Trafalgar Square. Cross the western end of the Strand and then that of Northumberland Avenue. Turn left into Whitehall.

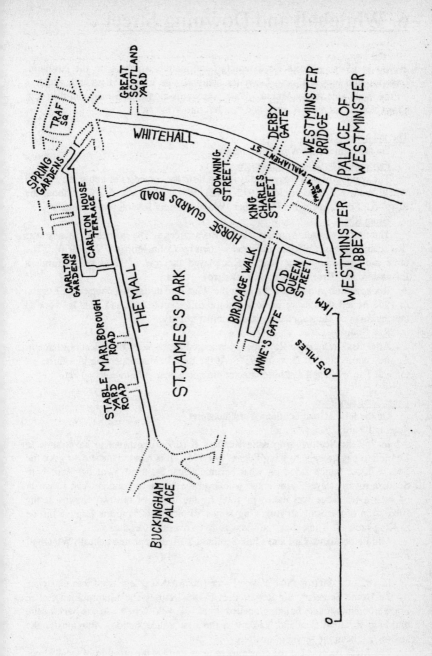

6. Whitehall and Downing Street

To Start

Go to Charing Cross Road underground station which is on the Northern, Bakerloo and Jubilee Lines. Leave the station by its Villiers Street exit, which is on the south side of the Strand. Walk westwards along the Strand and turn left. Cross Northumberland Avenue and turn left into Whitehall.

The Whitehall Theatre

On the right is The Whitehall Theatre.

Farce and The Whitehall Theatre

The coming of peace gave the British a taste for comedies of about the Second World War. R.F.Delderfield's (1912-1972) `Worm's Eye View', a farce about the Royal Air Force, opened in December 1945 and ran for several years thereafter.

Brian Rix

The first of the actor-manager Brian Rix's farces at The Whitehall Theatre was `Reluctant Heroes' (1950) which was written by Colin Morris (1916-1996). The farce ran for almost four years. Rix played the role of Gregory, a gormless Lancashire lad (Rix is a native of Yorkshire).

Rix appeared in over 100 farces in the West End during the course of 27 years. In 1978 he left the theatre while at the top of his profession and went to work as the chairman of Mencap, the mental disability charity.

Ray Cooney

After Rix's retirement Ray Cooney emerged as the West End's leading farceur. Cooney wrote his first farce in 1959. At the time he was appearing in a three-act farce at The Whitehall and his character did not appear until the second act.

Great Scotland Yard

On the left is Great Scotland Yard the street.

Scotland Yard

In 959 the Scottish king King Kenneth II (d.995) is meant to have come to London to pay homage to King Edgar (944-975). It is reputed that Edgar gave the Scot a house which stood on what became Great Scotland Yard off Whitehall. Scottish royalty stayed in the house whenever they came to London. The necessity of such a residence was ended in 1603 by the union of the two crowns at the succession of the Scottish king King James VI (1566-1625) to the English throne as King James I. Thereafter, the site was given over to other uses.

Middle Scotland Yard and Little Scotland Yard disappeared beneath Whitehall Place.

Peelers

In 1829 the Metropolitan Police Force (the Met) was legislated into existence by the Home Secretary Sir Robert Peel (1788-1850). The Metropolitan Police Force's commissioners building opened up at No. 4 Whitehall. At the back of the building, in Great Scotland Yard, was the first police station. Previously, the station had been the servants' quarters.

The Met's success led the government to encourage the creation of local forces throughout Britain.

Special Branch
A wave of Fennian terrorism in the mid-1880s led to the creation of the Special Irish Branch, which was subsequently renamed the Special Branch.

Literary Private Detectives
The creation of the Met's detective department in 1842 has led to it being possible to make a case for the character of Mr. Nadgett, in Charles Dickens's (1812-1870) `Martin Chuzzlewit' (1844), being the first proper private detective in English literature.

Whitehall
Whitehall the road takes its name from a royal palace which for the most part lay between the present road and the Thames.

`Whitehall' is the senior central Civil Service. Many of the ministerial buildings are located along or near Whitehall which stretches from Trafalgar Square almost to Parliament Square (the final section being known as Parliament Street).

Senior Whitehall civil servants are known as `mandarins'.

The Dame
The memory of the mandarin Dame Evelyn Sharp (1903-1985) of the Ministry of Housing & Local Government has achieved a reputation outside Whitehall through the diaries of the Labour politician Richard Crossman (1907-1974).

In his diaries Crossman referred to Dame Evelyn as `the Dame'. Sharp was devoted to public service and quite incorruptible. However, she believed politicians were to be guided rather than obeyed.

The Sausage Machine
It is an oft repeated criticism of Whitehall that the one activity it does unfailing well is to perpetuate itself - male, generalists educated at either Oxford or Cambridge make up the mass of its ranks.

Treasury Tags
In September 1995 the Treasury issued guidelines that Whitehall civil servants should write in clear and concise English. This was taken as meaning in part a ban on Latin tags, a legacy of the Civil Service's traditional domination by men whose education left them steeped in the Classics.

Decentralisation
In 1957 the London County Council adopted a policy of decentralisation, moving offices away from the centre of London. In the 1960s this was adapted as a government policy of decentralisation away from London; civil servants (especially the low grade ones) were sent out to the provinces. Fewer people now work in central London than was the case at the start of the 1960s.

The Admiralty
On the right is The Admiralty House (1788).

Parliamentary Counsel
On the right is the Parliamentary Counsel, the office of the government lawyers who draft most of the government's legislation. Parliamentary Counsel do not draft those bills relating wholly to Scotland, which has its own legal system.

The Parliamentary Counsel was instituted in 1869 during William Gladstone's (1809-1898) first ministry.

In March 1995 the Treasury invited outside tenders for work as Parliamentary draftsmen. This was the first such invitation.

Horse Guards

On the right is Horse Guards (1758).

In 1649 a guardhouse was erected in Whitehall Palace's tilt-yard.

As someone who had lost his father to the axeman, King Charles II (1630-1685) had a cautious aspect to his nature. In 1663 he established the Horse Guards in quarters adjoining Whitehall Palace. In 1665 a more substantial building was put up. The present Horse Guards building dates from 1758. (Only members of the royal family are permitted to drive through its central arch.)

The General Staff was headquartered in the building until 1872. Subsequently, it provided a home for both the London District and the Household Division.

The Banqueting Hall

On the left is the Banqueting Hall (1622), the principal remnant of Whitehall Palace.

Whitehall Palace

Whitehall Palace was sited between the riverside and Whitehall the modern road. From the middle of the C13th York Place, as the Palace was originally known, was the London residence of successive Archbishops of York.

Cardinal Wolsey (c1475-1530) became Archbishop of York in 1514 and spent lavishly on York Palace. In 1529 King Henry VIII (1491-1547) had Wolsey convey the Palace to the crown, renamed it Whitehall and moved the court's principal London residence downstream a hundred yards from the Palace of Westminster.

King James I (1566-1625) commissioned the architects Inigo Jones (1573-1652) and John Webb to design him a new palace. The Banqueting Hall was the only part of the design that was ever built, it being a replacement for one which had burnt down in 1619.

James's son was King Charles I (1600-1649). King Charles lost the Civil War. On 30 January 1649 he was beheaded on a platform in front of the Banqueting House's first floor. The bust of Charles on the building's exterior marks the approximate point from which he stepped out onto the scaffold on which he was executed.

(There is a model of the palace in The Museum of London.)

The Protestant Wind and The Revolution of 1688

Charles's son King James II (1633-1701) is reputed to have had the weathercock placed on the north end of the Banqueting House so that he could know when the wind was favourable for his son-in-law Prince William (later King William III) (1650-1702) to sail from The Netherlands.

In 1685, with King James's accession to the throne, William's wife Princess Mary (later Queen Mary II) (1662-1694) became the heir-apparent to the throne, she being James's first born daughter by his first wife Anne (d.1679). In June 1688 James's second wife, Mary of Modena (1658-1718), gave birth to a son. This meant that Mary was no longer the heir-apparent and gave William an incentive to actively involve himself in British politics, hence the weathercock.

The situation in Britain was tense because of James's wish to extend religious toleration so as to benefit his fellow Roman Catholics. Many Anglicans looked upon his actions with concern, as they thought they heralded the dawn of an era in which the monarchy would try to force the people of England to become Catholics, as had been the case during the reign of Queen Mary I (1516-1558). In November 1688 William invaded England - sailing with the `Protestant Wind' - and James, after putting up a brief resistance, fled from the realm. The events which followed led to, the Bill of Rights, the passage of the Triennial Act of 1694 and the birth of Western Parliamentary democracy.

In 1698 Whitehall Palace burned down as the result of a sheet being left to dry too close to a fire. All that remained was King Henry VIII's Wine Cellar (now under the Ministry of Defence Building) and the Banqueting Hall.

Whitehall Post-1698

After the fire in 1698, the crown granted out leases on much of its site to members of the aristocracy who then built town houses there.

Until the late C18th most government departments were small, and were housed in accommodation scattered across the West End. The only sizable governmental building was the Sir William Chambers (1726-1796) designed Somerset House (1786).

The ministers who headed the ministries were members of one or other of the Houses of Parliament. During the course of a working day they often had to be present in their Chamber, therefore, their ministerial offices needed to be near Parliament. As the Whitehall leases expired the government tended to hand the properties over to various offices of state.

The 1890s were a period in which the powers and responsibilities of government grew. As a consequence, there was a lot of building work done for the government around Whitehall.

The Banqueting Hall Post-1698

From 1698 until 1890 the Banqueting Hall was used as a royal chapel and then became the Royal United Services Museum. The government took back the Hall for official use and in 1963 it was opened to the public.

Dover House

On the right is Dover House, which houses the Scottish Office. (Dover is the far end of England from Scotland.)

In 1792 the 1st Viscount Melbourne (1745-1828) exchanged his house in Piccadilly for the Duke of York's (1763-1827) Dover House in Whitehall.

Gwydyr House

On the left is Gwydyr House (1772), the home of the Welsh Office. (Gwydyr is in Wales.)

Gwydyr House was built for Peter Burrell (1724-1775) the Surveyor-General of the Crown Lands. On his death it was inherited by his son the 1st Baron Gwydyr (1754-1820).

Gwydyr was the son-in-law of the the 3rd Duke of Ancaster (who was also the 6th Earl of Lindsey). The Lindseys' town houses have a higher survival rate than that of most other aristocratic families. The phenomenon appears to have been transferrable by marriage.

Since 1842 the building has housed government offices.

The Ministry of Defence Building

To the left is the Ministry of Defence Building (1959), which was designed by Vincent Harris (1876-1971) in 1913. Appropriately enough, in view of its present use, its completion was delayed by not just one World War but by two, the building being finished in 1959.

~~The Building sits on top of Whitehall's mini-bunker system, which stretches~~ from Downing Street to the Palace of Westminster. The Building is reputed to be mounted on a vast platform of rubber is intended to absorb some of the shock if it is ever bombed.

Downing Street

To the right, running eastwards off Whitehall, is Downing Street, which was built for Sir George Downing (c1623-1684), who was the Secretary of the Treasury from 1667 to 1671.

No. 10 Downing Street

In 1732 King George II (1683-1760) offered No. 10 Downing Street as a personal gift to his then Prime Minister Sir Robert Walpole (1676-1745). Walpole, with his experienced political judgement considering the jaded interpretation which backbench M.P.s might make of such royal generosity, accepted the gift on condition that the house was given to him in his official capacity and not in a private one. Therefore, when Walpole fell from power in 1742 he left the house for his successor as Prime Minister to occupy.

Many Prime Ministers have used No. 10 purely as an office, preferring to continue to reside in their own, often larger, town houses.

The street facade of No. 10 belies what is in fact a small office block, housing the Prime Minister's Private Office.

`Dear Bill'

The `Dear Bill' letters which appeared in the satirical magazine Private Eye were authored by John Wells and Richard Ingrams. In `Dear Bill', Sir Denis Thatcher, the husband of Margaret Thatcher the Conservative Prime Minister of 1979-90, was portrayed as a golf-obsessed, gin and tonic drinking, half-wit. The Bill was Bill Deedes, a former Conservative M.P., Cabinet member and editor of The Daily Telegraph newspaper, who is a golf-playing companion of Sir Denis.

The `Dear Bill' letters inspired the play `Anyone for Denis?' As a public relations exercise, the Thatchers attended a performance of the play. After the show there was a reception at No. 10 Downing Street for the cast. After the reception, John Wells came to the conclusion that the reality was more outlandish than the creation.

`Yes Prime Minister'

The television comedy series `Yes, Minister' (1980-6) and `Yes, Prime Minister' (1986-90) were major hits in the United Kingdom and overseas. The shows were based on the age-old formula of the servant who is cleverer than his master. Their stars were Paul Eddington (1927-1995), who played the dithering, vainglorious politician Jim Hacker, and Nigel Hawthorne, who played the scheming and manipulative mandarin Sir Humphrey Appleby.

In 1987 both Eddington and Hawthorne were made C.B.E.s (Commanders of the British Empire). When abroad, Eddington often found that foreign politicians were keen to meet Jim Hacker. At home Eddington was unwilling to allow the Conservative Prime Minister Margaret Thatcher to have any publicity shots with him. Eddington was a Labour voter and supporter of the Campaign for Nuclear Disarmament (C.N.D.), neither of which were causes which had received much endorsement from Mrs. Thatcher.

Humphrey

Humphrey the Downing Street cat arrived at No. 10 as a stray in 1988. Opinions as to his character vary. Some believe him to be capable of conducting a reign of terror over the local wildlife, others do not believe that he has it in his nature to do so.

In July 1995 Humphrey went missing. In September 1995 the Cabinet Office accepted that - in view of his history of kidney trouble - he was almost certainly dead. The newspaper stories that reported the beast's believed demise were accompanied by photographs of him. From these he was recognised. Humphrey had taken up residence three-quarters of a mile away at the Royal Army Medical College in Millbank.

In May 1997, following the Labour Party's victory in the general election and a subsequent report that Cherie Blair did not like cats, Humphrey found himself on the front of every newspaper being embraced by his new mistress in an effort to dispel any belief that his future residence at No. 10 might be in doubt

The Cabinet Secretary

The Cabinet Secretary is the most senior civil servant. The Cabinet Secretary is the Prime Minister's servant and, as such, s/he is not technically answerable to the House of Commons.

The office was instituted in 1915 by Prime Minister David Lloyd George (1863-1945) during part of his re-organisation of government during the First World War. The office was the de facto creation of Lord Hankey (1877-1963), who held it from 1916 to 1938.

Economical With The Truth

The office of Cabinet Secretary was brought into a degree of disrepute by the Conservative Prime Minister Margaret Thatcher's occasional use of the office's holders as fixers. As a result, during the `Spycatcher' book fandango of 1987-8 Lord Armstrong was made to look conceited in an Australian court room when he admitted that he had been "economical with the truth".

No. 11 Downing Street

No. 11 Downing Street is the official residence of the Chancellor of the Exchequer, the government's senior finance minister.

Until 1835 it was customary for the Prime Minister to be both First Lord of the Treasury (Prime Minister) and Chancellor of the Exchequer. After 1835 it became the usual practice for the two offices to be held separately.

No. 11 is physically far more spacious than No. 10. Whereas the Prime Minister's private residence is confined to a flat at the top of No. 10, No. 11 is still a town house. (Following the Labour Party victory in the May 1997 general election, the Blair family moved into No. 11 - execept for the Chancellor's official rooms - the new Chancellor, Gordon Brown, who is a bachelor, moved into the flat above No. 10.)

The Budget

The word Budget is a corruption of the French `bougette'. The original `bougette' was the leather bag in which Sir Robert Walpole (1676-1745) took his papers to the House of Commons.

Since the mid-C19th Chancellors of the Exchequer have taken their Budget speeches in the Budget box, a battered wood and leather case which is believed to have first belonged to the Liberal politician William Gladstone (1809-1898).

On the morning of each Budget it is customary for the Chancellor of the Exchequer to appear on the steps of No. 11 bearing the case which is held up by the side of her/his head to be photographed. At the Chancellor's side stands her/his spouse.

The only Chancellor to decline to use it was the Labour politician Jim Callaghan (subsequently a Prime Minister). (Callaghan was the only teetotal Chancellor of the Exchequer since 1945. However, despite having four Budgets he only put up the price of alcohol once.)

Denis Healey

The Labour government of 1974-9 initially continued the Conservative Prime Minister Edward Heath's economic conduct but soon sought to restrain spending. Chancellor Denis Healey's two 1974 Budgets were markedly different from one another. The spring one sought to squeeze manufacturing industry, whereas the November one sought both to use tax relief on stock appreciation to boost corporate liquidity and to use the easing of price controls as a means of reviving company profits.

In 1976, in response to the failure of a classical Keynesian approach to counter the prevailing inflation, Healey and (the now Prime Minister) Callaghan ditched thirty years worth of dogma and introduced a form of monetarism. (Peter Jay, who, with Sir Samuel Brittan, introduced monetarism to Britain, was the son-in-law of Callaghan.)

Popularly, Healey was best known for his bushy eyebrows. He became associated with the catchphrase `Silly Billy', which the impressionist Mike Yarwood came up with for his impersonation of Healey.

Richmond House

To the left is Sir William Whitfield's Department of Health Building (1988), which incorporates on its northern side Richmond Terrace (1822).

The Department of Health

Government figures published in August 1995 revealed that of all the Whitehall departments, the Department of Health had the highest rate of civil servants taking sick days (15 days a year as opposed to the national average of 8).

Aneurin Bevan

The Tredegar Medical Aid Society was founded in 1870. The Society was supported by voluntary contributions from the wages of the town's miners and steelworkers, and was run by volunteers. Aneurin Bevan (1897-1960), who was raised in Tredegar, served on its management committee prior to his election to Parliament as M.P. for Ebbw Vale in 1929. The Society acted as an inspiration for him when he was setting up the National Health Service (N.H.S.) after the Second

World War. Bevan welded the N.H.S. into being out of a ragbag of voluntary and local authority hospitals.

In March 1995 it was announced that the Society was going to be wound up. The size of its membership had declined to the point where - under new legislation covering friendly societies' audits - there was no real point in its continuation.

(In the 1930s the popular novelist A.J.Cronin (1896-1981) was employed by the Society as a doctor.)

Clive Frogatt

The physician Clive Froggatt was an adviser to five successive Conservatives Secretaries of Health and became known as `the tories favourite doctor'. Froggatt started his political career while a general practioner (G.P.) in Cheltenham. He came to the notice of the Conservative Party through work he was conducting on the future of general practice. He became the architect behind the planning of the G.P. contract and fundholding system. The reforms were aimed at breaking the power of the hospital consultants, who previously, were not accountable. Froggatt was a G.P. and thus not someone aspiring to become a consultant, therefore, he had no interest in preserving their privileges.

In 1990 Froggatt turned to using hard drugs, first cocaine and then heroin. In September 1994 the police arrested him and in April 1995 he was given a 12-month jail sentence, suspended for two years.

It emerged that Froggatt had been a heroin addict at the time that he was involved in formulating the health reforms. Subsequently, he espoused the view that his drug use may have made him more callous as to the consequences of the reforms than he might have otherwise been.

N.H.S. Managers

The profession of hospital manager mushroomed in the mid-1980s. Between the financial year 1986-7 and the financial year 1991-2 there was a 24-fold increase in the number of N.H.S. managers. In the view of the Conservative politician Brian Mawhinney this was indicative of how the N.H.S. had been "clearly undermanaged" prior to 1986. That is one interpretation, there is another.

Contracts

With more managers it became possible to generate more paperwork. In June 1996 it was reported that N.H.S. managers had drawn up a 17 000 page contract for the building of Walsgrave Hospital, Coventry.

The Cenotaph

In the centre of Whitehall is the Cenotaph (1920), which commemorates the Glorious Dead of the World Wars of 1914-8 and 1939-45. It was designed by the architect Sir Edwin Lutyens (1869-1944) and was first erected in plaster as a saluting point for the Allied Victory March of 1919. It was then rebuilt in stone and unveiled on 11 November 1920.

Remembrance Sunday

Remembrance Sunday takes place on the Sunday nearest to the 11th November. Members of the royal family, the government and opposition, and representatives of Commonwealth countries lay poppy wreaths around the Cenotaph. The flower was chosen for remembrance because after the First World War it was the first plant to spring up on the former battlefields of Belgium and

France. It is a symbol of vitality and regeneration. The two minutes' silence is observed at 11 a.m. in memory of the fallen.

The politician Lord Curzon (1859-1925) devised most of the Remembrance Day ceremonies.

Whitehall's End

To the right is a street sign which reads `Whitehall' on one half and `Parliament Street' on the other.

Parliament Square seems to have a particular effect on streets which run into it - they suddenly assume new identities - Birdcage Walk assumes the nom de route Great George Street, while Whitehall metamorphoses into being Parliament Street, and Victoria Street changes into Broad Sanctuary.

The cause of such name changes usually lies in the different sections of street lying on different properties. Prior to the burning down of Whitehall Palace in 1698, `Whitehall' and `Parliament Street' were separated from one another by a gate.

The Foreign Office Building

To the right is King Charles Street. On the north side of King Charles Street is the entrance to the Foreign & Commonwealth Office (1873).

The architect Sir George Gilbert Scott (1811-1878) won the 1868 competition for a new Foreign Office building with a Gothic-style design. Scott was an admirer of the work of Augustus Pugin (1812-1852) and the Foreign Office site was close to the Houses of Parliament. However, the then Prime Minister Lord Palmerston (1784-1865) overruled the decision and insisted that if Scott wished to retain the contract he should design a Classical building (it being seen as a cheaper style to build in than Gothic). Scott did as he was bid and produced the design for what is now the present building.

At the same time that Scott was working on the Foreign Office building, he was also designing the St.Pancras Station Hotel (1876) in King's Cross. He is reputed to have relieved his frustration over the matter of the Foreign Office building by stressing the Gothic element in the hotel's design.

The Foreign & Commonwealth Office

In the C19th the Foreign Office was the principal ministry, the Treasury was there to provide the financial wherewithal for its policies. Playing the Great Game of international relations was considered of far greater importance than whether or not to raise income tax by a ha'penny. With Britain's dropping down the world order by several pegs the diplomats have been called to order.

Within Whitehall's rarefied world-view, the Foreign Office is seen as being something of a different breed. Historically, there was a common attitude within the Foreign Office that, as an institution, it was best able to judge what policy it should execute; ministers, if they thought otherwise, were to be given about as much respect as the fairy on the top of the Christmas tree.

The Foreign Office has long laboured under the stigma of being so keen to woo foreign powers that it has been more than happy to subordinate Britain's interests to its own gratification.

New Scotland Yard

On the left, down Derby Gate, can be seen old, Norman Shaw (1831-1912) designed New Scotland Yard (1890). (The site had originally been intended to accommodate an opera house. However, the cost of sinking foundations into ground only recently reclaimed from the Thames had proved too great and the project had foundered.)

The senior police officers were accommodated in offices on the lower floors. The more junior a policeman was the more flights of stairs he had to climb.

In 1958 Joseph Simpson (1909-1968) became the force's Commissioner. He was the first person to be appointed to the position who had risen to it from the ranks.

In 1967 the Met moved to the present New Scotland Yard which is on a site between Victoria Street and Broadway.

The Treasury

On the right is the Treasury Building (1912), which being on the corner of Parliament Square and Great George Street, used to have an alternative name - Goggs, the building having originally been known on maps as Government Offices, Great George Street.

There is tale that the building was designed to be a set of government offices in Bombay but that, due to a mix-up, the Indians ended up with the building that should have been the British Treasury. The Treasury building's interior character is said to be most un-British.

The Treasury is not renowned for the financial acuity with which it handles its own affairs. The Cabinet Office had to take over the Treasury's centre for information systems, the C.C.T.A., after it emerged that the Treasury had been unable to balance the centre's figures for several years.

Sir Terence Burns

Sir Terence Burns the Permanent Secretary to the Treasury is an unusual figure among Whitehall's senior mandarins, he having had a substantial career in academia before entering the Civil Service.

In 1976 Burns became the director of economic forecasting at the University of London's London Business School and a member of the Treasury's Economic Panel. His accuracy as a forecaster impressed Nigel Lawson and other Thatcherites. Therefore, after the Conservative victory in the 1979 general election, Burns was offered the Civil Service position of the Treasury's Chief Economic Adviser. In 1991 he was appointed Permanent Secretary to the Treasury.

To Finish

Turn left and walk eastwards along the north side of Bridge Street. On the left is Westminster underground station, which is on the District and Circle Lines.

To Continue

Cross Bridge Street to the southern side of that road's juncture with St.Margaret Street, which is on the northern end of Parliament Square's eastern side.

7. The Houses of Parliament and Buckingham Palace

To Start

Go to Westminster underground station, which is on the District and Circle Lines. Use the subway to cross under Bridge Street. Ascend to Bridge Street and then walk west to where the road enters Parliament Square.

Westminster Bridge

To the left is Bridge Street which leads to Westminster Bridge.

The first recorded reference to the Horseferry ferry dates from the C16th. The ferry was the property of the Archbishops of Canterbury, who resided on the south side of the river in Lambeth Palace. The first Westminster Bridge was opened in 1750.

The Shape of London

London is longer east-west than it is north-south. This is probably because during its initial growth communications were hampered by the limited number of river crossings.

The Palace of Westminster

The Houses of Parliament meet in the Palace of Westminster, a building which is still legally a royal palace. A palace has stood on the site since King Edward the Confessor (c1003-1066), the last of the Anglo-Saxon kings, built one there in the C11th.

New Palace Yard (on the site's north-west corner) takes its name from a late C11th plan that never progressed beyond the completion of Westminster Hall (1099).

Parliament 1265-1529

During the reign of King Edward III (1312-1377) the two Houses of Parliament were separated from one another and began to develop their own distinct identities. The Commons's sessions were held in the Chapter House of Westminster Abbey. The Lords remained in the Palace of Westminster, occupying a chamber in the site's southern portion.

The Woolsack

In the House of Lords, the Lord Chancellor, in his/her capacity as the Speaker of the House, sits upon the woolsack, a reminder of how important the wool trade was to England's prosperity. This practice is meant to have originated during the reign of King Edward III (1312-1377).

Money Bills

In 1407 King Henry IV (1366-1413) assented to the principle that money grants should originate in the Commons. The House's dominance in financial matters was by no means firmly established right away. Nearly 300 years later the Lords still felt able to interfere in money bills. Eventually, the two Houses agreed to accept one another's dominance in particular spheres, the Lords choosing justice (the Law Lords are the highest court in the land). It was upon the Commons's ability to hold the government to financial ransom that its eventual political dominance was based.

Parliament 1529-1834

In 1512 the Palace was damaged by fire and the subsequent repairs which were carried out were only partial. In 1530 King Henry VIII (1491-1547) saved himself the expense of further building work by moving the court a few hundred metres downstream from the Palace of Westminster to Whitehall. He left behind the judiciary and the legislature. (Until 1882 the principal courts for England and Wales sat in Westminster Hall during the legal term.)

St.Stephen's Chapel

One of the means by which the Reformation was wrought was the Chantries Act of 1547 which ruled that all religious services must occur in public places, this was done so that their doctrinal orthodoxy could be monitored by the state. As a result all private chapels were deconsecrated, including those in royal palaces. As a result, Westminster Palace's St.Stephen's Chapel became a secular room.

The Commons moved their meetings back into the Palace in 1547, taking up residence in St.Stephen's. The Commons's seating arrangement is reputed to be descended from the lay out of the chapel's choir stalls. The custom of M.P.s bowing to the Speaker's chair is thought to derive from the chair having been placed where the altar had been and the first M.P.s being inclined to genuflect towards altars.

November 5th and The State Opening of Parliament

Each autumn the State Opening of Parliament marks the opening of the Parliamentary session. The Opening involves the Commons being formally summoned from their Chamber (by Black Rod) to hear the Queen's Speech in the House of Lords. In the Speech, the Sovereign reads out the government's intended legislative programme for the forthcoming year.

Present in their official capacity are a range of bizarrely titled officials from both the Palace of Westminster and the Royal Household - e.g. Black Rod, the Howard Pursuivant Extraordinary, and Bluemantle Pursuivant.

On the eve of the State Opening, the Yeomen of the Guard carry out a ceremonial search of Parliament's cellars. The custom is meant to derive from the discovery of the Gunpowder Plot of 1605. The Plot was a conspiracy by fanatical Catholics to assassinate King James I (1566-1625) and all those who were attending the Opening. (The Yeomen's task has been made relatively easy by the fact that Parliament's cellars are no longer rented out to plotters wishing to overthrow the existing political order.) The first recorded instance of such a search was in 1641, at a time when political tension was mounting prior to the outbreak of the Civil War.

The Catesbys

The Catesby family have made something of a habit of forfeiting their estates, having done so in 1265, 1485, and 1605. In the last instance it was for Robert Catesby's (1573-1605) involvement in the Gunpowder Plot which did for them. The resulting Bill of Attainder on the family technically continued to be in operation until the 1970s, its provisions legally prohibited the Catesbys from voting. However, the family were unaware that the measure was still in force and had been leading an ordinary civil life for several generations.

Celebration of November 5th

Since King James I's reign it has been a tradition to celebrate November 5th and Parliament's delivery from the Gunpowder Plot with bonfires. The celebration, despite its origins, has long been free of any sectarian character. Fireworks did not become a feature until the High Victorian era when the government ended its own monopoly on the manufacture of gunpowder.

The introduction of the Fireworks Code in 1976 led to some varieties of firework being phased out. As a result, many young children take more interest in Hallowe'en than used to be the case.

(In the C18th the celebration of 5th November was by no means to do solely with the discovery of the Gunpowder Plot. King William III's (1650-1702) landed in Britain at Torbay on 5 November 1688, thus starting the Revolution of 1688. William was the hero of Nicholas Rowe's (1674-1718) play `Tamerlane' (1701). For more than a century the play was performed in commemoration of the Dutchman's arrival.)

The Monarch and The House of Commons

In 1642, during the political troubles that led up to the outbreak of the Civil War, King Charles I (1600-1649) and a troop of soldiers entered the Chamber of the House of Commons in order to try to arrest five particularly troublesome M.P.s. The Commons had been forewarned of the king's intention and the five had left the House before Charles's arrival. Upon his entry into the Chamber, the king was informed by the Speaker of the House that "the birds have flown". Since that occasion the Sovereign only formally enters the Chamber with the House's permission; the visit made by King George VI (1895-1952) in 1950 to inspect the repairs carried out after the Chambers's wartime bombing was a rare instance of such.

The Fire of 1834

Most of the medieval palace was burned down during the night of 16 October 1834. Like a true professional, the artist J.M.W.Turner (1775-1851) took sketches of the fire which he subsequently worked up into paintings. (The conflagration was caused when a fire of tally sticks got out of control. Tally sticks were pieces of wood used to record receipts for payments to the Treasury; notches were cut in the sticks recording the amount of money paid. In 1826 they had been superceded by the use of indented cheques.)

The only parts of the old Palace to survive the fire were the Cloisters, the Jewel Tower, St.Mary Undercroft (St.Stephen's crypt), and Westminster Hall.

Parliament 1834-Present

The architect Charles Barry (1795-1860) was selected to design the new palace. Much of the building's distinctive character derives from his decision to have Augustus Pugin (1812-1852) assist him. Pugin's decorative work both stressed Parliament's Medieval origins and sought to create a level of architectural harmony with the neighbouring Westminster Abbey. It is his details which help give this archetype of Victorian Gothic building its power.

Building work was started in 1840. The Lords moved into their new Chamber in 1847 and the Commons into theirs five years later. The building was finished in 1888.

Office Space
Barry did not plan offices for M.P.s within the Palace. Offices tend to be shared with other M.P.s and are, for the most part, located either on the south side of the river or on the river-side of Whitehall. Compared to most western Parliamentary representatives, British M.P.s are very underresourced.

Atmosphere
The Palace of Westminster is reputed to be a world apart from London. During the winter the building is said to smell of toast (in view of the Commons usually not starting its business until mid-afternoon, this may just be basic detection).

The Commons Chamber
The government of the day sits to the Speaker's right and Her Majesty's Opposition to the left.

The Commons Chamber has 427 seats. There are 651 M.P.s. The spaces used by various official functionaries and the Press Gallery could be seconded to provide more seating, however, unlike the mass of backbench M.P.s, the functionaries and the press are of use in the daily running of Parliament and government.

In 1941 the Commons's Chamber was wrecked as the result of aerial bombardment. After the war, Sir Giles Gilbert Scott (1880-1960), an architect deeply versed in the Gothic Revival style, was commissioned to rebuild the Commons. In 1950 the Commons returned to their own Chamber.

Big Ben
The intended bell was cast near Stockton-on-Tees and then transported to London. Before being placed in the Clock Tower, the bell was tested in New Scotland Yard; it cracked. The Whitechapel Bell Foundry used the original bell's metal to cast a smaller bell which became Big Ben. In July 1859 the bell rang out for the first time.

The derivation of Big Ben's name is uncertain. There are two leading contenders for its origin. The first is Sir Benjamin Hall (1803-1867), a rather fat man, who supervised the bell's installation. (Hall's wife Augusta (1802-1896) wrote `The First Principles of Good Cooking' (1867), a noted cookbook of the era. Lady Hall's culinary expertise may have contributed to her husband's `bigness'.) The other is Benjamin Caunt (1815-1861), a popular boxer of the day, whose nickname was Big Ben.

(The Clock Tower's belfry is lit whenever Parliament is sitting after dark.)

The Members' Lobby
The Members' Lobby only became limited to M.P.s and certain journalists after a terrorist attack in 1884. The Lobby reporters include the representatives of national daily newspapers and weeklies, provincial newspaper chains, and assorted radio and television journalists, at any given juncture a couple of hundred journalists have access to it. Anything which is said by a politician in the Lobby has an automatic anonymous attribution given to it unless the politician wishes to be associated with the statement; the purpose of this informal rule is to encourage politicians to speak more freely than they might otherwise do.

Manipulation of Print Journalists
In terms of media manipulation, politicians are reputed to be most wary of those journalists who work for provincial newspapers. This is because Fleet Street

newspapers have to be distributed nationally overnight, therefore, their journalists have to meet very tight deadlines. Therefore, if a politician wishes to leak a story, the national newspaper journalists have only a short time in which time to write it up and may not have the time to assess its true character. For an individual newspaper to fail to publish the story might make the paper appear to be lacklustre in comparison to its rivals. In contrast, regional newspapers, with their local distribution patterns, do not have to go to press so early, so their journalists have an extra two or three hours in which to mull over a story and to follow leads which may cast a different light upon it.

Back To Basics

In October 1993 the Conservative Prime Minister John Major launched his Back To Basics campaign. The campaign was intended to portray the Conservatives as being the political party which stood for family values and morality. In the months that followed public disclosure of the private conduct of various Conservative M.P.s gave consistent lie to such.

The crescendo was reached with the death in February 1994 of Stephen Milligan M.P. (1948-1994), a promising politician who died foolishly. He managed to suffocate himself upon his own kitchen table while engaging in a rather bizarre form of masturbation

In April 1994 M.P.s voted to ban journalists from the Commons's Riverside Bar unless they were the escorted guest of an M.P.. M.P.s felt that journalists had been overstepping the mark in their reports of M.P.s' private lives and that journalists had failed to view conversations which had taken place in the Riverside Bar as having the same `unattributability' as those which took place in the Members' Lobby. (Before entering Parliament, Milligan had himself been a radio journalist.)

Liquid Refreshment

The Kremlin

Until the 1987 general election the Labour M.P.s from the constituencies of north-eastern England were largely poorly-educated, trade union sponsored men who were native to the region. At Westminster, they tended to drink together in the Strangers' Bar, which as a result was nicknamed The Kremlin.

Robert Maxwell

During the 1960s Robert Maxwell (1923-1991), the disgraced newspaper owner, was a Labour M.P.. When Maxwell was Chairman of the House of Commons Catering Committee, he managed to generate a profit by selling the Commons's excellent wine cellar to himself.

Baiting

M.P.s are skilled in baiting one another across the floor of the Commons.

In 1981 Geoffrey Dickens (1931-1995), a Conservative M.P., in an attempt to control the story, informed the press that he had had a dalliance with a lady who was not his wife. Dickens had met the woman at a tea dance. When one of the journalists asked him how his wife felt about the matter, the M.P. suddenly realised that he had not yet told his wife about it. Thereafter, Dickens, when speaking in the Chamber, was baited from the Opposition benches with cries of "Slow, slow, quick, quick, slow".

Quentin Davies the Conservative M.P. for Stamford & Spalding was fined £1500 under the Protection of Animals Act of 1911 for cruelty to sheep after a flock starved to death on his property. As a result, when he rises to speak in the Commons a chorus of baaing often breaks out from the Opposition benches.

Hours

From Monday to Thursday, the House of Commons meets at 14:30 p.m., and on Fridays earlier. The supposed reason is to allow Ministers to execute their departmental duties and M.P.s to sit on Committees. In 1967 there was an experiment with morning sittings but the experience did not lead the Commons to adopt the practice.

Prime Minister's Question Time

The practice of Prime Minister's Question Time emerged in the 1880s. In 1953 it was timetabled for its present slots on Tuesdays and Thursdays because of the infirm condition of Winston Churchill (1874-1965) the then Conservative Prime Minister.

Prime Minister's Question Time can seem a rather absurd procedure. It has survived largely because of its basic usefulness to whoever is the incumbent premier. A Question Time in which the Prime Minister performs well has a marked effect in boosting the morale of his/her own party; it keeps the various Whitehall departments in a condition of being able to regularly brief No. 10 Downing Street on their activities at very short notice; it allows the legislature to grill the executive without the executive having to give much away, which might prove the case with some other form of interaction.

Perhaps one of the strangest aspects of the practice is the way in which M.P.s ask the Prime Minister to list his/her engagements, a question that may be asked separately by several different M.P.s; this is because the form of the question allows the M.P. to then ask the Prime Minister a supplementary question on anything s/he wishes.

Interhouse Activities

Bridge

George Murray 10th Duke of Atholl (1931-1996) successfully captained the House of Lords bridge team in a number of matches against the bridge team of the House of Commons. This led the bridge playing Labour M.P. John Silkin (1923-1987) to make dark mutterings about the Lords having "too much time to practice" and that the Upper Chamber should be abolished.

The Hereditary Peerage

There are just under 780 hereditary peers and just over 400 life peers.

Just under 170 peers describe themselves as cross-benchers and just over 220 claim to have no political allegiance. (In the mid-1960s there were only a few cross-benchers.)

The hereditary factor draws people into Parliament from diverse backgrounds. That the present system should have drawn into the legislative process the present and 4th Earl Russell, a distinguished academic historian, is an argument in its favour. Lord Russell favours reform of the House of Lords.

Some families have a number of separate peerages. The Barings has four separate peerages - Ashburton, Cromer, Northbrook, and Revelstoke. The Baring family's original wealth and prominence was derived from Barings the merchant bank.

Lords of the Jungle
(Tarzan's ancestral title was the Barony of Greystoke.)

Communists
The 2nd Baron Milford (1902-1993) was the first Communist to sit in the House of Lords. When taking his seat Milford gave a speech in which he called for the Abolition of the House. Milford was a scion of the Philipps family, a group of brothers who were prominent as businessmen during the first half of the C20th.

U.F.O.s
For many years the 8th Earl of Clancarty (1911-1995) was a leading exponent of the existence of U.F.O.s. Clancarty believed that the craft did not come from Outer Space but rather that they came from a subterranean civilisation. He believed that the U.F.O.s passed to and from their civilisation to ours by means of tunnels at the North and South Poles, among other places.

David Lloyd George
As an M.P., the Liberal politician David Lloyd George (1863-1945) was unsurpassed in his expression of derision and scorn for the House of Lords. Lloyd George's generosity in giving out titles was in part an expression of his contempt for the peerage. The Liberals broke the political power of the Lords with the Parliament Act of 1911. By the time of the First World War sliding scale operated between £15 000 for a baronetcy (a hereditary knighthood) and £100 000 for a Viscounty.

Lloyd George's coalition ministry fell in 1922 because the rank and file of Conservative M.P.s felt they could have power without him. He played into their hands by forwarding a number of names for peerages on the 1922 Birthday Honours list which were regarded as being totally unsuitable. Among the recipients of honours which helped engender the scandal were the furniture retailer Samuel Waring (1860-1940) and the butcher William Vestey (1859-1940). After Lloyd George's fall abuse of the honours system continued. The Honours (Prevention of Abuses) Act was passed in 1925.

Lloyd George remained an M.P. until January 1945 when he accepted Winston Churchill's (1874-1965) offer of an earldom. This action caused an outcry. After decades of savagely criticising the House of Lords, Lloyd George appears to have accepted the peerage as a gesture for Frances Stevenson (1888-1972), his second wife. She had been his mistress since 1912 but they had not wed until 1943 after the death of his first wife, whom Lloyd George had refused to divorce.

(John Grigg wrote a notable biography of Lloyd George. Appropriately enough, for Lloyd George's biographer, Grigg disclaimed his own peerage, as Lord Altrincham, in 1963.)

Miscreants
From time to time, individual members of the hereditary peerage are the subjects of news stories which arise from the miscreant money-making activities. In February 1996 3rd Lord Brocket was jailed for five years after admitting taking part in a fraudulent £4.5m insurance claim made in May 1991 involving a number of classic cars. In June 1996 a court in Tampa, Florida, sentenced the 12th Duke of Manchester to 33 months' imprisonment after he had attempted to defraud the Tampa Bay Lightning ice hockey team.

The 6th Earl of Effingham (1905-1996) inherited his peerage in 1946. However, no estates came with the title. During his life the Earl was the subject of a number of newspaper reports which were about his being arrested.

In the late 1960s Effingham was associated with the East End gangsters the Kray brothers. He served as a director of their Esmeralda's Barn nightclub. In 1969 he appeared as a witness during Ronnie Kray's (1933-1995) trial for murder. (The Krays sometimes referred to him as Effing Effingham.)

Effingham made his maiden speech in the Lords in 1967. He went on to acquire a certain notoriety within the House both for being a frequent attender (i.e. a frequent collector of the attendance allowance) and for seeking to drum up business from his fellow peers for a travel agency with which he was associated.

On occasion the news stories arise from their love lives. In March 1994 5th Baron Monkswell was imprisoned for seven weeks after attacking his mistress's psychotherapist with a spanner.

Lord Kagan

Members of the life peerage are capable of malefactions.

Joseph Kagan (1915-1995) was a successful textile manufacturer. In 1956 Kagan invented the Gannex raincoat. He befriended the Labour politician Harold Wilson (1916-1995), through one his factories being in Wilson's Liverpool constituency, and became an influential social figure at No. 10 Downing Street when Wilson became Prime Minister. Kagan was knighted in 1970 and was made a peer as Lord Kagan in the `lavender' Honours List of 1976.

In December 1979 a warrant was issued for Kagan's arrest relating to various financial irregularities. In 1980 he was arrested, tried, found guilty, and fined and sentenced to ten months' imprisonment. While Kagan was in prison, he was stripped of his knighthood by the Queen. However, to have deprived him of his life peerage would have taken an Act of Parliament and the matter was not felt to be of sufficient importance to warrant such a use of Parliamentary time. A few months after his release, Kagan took up his seat in the Lords and continued to attend the House regularly up until his death.

Westminster Hall

From the late C13th until 1825, the chief courts of English law sat in Westminster Hall during the legal term. Out of term, during that period, they sat at a variety of other places.

After Parliament was burned down by fire in 1834 it was decided to relocate the superior courts nearer to the Inns of Court. The Royal Courts of Justice (1882) in the Strand were built to provide permanent year-round accommodation. The Royal Courts received the courts which had previously been housed in Westminster Hall, Lincoln's Inn, and the Doctors' Commons.

Direction

Walk to the southern end of Parliament to the Victoria Tower (the other tower).

Cross over Abingdon Street to the western side of the road which faces Parliament.

The Victoria Tower

In front of you is the Victoria Tower, which holds the principal Parliamentary archive. Its possessions include a master copy of every public Act of Parliament since the end of the C15th. It houses a great collection of miscellania generated by centuries of litigation and legislation.

College Green

The grassed area behind you, opposite the Victoria Tower, is College Green, a.k.a. Abingdon Green, which is frequently used as a location on which television political commentators either deliver material to camera or interview politicians. The site's telegenic attraction is that it enables the Palace of Westminster to be used as a backdrop. The site is owned by the Parliamentary Estate. It is the turfed roof of an underground car park which was built in the mid-1960s.

The Jewel Tower

The old building to the north of College Green is the Jewel Tower, which from 1621-1864 served as the Lords Record Office.

(Behind the Jewel Tower are Westminster School and Westminster Abbey.)

Direction

Walk back towards Parliament Square.

Old Palace Yard

The area to the left is Old Palace Yard. The Yard, which is now open on two sides, used to be a yard enclosed within the Palace of Westminster. The Yard was the scene of a number of notable executions, including that of the Gunpowder Plotter Guy Fawkes (1570-1606) in 1606.

St.Margaret Westminster

On the corner of St.Margaret Street and Parliament Square is the Church of St.Margaret Westminster.

The church was founded in the C12th by an Abbot of Westminster to provide for the spiritual needs of Westminster Abbey's tenants and servants. In 1189 Pope Clement III declared the church to be exempt from the jurisdiction of the Bishop of London.

In 1614 the House of Commons made St.Margaret Westminster their parish church.

In 1840 the parish again became part of the diocese of London.

Direction

Walk along the southern side of Parliament Square to Westminster Abbey.

Westminster Abbey

Westminster Abbey is the popular name of the Collegiate Church of St.Peter in Westminster.

The Abbey was built on Thorney Island, surrounded by the Thames, Tyburn Brook and a marsh. It was consecrated in 1065. Until the Reformation it was a Benedictine abbey.

In 1540 the monastery was dissolved, however, the Abbey's royal associations helped it survive (it could easily have been stripped for building materials). It became the cathedral for the new diocese of Westminster; some of its revenues were transferred to St.Paul's Cathedral (hence the phrase `to rob Peter to pay Paul'.)

In terms of the organisation of the Church of England, Westminster Abbey is a `royal peculiar'. It operates under the jurisdiction of a Dean and Chapter and is subject only to the Sovereign.

The towers (c1739) at the building's western end were late additions. They were designed by Nicholas Hawksmoor (1661-1736).

The Rev. Arthur Penrhyn Stanley (1815-1881), Dean of Westminster during the years 1864-81, promoted the Abbey as `the sanctuary of the English people' rather than just of the Church of England.

The Chapter House

The Abbey's Chapter House is where the House of Commons met after it was separated from the House of Lords during the reign of King Edward III (1312-1377). The Commons held its meetings there until 1547, when it moved to St.Stephen's Chapel in the Palace of Westminster. From c1550 to 1865 the Chapter House served as a state archive.

Coronations

Every English Sovereign since King Harold (c1022-1066) (with the exception of King Edward V (1470-1483) and King Edward VIII (1894-1972)) has been crowned in Westminster Abbey.

Hereditary Office Holders

A few offices at court are hereditary. The coronation provides some of the hereditary office holders with roles to execute.

The Earl Marshal plays a central role in the ceremony's organisation. The office has long been in the possession of the Howard Dukes of Norfolk, most of whom have been Roman Catholics. The coronation can be said to be one of the most Anglican of ceremonies, as the new Sovereign swears to act as the Defender of the Faith.

During the coronation, the hereditary Champion calls upon anyone seeks to dispute the new Sovereign's claim to fight him. The office has long been held by the Dymoke family of Scrivelsby, Lincolnshire.

The Dukes of St.Albans hold the office of hereditary Grand Falconer. The 12th Duke (1874-1964) proposed taking a live falcon to Queen Elizabeth II's coronation in 1953. He was told that he should bring a stuffed bird or nothing. St.Albans chose not to attend the ceremony.

Some roles are executed by people who have inherited or bought particular lordships of manors. The lordship of Worksop carries with it the right to support the Sovereign's right arm at his/her coronation (provided that the Earl Marshal's Court of Claims has judged the holder of the Lordship to be `fit and proper' to do so). In July 1994 the lordship was sold at auction. It was bought for £40 000 by John Hunt, a retired businessman.

The Coronation Chair

The Coronation Chair in Westminster Abbey is the oldest dated piece of furniture in Britain. It was made by the king's painter Walter of Durham.

The Chair was first used in a coronation in 1399 when King Henry IV (1366-1413) was crowned. It has been used in every coronation since the C15th, with the exception of that of Queen Mary I (1516-1558). She considered the chair to have been tainted by the Protestantism of her predecessor (and younger brother) King Edward VI (1537-1553).

The Coronation Chair has left the Abbey only three times: for the installation of Oliver Cromwell as Lord Protector (1599-1658) in Westminster Hall, and for safety during the two World Wars.

The Stone of Scone

The Stone of Scone is a 336 lb. lump of yellow sandstone which became a talisman of Scottish nationhood.

In 1296 King Edward I (1239-1307) of England took the stone to England and placed it in Westminster Abbey the following year.

The Stone was taken from Westminster Abbey by young Scottish nationalists in December 1950. It was recovered from the ruined high altar of Arbroath Abbey and returned to Westminster Abbey in April 1951.

In November 1996 the Stone was moved to Scotland. It will be brought back to the Abbey temporarily for any future coronations.

Memorials and Graves
Royal Graves

From 1269 until 1760 royalty were buried in Westminster Abbey.

Westminster Abbey underwent extensive reshaping as the result of King Henry III's (1207-1272) desire that the remains of the last of the Anglo-Saxon kings, King St.Edward the Confessor (c1003-1066), should have a resting place commensurate with his canonised status.

On St.Edward's Day (13th October), Catholic pilgrims visit the shrine of St.Edward the Confessor.

The Chapel of Henry VII was started by the Tudor king (1457-1509) to commemorate his Lancastrian predecessor King Henry VI (1457-1509). This was a means of underlining the Tudors' legitimate succession to the House of Plantagenet as kings of England. (It was in large part Henry VI's political incompetence which had allowed the Wars of the Roses to start in 1455. However, he had been very pious.)

The work on the Chapel was not finished at the time of King Henry VII's death. When King Henry VIII finished the chapel, he chose to dedicate the chapel to his father, Henry VII.

Royals Buried Elsewhere

The kings buried in Old St.Paul's Cathedral in London included King Aethelred the Unready (c986-1016). A number of kings are buried beneath the choir of Winchester Cathedral.

What was the London Post Office in King Edward Street in the City of London is built over the burial site of both Queen Margaret (c1282-1312), the consort of King Edward I, and Queen Isabella (1292-1358), the consort of King Edward II.

King Richard III (1452-1485) is probably buried under Leicester city centre.

Other royals are buried in France.

The Percies

Below the Chapel of St.Nicholas is the vault of the Dukes of Northumberland; the Percies are the only family with the right of sepulture in Westminster Abbey.

Memorials and Graves of Notables

Many people are commemorated by memorials in the Abbey rather than being physically buried in it.

The historic standing of a number of professions can be gauged by when their foremost members started to be commemorated or interred in Westminster Abbey. Medicine as a profession was not held in any particular social regard until the late C19th. Originally, the surgeon and anatomist John Hunter (1728-1793) was buried in the Church of St.Martin-in-the-Fields. In 1859 his remains were removed to Westminster Abbey. (Another sign of the social rise of medicine came in 1887 when Joseph Lister (1827-1912), the pioneer of antiseptic surgery, became the first doctor to be ennobled.)

Engineers

In the north aisle of the Abbey's nave is Engineers' Corner. There there are memorials to the likes of Isambard Kingdom Brunel (1806-1859), John Smeaton (1724-1792), George Stephenson (1781-1848) and his son Robert Stephenson (1803-1859), Thomas Telford (1757-1834), and James Watt (1736-1819).

Poet's Corner

As a royal official the poet Geoffrey Chaucer (c1340-1400) was buried by the east wall of the south transept of Westminster Abbey. He was the first writer to be buried in Westminster Abbey. Subsequently, other writers sought to be interred near him. As a consequence that part of the Abbey became known as Poet's Corner.

The delay between a writer's death and her/his receiving a memorial in the Corner was often the result of an unconventional life casting, to the eye of the current Dean of Westminster, a shadow over the individual's candidacy. With time, the writer's work tended to be remembered more than the life and so a writer's reputation was commemorated if not necessarily her/his person.

The monument to William Shakespeare (1564-1616) in Westminster Abbey was not erected until 1740, over 120 years after the dramatist's death.

The playwright Ben Jonson (c1573-1637) lived in the residential part of Westminster Abbey's precincts, and was buried in the Abbey. He declared that "Six feet by two feet wide is too much for me; two feet by two will do for all I want." The Dean obliged him by burying him standing upright.

Painter

Sir Godfrey Kneller (1646-1723) (buried at Kneller Hall) is the only artist to be commemorated in the abbey. (There are plenty of painters in St.Paul's Cathedral.)

Soldiers

Buried in the Abbey are a number of soldiers who helped maintain royal dynasties. The 1st Duke of Albemarle (1608-1670) has a grand tomb in the south aisle of the Chapel of Henry VII. Albemarle has four monarchs and a royal consort buried underneath him. King Charles II (1630-1685), Queen Mary II (1662-1694), King William III (1650-1702), Queen Anne (1665-1714), and Prince George of Denmark (1653-1708) were all indebted to the Duke for his part in the overthrow of the English Republic and the Restoration of the monarchy in 1660.

Field Marshal George Wade (1673-1748) took a leading part in suppressing the Jacobite Rebellion of 1745.

The Unknown Warrior

The Unknown Warrior was buried in Westminster Abbey on Armistice Day 1920.

The Undercroft Museum

Westminster Abbey's Undercroft Museum has Europe's oldest death mask - that of King Edward III (1312-1377).

The effigies of the politician Pitt the Elder (1708-1778) and the naval hero Lord Nelson (1758-1805) were included as attractions rather than for any funeral reason.

The Abbey Garden

The walled garden of Westminster Abbey is reputed to be the oldest walled garden in England.

William Caxton

William Caxton's (c1422-1491) original printing press (1477) was set up in Westminster Abbey. In 1483 he moved to premises in the neighbouring Almonry.

(It was Caxton's apprentice Wynkyn de Worde (d.1535) who established the first printing press in Fleet Street. De Worde was buried in St.Bride Fleet Street.)

Westminster School

When you leave Westminster Abbey, to the left is Westminster School, one of the country's leading public schools.

A monastic school is mentioned in the C14th. The Benedictine monastery of Westminster Abbey was dissolved by King Henry VIII (1491-1547).

Westminster School, properly St.Peter's College, Westminster, was refounded by Queen Elizabeth I (1533-1603). The school was continued under headmastership of Alexander Nowell (c1507-1602). The School's Great Hall was part of the monastery's dormitory building.

The Public Schools Act of 1868 made Westminster School financially and administratively independent of Westminster Abbey. The Dean and Chapter were replaced by a new board as its governors.

Public Schools

During the C18th the aristocracy began to send their sons to certain schools. The word `public' refers to a choice of some either having their child educated at home privately or having the child educated in a school publicly.

A factor in the decision of the aristocracy to send their sons to public schools may have been a change in the nature of English society. In the wake of the Revolution of 1688, Parliament began to meet in London every year rather than just when the Sovereign needed to raise some money. With Parliament meeting annually aristocrats began to spend every winter in London, where they began to socialise more with one another than had hitherto been the case. Initially, those few who had been educated together had an advantage in already knowing one another. With the C18th's progress an increasing number of aristocrats chose to send their sons to the `public' schools to give them the advantage of mixing with the sons of other aristocrats.

Those who attended the schools and who were not of aristocratic backgrounds themselves had an advantage when it came to building careers for themselves, they were able to call on their schoolfellows and the fathers of their schoolfellows to help pull strings for them. The schools became ever more attractive. This led to new schools being founded by enterprising schoolmasters who, while they could not rival the major schools for social prestige, could seek to provide a near identical education and instil much the same ethos in their pupils.

Direction
Cross Broad Sanctuary and walk along Storey's Gate.

Broad Sanctuary
The Broad Sanctuary was next to Westminster Abbey. Queen Elizabeth I (1533-1603) permitted only debtors to claim sanctuary there, while her successor, King James I (1566-1625), abolished the right of sanctuary there altogether in 1623.

Methodist Central Hall
On the left, at the southern end of Storey's Gate, is Methodist Central Hall (1911).

Direction
Turn left into Old Queen Street.

The Spicer House
On the right, at No. 20 Old Queen Street, is the Spicer House (1904). The Frank Tromp designed building is a rare example of a town house in the Arts & Crafts style.

Direction
At the end of Old Queen Street, turn right into Queen Anne's Gate.

Queen Anne's Gate
On the left is a statue of Queen Anne (1665-1714).

Reputedly, the statue was made to commemorate the queen's part in promoting the Fifty New Churches Act of 1711. The measure was intended to provide the financial wherewithal to build new churches in London to minister to the religious life of the growing city. The statue was to have been erected on top of a column in front of the Church of St.Mary-le-Strand (1717), the first of the new churches to be built.

Until 1873 Queen Anne's Gate was two separate closes. The western portion, Queen Square, was built in the early C18th, and the eastern one, Park Street, in the late C18th. The wall which divided them was adjacent to where the statue of Queen Anne now stands.

Direction
Continue to the end of Queen Anne's Gate.

The National Trust

The large grey building (which is out of character with the rest of the street), at No. 36 Queen Anne's Gate, is the headquarters of the National Trust.

The National Trust for Places of Historic or Natural Beauty was founded in 1895 by the social reformer Octavia Hill (1838-1912), Sir Robert Hunter (1844-1913) the Solicitor to the Post Office, and Canon Hardwicke Rawnsley (1851-1920) a Lakeland clergyman (and friend of the children's author Beatrix Potter). They founded the Trust to protect open spaces from urban and industrial engulfment, the government having refused to involve itself in the preservation of beauty spots and ancient monuments.

The National Trust's first acquisition was made in March 1895 - Dinas Oleu, a clifftop above Barmouth in Wales.

The Trust is a private body and has never been part of the state. The Trust Act of 1907 gave the Trust a privilege unique in English law - it has the right to petition Parliament directly if all other channels have failed it. This right was justified on the grounds that it is the only private organisation in Britain that is able to declare its land inalienable. The right to petition Parliament was used in 1967 - with respect to the Trust's property at Saltram in Devon - but Parliament failed to concur with the Trust's opinion. In April 1994 the Trust announced that it was considering using its right to petition again in view of the threat posed to a number of its property's by some of the government's road-building schemes.

In the 1920s the growth of interest in architecture, particularly Georgian architecture, gave the Trust a new range of ambitions. In 1931 it was given Montacute, a palatial country house in Somerset. Looking after such a building whetted the Trust's institutional palate. However, its management appreciated that it would be administrative suicide to accept such buildings without the financial means to underwrite the support of their fabric. Thus was born the Country Houses Scheme. Under the Scheme, a family may give their house to the Trust, and retain for themselves and their heirs the right to live in it, so long as they hand it over with an endowment of investments or land to provide for its upkeep and maintenance.

The prolonged agricultural depression between the World Wars and the economic crash, as well as death taxes, helped part much of the aristocracy from the full ownership of their ancestral seats.

The National Trust has become one of the largest landowners of land in the United Kingdom. It owns more than 500 000 acres.

The 1930s saw the birth of mass car ownership. In the 1950s and 1960s the leisure use of cars meant that a growing number of people were able to visit a greater number of sites. This led to the growth of the Trust's mass membership.

In November 1995 the Trust bought No. 20 Forthlin Road, Allerton, Liverpool. The 1952-built terraced-house, a former council property, was the childhood home of the Beatle Paul Macartney. It was where Macartney, John Lennon (1940-1980) and George Harrison practiced.

Direction

Walk down the alley between Nos. 34 and 36 Queen Anne's Gate.

Turn right into Birdcage Walk.

Birdcage Walk

Birdcage Walk was established by King James I (1566-1625) and enlarged by his grandson King Charles II (1630-1685).

The Grand Falconer

The Dukes of St.Albans hold the hereditary office Grand Falconer. Until 1828 only members of the royal family and the Grand Falconer could drive down Birdcage Walk in St.James's Park. (The Dukes are descended from one of King Charles II's bastards.)

St.James's Park

St.James's Park is the oldest of the royal parks in central London. Originally, it was a marshy meadow owned by the leper hospital of St.James. In 1532 the land was drained and layed out by King Henry VIII (1491-1547) as a deer nursery linking the palaces of St.James and Whitehall.

The lake was originally a set of ponds. These were joined up to form a canal (a rectangular ornamental lake) by the French landscape designer Le Notre.

The park was very much King Charles II's (1630-1685) pleasure ground. He used the canal for swimming in. His interest in ornithology is remembered in the names Duck Island and Birdcage Walk.

In the late 1820s the architect John Nash (1752-1835) turned the formal canal into an informal lake.

Direction

Turn left into Horse Guards Road.

The Cabinet War Rooms

On the right are the Cabinet War Rooms, which were opened to the public in 1984.

The complex is below a building in Great George Street, which runs parallel to Downing Street to the west of Whitehall.

Winston Churchill the Domestic Politician

As a domestic politician Winston Churchill (1874-1965) made numerous errors during his career. He was distrusted by many tory M.P.s because in 1900 he had started his Parliamentary career as a Conservative, in 1904 he had become a Liberal and in 1924 a Conservative again. He earned the lasting hatred of large portions of the working class while Home Secretary; he was regarded as having authorised the use of troops against striking miners at Tonypandy in November 1910 (the troops arrived after members of the Metropolitan Police had virtually dispersed a crowd of miners). His handling of both the Dardanelles campaign during the First World War and the General Strike of 1926 was poor. In 1935 he opposed the Government of India Act. He managed to back King Edward VIII (1894-1972) during the Abdication Crisis of December 1936.

In the Norway debate of April 1940 many Conservative M.P.s voted against Prime Minister Neville Chamberlain (1869-1940) in order to scare the government. These M.P.s did not want Chamberlain to resign and they certainly did not want to see Churchill succeed him. Chamberlain resigned and Churchill succeeded him. As a result, the new Prime Minister found that large sections of his own party were hostile towards him. But for Chamberlain's assistance during the summer of 1940, serving loyally as Lord President of the Council, Churchill might not have survived in office.

Until 1940 Private Offices existed in the Service Departments but not at No. 10 Downing Street. In September 1939 Churchill had become First Lord of the Admiralty, where he had a Private Office. In May 1940, when he became Prime Minister, he took his Admiralty Private Office with him to No. 10 to guard against the possibility that his actions being undermined by some of the Downing Street civil servants who might have felt a greater loyalty to his predecessor as Premier than to him.

Pamela Harriman

Pamela Harriman (nee Digby) (1920-1997) married Randolph Churchill (1911-1968), Churchill's eldest son, in October 1939. Her vitality and her capacity for adultery did much to foster the Anglo-American alliance during the Second World War. She was able to help persuade a number of President Roosevelt's senior emissaries that there was plenty of fighting spirit left in Britain. (Subsequently, she moved to the United States, became an American citizen and involved herself in Democratic politics. She was appointed an ambassador by the Clinton administration.)

St.James's Park Lake

On the left is St.James's Park Lake. The wide variety of species of bird present on the lake owes much to King Charles II's (1630-1685) interest in ornithology. Many were effectively exiles from their native habitats as he himself had been after his father lost the Civil War.

Charles's nephew King William III (1650-1702) had a hide on the island in St.James's Lake, which he used for bird-watching.

Pelicans

There have been pelicans on the lake in St.James's Park since the 1660s. The colony is descended from a gift from a Russian Ambassador. In a way, they are harbingers for all the unnecessary spilling of blood during the Crimean War of 1854-6. They were a sign that the Tsars of Muscovy were thinking of heading south for that dream of a warm water port; if the gift had been of a colony of Artic terns then history might have been altogether less dramatic.

(In March 1996 it was reported that a pelican was living wild at Enfield, north London.)

Seagulls

Seagulls are Artic birds. They are a not uncommon sight in the parks of central London. The birds are a sign of London being a maritime city.

Gulls began living further inland than London during the 1950s. This seems to have been a result of the development of the practice of using landfill as a means of rubbish disposal. The rubbish was exposed for long enough, before being covered, to allow the birds an opportunity to exploit it as a food source.

Quarks

A quark is the cry of a seagull; the writer James Joyce (1882-1941) used the word in `Finnegan's Wake' (1939); in turn, the American physicist Murray Gell-Mann used it to describe the particle which is fundamental building block of all matter.

Cormorants

Cormorants are increasingly leaving their coastal habitats and moving to inland freshwater habitats, much to the ire of anglers.

The cormorant is one of the world's oldest forms of bird. They are capable of flying in high winds which are too strong for `younger', more sophisticated species of bird to risk flight in.

Twitchers

Ardent bird-watchers are known as twitchers. Twitchers will happily traverse the breadth of the country at a moment's notice if it means that they have the chance of catching sight of a species of a bird that they have not seen in Britain before.

The Scilly Isles, off the coast of Cornwall, are a regular destination for twitchers, because it is where North American birds, which have been blown across the Atlantic, are most likely to be spotted.

In order that twitchers can be kept up-to-date minute-by-minute, many of them subscribe to one of a number of rival paging services which do nothing else but pass on news of the latest sightings of rare birds.

Horse Guards Parade

On the right is Horse Guards Parade.

Trooping The Colour

Each year, on the Saturday nearest 11th June, Horse Guards Parade hosts the Trooping the Colour ceremony on the Sovereign's Official Birthday Parade. The custom originated in the military custom of trooping (or carrying) flags and banners in front of soldiers, thereby familiarising them with the colours around which they would be expected to rally on the battlefield. The ceremony was first performed in 1755 and has taken place regularly since 1805.

A Former Car Park

For the most part, mandarins are suburban creatures. Many of them travel through the inner city safely encased in trains which deposit them at Waterloo, Charing Cross, and Victoria.

Others are so bold as to drive to work. In June 1994 the power of the mandarins was exercised - they succeeded in retaining their privilege of parking their cars on Horse Guards Parade, the National Heritage Minister Peter Brooke having had the audacity to suggest that one of London's great vistas should be properly enjoyed by Londoners and visitors to the city.

In March 1997 the mandarins were vanquished.

Downing Street

On the right to the south of Horse Guards Parade is Downing Street.

The Admiralty

On the right to the north of Horse Guards Parade is The Admiralty.

The Citadel

On the right, at the western end of The Admiralty is a breeze block building - the Citadel (1942), which was built during the Second World War in order to house particularly sensitive communications equipment which the Admiralty was using. Its breeze blocks, although largely covered by foliage, have, in view of their setting, a slightly incongruous air about them.

Direction

Turn left into The Mall.

The Mall

In the 1660s there was a fad for the game of `pail-mail'; in Italian `palla' means ball and `maglio' mallet. The game contained elements of both golf and croquet.

Both The Mall and Pall Mall derive their names from the game.

The original pail-mail pitch was in The Mall. Dust created by passing coaches effected the play. To avoid this problem, a new road was lain out in 1661 to the north which became known as Pall Mall.

The Institute of Contemporary Arts - The I.C.A.

Across the Mall at the western end of the eastern section of Carlton House Terrace is the Institute of Contemporary Arts. The I.C.A. caters to virtually all of the arts.

In the 1930s the idea of London having a Museum of Modern Art was being mooted by the American collector Peggy Guggenheim and the British art critic Herbert Read (1893-1968). After 1945 the concept was resuscitated by E.C. (Peter) Gregory, Roland Penrose (1900-1984), and Peter Watson (the patron of the literary magazine `Horizon').

The Institute has always maintained a virtually independent existence.

Sir Herbert Read

Sir Herbert Read metamorphosed from a being civil servant who cared for ceramics into the impassioned herald of Modernism. Not having trained as a painter, proved a freedom for Read. It allowed him to move intellectually further than the painter-critic Roger Fry (1866-1934) had been able to - Read was not bound by the artistic training which ultimately came to hold back Fry in his appreciation of new art.

Sir Herbert Read was an anarchist who sent his children to Catholic public schools and a libertarian who in 1952 accepted a knighthood. This behaviour stemmed from his being prepared to give way to the opinion of his second wife Margaret Read (1905-1996), whose views he respected. Lady Read's desire to become `Lady' Read stemmed from her wish to receive decent service when she went to the local garage.

Admiralty Arch

At The Mall's eastern end is the Admiralty Arch (1910). Beyond the Arch, to the left, is Trafalgar Square.

Admiralty Arch, which can reasonably be mistaken for a viaduct, was created as part of the remodelling of the Mall as a memorial to Queen Victoria (1819-1901).

In January 1996 the Admiralty Arch was put up for sale. Various former senior naval officers voiced their disquiet at such a state of affairs. As a result, the Conservative Prime Minister John Major made it known that the building would stay in government use.

Direction
Walk westwards along the south side of The Mall to Buckingham Palace.

Buckingham House
Queen Anne (1665-1714), when a young minor princess, had a crush on John Sheffield 1st Duke of Buckingham (1647-1721). By the time she succeeded to the throne in 1702, she had long outgrown that youthful phase of her life, however, Buckingham does not seem to have been aware of this and viewed himself as a great royal favourite. Anne seems to have humoured him. The politicians who acted as her ministers often had problem of dealing with the duke's pretensions and general high view of himself, after which they had a lot less energy to confront the queen with.

Buckingham Palace takes its name from this Duke of Buckingham. The Palace has grown out of rebuildings of the town house (1705) which he had built.

In 1761 King George III (1738-1820) bought the house from the Sheffield family. In 1775 the king gave it to his wife Queen Charlotte (1744-1818) (she in turn gave up Somerset House, the traditional palace of the king's consort). The couple occupied it as a private residence. In 1818 the queen left it to their son the Prince Regent (the future King George IV) (1762-1830).

Upon succeeding to the throne King George IV decided that Carlton House, his pet architectural project in London, was not grand enough for him now that he was a monarch. From 1821 to 1830 Buckingham House was remodelled by the architect John Nash (1752-1835). Upon the accession of King William IV (1765-1837), Nash, who had gone over budget, was replaced on the project by Edward Blore (1787-1879), who did not finish the work within William's 1830-7 reign.

Having grown up in Kensington Palace, Queen Victoria (1819-1901) sought to mark her accession as queen in 1837 by taking up residence in Buckingham Palace, making it the offical royal residence. However, she spent much of her reign, especially after the death of her husband Prince Albert (1819-1861), living away from London.

The Royal Standard
At a glance it is possible to see whether the present queen is in residence, if she is then the Royal Standard flag is flown above Buckingham Palace.

The Royal Standard is the personal property of the Sovereign. It may be flown only where the monarch is residing. (`The Royal Standard' is a popular name for pubs - none of which are allowed to fly it.)

The Royal Collection
The Lost Collection of King Charles I
King Charles I (1600-1649) had poor political judgement (he lost the Civil War and then had his head chopped off) but he did have an excellent eye for paintings and built up one of the great art collections of C17th Europe. The king's aesthetic indulgence was one of the characteristics which separated him from his political critics. When the English Republic was established in 1649 the royal art collection was sold off to eager continental purchasers.

The Queen's Gallery
In honour of his father King Charles II (1630-1685) half-heartedly tried to restart the royal collection, commissioning the painter Sir Peter Lely (1618-1680) to buy a series of drawings by Michaelangelo, Raphael, Leonardo Da Vinci, and

Holbein. (These were largely from the collection of Lord Arundel (1585-1646), one of the great collectors of early C17th England.) They were stored in a bureau and soon forgotten about. Over forty years later, during the reign of King George II (1683-1760) the bureau, by then in Kensington Palace, was re-opened and the trove discovered.

George II's heir-apparent, Frederick Prince of Wales (1707-1751), developed an interest in painting and became an active art buyer. The Prince bought the collection assembled by the physician Dr. Richard Mead (1673-1754). Frederick's son, King George III (1738-1820), bought on a sufficiently large-scale that his failures in judgement did not stop a solid collection being amassed.

Prince Albert (1819-1861), Queen Victoria's husband, had the Royal Collection put in order.

The Queen's Gallery opened to the public in 1962. It displays works of art which are in the Royal Collection. (It is in Buckingham Palace's grounds and is accessible from Buckingham Palace Road.)

The Royal Collection Trust

The Royal Collection Trust is the Queen's trading business. The Trust has a subsidiary, Royal Collection Enterprises, which administers souvenir sales and admissions at Buckingham Palace, the Queen's Gallery, and Windsor Castle. The Trust's profits are spent on the restoration work at Windsor Castle and on the Royal Collection.

In July 1996 it was announced that the summer opening of Buckingham Palace would be continued until 2000. Previously, the five-year experiment had been due to end in 1998. The revenue raised will go to the Royal Collection Trust.

Garden Parties

The guests at royal summer garden parties are, for the most part, ordinary men and women from throughout Britain, who have made some form of contribution to society.

Guests have been allowed to take their 18 to 25-year-old daughters since the late 1950s. This was a sop after the Queen stopped the presentation of debutantes at court. In 1993 guests were allowed to take a partner of their choice. There was no specification that the partner had to be of a different sex. In 1994 the privilege was being extended to guests' sons in the 18 to 25 age bracket.

In February 1996 it was announced that, for the first time since 1972, the London Borough of Hackney would be sending representatives to one of the Queen's garden parties. The invitations had been sent annually by the Palace but the borough council, because of its ardent left wing agenda, had chosen not to send representatives.

Fox Flamingo Frenzy

In February 1996 it was reported that an urban fox had either killed or scared to death six flamingoes which lived on an ornamental pond in the gardens of Buckingham Palace. This was in spite of the fact that the Palace's grounds are surrounded by a tall brick wall which is topped off by barbed wire.

(Llamas have a reputation for attacking foxes. As a result, some sheep farmers have bought them and put them in with their flocks as a protection against losing lambs to foxes. However, your average llama would probably regard Buckingham Palace gardens as a smorgasbord rather than as a field of valour upon which to be chivalrous to flamingoes.)

Dwarf Dogs

There are seven royal dogs. The corgis are Flora, Kelpie, Pharos, Phoenix, and Swift and the dorgis (corgi/daschund crosses) are Brandy and Harris. Collectively, they and the Queen Mother's beasts have as bad a reputation as any C16th Ruler of All The Russias could wish for. In May 1989 Chipper, one of the Queen's dorgis, was assassinated by the Queen Mother's corgis. In August 1994 news leaked of the Queen's animals had been `hounding' a police alsatian.

`Corgi' is Welsh for `dwarf dog'.

The Civil List

The Civil List was established in 1689. The crown vested its property in the Crown Estate (the profits of which go to the Exchequer) in return for receiving a Parliamentary voted sum of money each year.

In 1991 the crown and Downing Street struck a ten-year deal over the Civil List, by which the Queen receives £7.9m p.a.. (In February 1993 the Conservative Prime Minister John Major announced that the Queen had agreed to be taxed on her private income.)

Royals

George III

King George III (1738-1820), is about the only pre-C20th example of a British king who had a virtuous domestic life.

His sons had numerous mistresses and fathered hordes of bastards.

The royal family became bourgeois during the reign of Queen Victoria (1819-1901).

Queen Victoria

During the late 1860s and early 1870s there was a wave of Republicanism in England. This appears to have started waning in 1872 after a thanksgiving service was held at St.Paul's Cathedral, which Queen Victoria attended, to give thanks for the recovery of the Prince of Wales (later King Edward VII) (1841-1910) from typhoid.

The popular image of Queen Victoria is one that was largely created during the final years of her reign by the Conservative Prime Minister Benjamin Disraeli (1804-1881). In 1877 Disraeli had her crowned Empress of India.

The Duke of Edinburgh

The Duke of Edinburgh is the husband of the present Queen. He has something of a reputation for trying to make jokes which turn out to be indiscreet remarks. On a tour of China in 1986 he described Beijing as "ghastly". In August 1995 he asked a driving instructor in Oban, Scotland "how do you keep the natives off the booze long enough to get them past the test?"

In November 1995 the Duke entered the debate over the French government conducting underground nuclear weapons on Mururoa atoll in the Pacific. On a visit to New Zealand where the tests were opposed. The Duke, in his capacity as President of the World Wide Fund for Nature, backed a call for an assessment of the effects of the tests. Previously, the British Conservative Prime Minister John Major had backed the right of the French to carry out the tests.

(Perhaps the Duke's interest in the affairs of the region was influenced by his being an object of worship for a native cult on the South Pacific island of Tanna.)

The Royal Surname

Princes of the Royal Blood do not have a surname. However, the royal family does have a surname for those members who are not Princes of the Royal Blood.

Until the First World War the royal family were, thanks to Prince Albert (1819-1861), the Saxe-Coburg-Gothas. In 1917 King George V (1865-1936) changed the family's name to Windsor in order to alleviate the anti-German sentiment then being focussed on them. (From time to time, Britons are given to referring to the royal family as `Germans'.)

In April 1952 a declaration in Council was made that the Queen and her children would be known as the House of Windsor.

The Constitution

The Prime Minister and The Sovereign

The Prime Minister has a weekly audience with the Sovereign.

The Sovereign has two prerogative powers which are potentially of great political import - the power to appoint a Prime Minister and the power to dissolve Parliament.

Emergency Powers

In an emergency, the Sovereign's residual powers enable her/him to overrule Parliament and govern by means of Orders of Council.

Under the terms of the Emergency Powers Act of 1964, a state of emergency does not have to exist for the Sovereign to be able to declare that such a state is extant.

John Prescott

John Prescott M.P., the Deputy Leader of the Labour Party, is by no means a royalist although he has been known to express his appreciation of the Queen's political skills. On one occasion, to please some members of his constituency party, he accompanied them to a gathering where the Queen was present. Prescott and the people from his constituency party were placed in the receiving line. As the Queen walked down the line the Labour Party members each bowed or curtsied to her in turn; the M.P. was resolute that he would do no such thing. When the Queen got to him, she whispered something. He could not quite catch what she said. She whispered it again. He leant forward to try to catch what she was saying - a move, he soon realised, not so very dissimilar from a bow.

Elizabethans

Many of the British public who find the crown a tolerable institution are `Elizabethans' rather than monarchists. Elizabethans regard the crown as an office which is justified through its holders' execution of it rather than as something that has a right to exist of itself.

Constitution Hill

Between the Green Park and the wall which runs along the north-east side of the Buckingham Palace's grounds runs Constitution Hill. In almost any other country this street name would refer to a momentous political development. In Britain, with its unwritten constitution, the name refers to King Charles II's (1630-1685) partiality for taking a `constitutional' walk for the sake of his health. (The incline is so slight that `Hill' is something of an overstatement.)

During the 1840s three separate assassination attempts were made on Queen Victoria's (1819-1901) life along this stretch of road. This helps explain her disinclination, after the death of her husband Prince Albert (1819-1861), to reside more than briefly at Buckingham Palace. Instead, she chose to spend most of her time at Windsor Castle.

Direction
Cross to the northern side of The Mall. Turn right and walk back along The Mall.

Walk to the junction of The Mall with Stable Yard Road.

Lancaster House
The building to the west (left) of Stable Yard Road is Lancaster House.

Lancaster House acquired its present name early in the C20th. In 1807 Frederick Duke of York (1763-1827) moved into Godolphin House, which was in the Stable Yard of St.James's Palace. On the death in 1817 of his niece Princess Charlotte (1796-1817), the Duke became the heir-apparent to the throne. Both he and his elder brother King George IV (1762-1830) felt he should have a residence commensurate with his new status. In 1825 work on a Benjamin Wyatt (1775-1855) designed house was begun.

In 1827 the Duke died deeply in debt while the building work was still in progress. The government tidied up his estate and in 1842 sold the house to the immensely wealthy 1st Duke of Sutherland (1765-1833), who had been one of the Duke of York's leading creditors. The building became known as Stafford House, one of Sutherland's titles being the Marquisate of Stafford. Stafford House became one of the great venues of C19th aristocratic London; its brilliance glowed all the brighter because under Queen Victoria (1819-1901) the court played a limited role in the capital's social life.

In 1913 a lease on the House was given to the nation by Sir William Lever Lord Leverhulme (1851-1925) the soap magnate. The house was renamed Lancaster House in honour of his native county of Lancashire.

After the Second World War, many of the constitutional conferences which were held prior to a British territory achieving independence took place in either Lancaster House or Marlborough House.

Lancaster House currently serves as a government reception centre.

Clarence House
The bestuccoed building to the east (right) of Stable Yard Road is Clarence House.

The Duke of Clarence (1765-1837) was the next younger brother to the Duke of York (1763-1827). Clarence succeeded their brother King George IV in 1830, becoming King William IV. Like George, Clarence was partial to the work of the architect John Nash (1752-1835). As king, William continued to reside there because the work on Buckingham Palace was unfinished.

The house was the residence of Queen Elizabeth II prior to her accession as Sovereign in 1952, since when it has acted as the home of her mother the Queen Mother.

Direction

Cross Stable Yard Road and continue up The Mall. Walk to the junction of The Mall with Marlborough Road.

St.James's Palace

The brick building to the west (left) of Marlborough Road is St.James's Palace, the court's statutory seat. All foreign ambassadors in London are still officially posted to the Court of St.James's.

In the Middle Ages, the marshy ground on which St.James's stood was physically isolated from London. As such, it was well suited to being a lepers' hospital.

King Henry VIII (1491-1547) acquired the property and had a house built on it for his wife Anne Boleyn (c1507-1536). With the burning down of Whitehall Palace in 1698 the court needed a palace which was physically convenient for both Westminster and Kensington Palace, where the court proper resided. Thus, St.James's became the official royal residence, the palace which was used for court functions such as levees. Queen Anne (1665-1714) and her Hanoverian successors tended to follow King William's III (1650-1702) example of living at Kensington and using St.James's for functions.

The last members of the royal family to live in St.James's Palace for many years were two of King George III's (1738-1820) sons - the Duke of York (1763-1827) and the Duke of Clarence (the future King William IV) (1765-1837). On King George IV's (1762-1830) accession in 1820, the new king supplied his brothers with the financial wherewithal to start building their own grandiose town houses (Lancaster House and Clarence House).

With Queen Victoria's accession in 1837, and her decision to make Buckingham Palace the official royal residence, a number of court functions were transferred to Buckingham Palace. However, St.James's remained the crown's statutory seat.

Many of the bricks of the Palace's exterior were, until the 1930s, part of Beaudesert, a Jacobethan mansion in Staffordshire. Beaudesert was put up for sale in 1924 and was only sold a decade later when it was purchased by house-breakers who stripped it systematically of its saleable items.

Prince Charles

On the breakdown of his marriage in 1992, Prince Charles moved from Kensington Palace to St.James's. Princess Diana remained in Kensington Palace.

The Chapel Royal

The bestuccoed building to the east (right) of Marlborough Road is the Chapel Royal (or Queen's Chapel), which was built as a private chapel for the Catholic Infanta Maria of Spain whom the then Prince Charles (later King Charles I) (1600-1649) was expected to marry. The building was completed for the French Catholic Queen Henrietta Maria (1609-1669), whom he actually married.

Marlborough House

The brick building to the east of the Chapel Royal is Marlborough House (1711), on a site which was previously occupied by a Capuchin Friary. The Friary was established to help serve the religious needs of Queen Henrietta Maria.

The original two-storey brick Marlborough House was built by the architect Sir Christopher Wren for (1632-1723) John Churchill 1st Duke of Marlborough (1650-1722), the victor of the Battle of Blenheim (1704). The house was built with Dutch-made bricks, which had been used as ballast for the ships that ferried supplies and men to The Netherlands to help provision the Duke's army.

That the House is approached from the side rather than from the front, as Wren's plan intended, stems from the behaviour of Sarah Churchill Duchess of Marlborough (1660-1744), the duke's wife.

Blenheim Palace, the Marlborough's country seat in Oxfordshire was designed by the architect (and playwright) Sir John Vanbrugh (1664-1726). The duchess treated Vanbrugh in appalling manner, both failing to pay him money he was owed and barring him from entering Blenheim's grounds after she had promised him he could have a residence there. Vanbrugh sought redress and informed Sir Robert Walpole (1676-1745) the Prime Minister of what had happened. Walpole straightened Vanbrugh financially and then chose to avenge the man by waging his own vendetta against the duchess, with whom he had had no love lost to start with. Marlborough House proved the means for his vengeance.

Wren's plan for Marlborough House required two houses on Pall Mall (on what is now the site of the United Oxford & Cambridge University Club) to be acquired and torn down so that the House could have a formal entrance onto Pall Mall. For the interim, the House's entrance was a gateway to its south into Green Park. Walpole had King George I (1660-1727) revoke the duchess's right to have carriages driven into the park thus stopped her using the gateway. Next Walpole had the leases on the two houses on Pall Mall, the freeholds of which were owned by the crown, extended. He then had the lease of one house transferred to his brother and that of the other to one of his sons, giving the duchess two Walpoles as her neighbours and leaving her with no choice other than to convert her tradesmen's gate into the House's principal entrance.

In 1817 the Churchills' lease on Marlborough House expired and, despite heavy hints by the family, the property reverted to the crown. Since then its prinicipal use has been to house assorted royals, the likes of King Edward VII (1841-1910) and his Danish wife the immensely popular Queen Alexandra (1844-1925), their son King George V (1865-1936) and his wife Queen Mary (1867-1953).

After the Second World War many of the constitutional conferences which were held prior to a British territory achieving independence took place in either Marlborough House or Lancaster House.

<u>Bricks As Ballast</u>

Some of East Coast America's oldest buildings were built with English-made bricks, which had acted as ballast for ships on their way out to the colonies. An example is Warner Hall, near Yorktown, Virginia, which was built in the C17th.

<u>Direction</u>

Continue along The Mall.

About 20 metres after the stucco of Carlton House Terrace starts, there is a small flight of steps. Ascend these.

King George VI

At the top of the steps is a martial statue (1955) of King George VI (1895-1952), the father of the present Queen.

During the Second World War King George was careful to make sure that his bath water at Buckingham Palace was never more than five inches deep when he took a bath. This was a measure to save the energy that would have otherwise been used to heat more water. (Perhaps he should have been sculpted with a loofah rather than a sword.)

Direction

Pass his Majesty and turn right into Carlton Gardens, which metamorphoses into Carlton House Terrace.

Carlton House

Carlton House was demolished in 1826. The John Nash (1752-1835) designed Carlton House Terrace (1832) occupies what was its site.

The original Carlton House (1709) was built for Baron Carleton (d.1725). The baron was a younger son of the Boyle family (he was the uncle of the architect-earl the 3rd Earl of Burlington (1694-1753)).

In 1732 Frederick Prince of Wales (1707-1751) bought the House. The Prince's widow, Princess Augusta (1719-1772), used it as her residence until her own death. King George III (1738-1820) granted it to his eldest son the future King George IV (1762-1830).

The Prince Regent was very interested in architectural matters and experimented both at Carlton House and on his Pavilion at Brighton. The Prince's London operations were given greater scope when he bought the neighbouring Warwick House in 1792.

The building work did not stop until after he had ascended the throne in 1820.

In 1826 the House was dismantled and its materials and fittings were cannibalised for contemporary building projects. The columns of the central portico of the National Gallery (1837) were originally part of it.

The Marquis of Curzon

On the right, at No. 1 Carlton House Terrace, was the town house of the politician the Marquis of Curzon (1859-1925). For most of his adult life, it was widely assumed that he would become Prime Minister.

In 1923 King George VI (1895-1952) chose the Conservative M.P. Stanley Baldwin (1867-1947) as Prime Minister rather than Curzon who was regarded generally as the front runner for the position. The king told Curzon that he felt it was proper that the premier should be in the same House as the mass of the opposition. Curzon sat in the Lords where, at the time, the Labour Party was virtually unrepresented. King George may have done the nation a considerable political service as Curzon's haughtiness meant that he was temperamentally ill-equipped to deal with the social unrest which existed in Britain during much of the 1920s.

Curzon's high opinion of himself is testified to by a remark which he made as a young man, and for which he is now best remembered, "My name is George Nathaniel Curzon. I am a most superior person".

(There is a bronze statue of the "most superior" Curzon on the corner of Carlton Gardens and Carlton House Terrace.)

The Royal Society

On the right, at No. 6 Carlton House Terrace, is the Royal Society.

From 1648 to 1659 meetings to discuss natural philosophy were held in the rooms of Dr. John Wilkins (1614-1672) of Wadham College, Oxford. From 1659 the meetings took place at Gresham College in Broad Street, London. In 1660 a Society was formally instituted. In 1662 King Charles II (1630-1685) granted the Society a charter.

In 1665 the Royal Society published its first `Philosophical Transactions'.

The Society sponsored a number of exploratory expeditions. In 1768-71 the navigator Captain James Cook (1728-1779) and the scientist Sir Joseph Banks (1743-1820) sailed to the Pacific to observe the transit of Venus. In 1845 the Society organised the explorer Sir John Franklin's (1786-1847) expedition to try to find the north-west passage. Franklin did not return.

In 1945 the Society admitted women as fellows. In the mid-1990s barely one-in-twenty of the 1100 Fellows of the Royal Society (F.R.S.s) was a woman.

In the late 1960s it was still unusual for an industrial scientist to be elected to the Royal Society. This is now less the case than it was.

An accusation sometimes made against the Society is that it tends to be dominated by the Golden Triangle of British Higher Education - London-Oxford-Cambridge.

The Duke of York's Column

At the junction of Carlton House Terrace with Waterloo Place stands the Duke of York's Column (1834).

The Duke of York (1763-1827) was the second son of King George III (1738-1820). The duke died deeply in debt; one wag said that on top of his column he would at least be out of the reach of his creditors.

The money for building the column was raised by every officer and soldier in the British Army forfeiting one day's pay; this was in line with the old army tradition of `being volunteered'. The duke's gaze is reputed to rest on what was then the War Office building in Whitehall.

The soldier-duke had not been a dashing victorious commander. Rather, he had been a thorough administrator whose labours had done much to improve the lot of the ordinary individual soldier and of the standing of the Army in society in general.

(It was once possible for members of the public to climb up a series of steps within the column. This was stopped after rather too many people declined to use the same method to descend.)

The Crown Estate Office

On the right, at No. 13 Carlton House Terrace, is the Crown Estate Office.

In 1760 King George III (1738-1820) handed over the profits of the crown's estates to Parliament. In return, he received the financial provision of the Civil List. Those estates now form the Crown Estate.

The Crown Estate is neither owned by the government nor is it the private estate of the monarch. Any profits from it go to the Exchequer. It encompasses valuable portions of central London, Windsor Great Park, and numerous other commercial and agricultural properties throughout Britain.

Direction
Continue to the end of the Terrace. On the left is a small flight of steps. Descend these. At their bottom turn right into Spring Gardens.

The British Council
The modern building on the right, at No. 10 Spring Gardens, is the British Council.

The British Committee for Relations with Other Countries first met in 1934. The Committee was established to promote a wider international knowledge of British life, thought, and culture. It became the British Council.

Spring Gardens
A `spring' was a plantation. Planted leisure gardens in the mid-C17th consisted of just trees and walks.

The London County Council
No. 10 Spring Gardens was the centre of London government, it being the home first of the Metropolitan Board of Works and then of the London County Council.

Parishes
The system of London government outside of the City of London is built upon the parish, a system which stretches back centuries.

(A manor is an area of land. Often it will have a high degree of overlap with a parish. A lordship of a manor consists of a series of rights within its manor, these rights vary from instance to instance. The lordship of the manor of Hampstead had the right of deodand - in the event of a suicide taking place within the lordship, all the belongings of the suicide fell to the the lord of the manor. The Metropolitan Board of Works purchased lordships whenever it felt able to justify the return for the money involved. In 1870 the Board felt it was worth paying the Maryon-Wilson family £45 000 for the lordship of the manor of Hampstead.)

Beating The Bounds
Beating the bounds is a practice whereby boys would have the bounds of their parish instilled into them. On a given day each year they would be walked around the edge of the parish and at a number of points a ceremony - such as singing, or the boys whipping a stone or tree with small branches, or indeed the boys themselves being lashed - would be performed to help the children remember that site and thus the bounds of their parish.

Ends
When a placename includes the word `End', it is usually a reference to the `edge' of the parish, i.e. where the parish ended. Thus, the West End grew out of the west edge of the City of London.

The Bills of Mortality
From the C16th on, the Company of Parish Clerks compiled the weekly Bills of Mortality. The Bills were started in response to the impact that the plague had had on public health. They recorded deaths in over 100 parishes in and around

London. The Bills were a means of monitoring the size of the population in London and in the districts near the city.

The Bills of Mortality became a de facto form of greater London. Legislation which dealt with matters which affected the whole of London, and its satellite townships and villages, was often binding within the Bills. (In 1836 the Bills of Mortality were superseded by the returns to the Register General.)

(An alternative to the Bills for London-related legislation was a stated radius of miles from the city.)

The Metropolitan Board of Works

Citywide government was induced by the fact that by the mid-C19th there was a danger that if London's population did not drown in its own filth then it would be poisoned by diseases which that filth harboured.

In 1856 the Metropolitan Board of Works was set up. Originally, the Board had 45 members. Three were appointed by the Common Council of the City of London and the rest by either parish vestries or district boards. The district boards were made up of groupings together of small parishes.

The Board had limited powers and its having to co-exist with the vestries meant that it was continuously the subject of adverse criticism. However, it did secure a number of achievements: it constructed many of the West End's principal avenues, it created a citywide drainage system, it built the Thames Embankment, and it preserved a number of London's open spaces, e.g. Hampstead Heath.

The London County Council - The L.C.C.

In 1889 the London County Council superseded the Board. The Council covered not only the Board's domain but also received additional sections of Middlesex, Kent and Surrey.

The L.C.C. was the first metropolitan authority to be directly elected by Londoners.

Politics

But for an interlude in 1895-8, the Liberals (or Progressives) controlled the Council from its formation until 1907. The 1907 elections were bitterly contested and ended in the return to power of the Conservatives (or Municipal Reformers). The Conservatives controlled the Council until 1934. They closed the Works department and stopped the Thames steamboats. In 1934 Labour won control of the Council.

To Finish

Leave Spring Gardens by its exit which enters Whitehall. Cross Whitehall and then Northumberland Avenue and then turn right into the Strand. Walk eastwards to Charing Cross underground station which is on the Northern, Bakerloo and Jubilee Lines.

To Continue

Leave Spring Gardens by its exit which enters Whitehall. Cross Whitehall and then Northumberland Avenue and then turn right into the Strand. Walk eastwards to Charing Cross underground station which is on the Northern, Bakerloo and Jubilee Lines. Take the underground to Marble Arch, which is on the Central Line.

8. Oxford Street and Regent Street

To Start

Go to Marble Arch underground station, which is on the Central Line. Leave the Marble Arch subway system by Exit 4, which comes up by Speaker's Corner.

Hyde Park

Together, Hyde Park and Kensington Gardens make up the largest of the central London parks, occupying nearly an unsquare, square mile of greenery.

The land from which Hyde Park was made belonged to Westminster Abbey until 1536 when King Henry VIII (1491-1547) acquired it by an exchange of estates. The king turned his new property into a deer park (deer remained a feature of the park until the middle of the C18th). It is not altogether clear when the park was opened to the public, although King Charles I (1600-1649) was probably responsible for it in the 1630s.

In the early C19th iron railings replaced the wall which had hitherto enclosed Hyde Park. In the mid-C19th the railings at the park's eastern end were moved back in order to accommodate a broadening of Park Lane.

Marble Arch

The presence of the arches Marble Arch (1827) and Hyde Park Corner (1828) are accepted by most Londoners without question, few probably ever wonder why the arches stand where they stand. Both owe their existence to the efforts of King George IV (1762-1830) to beautify the city.

Originally, Marble Arch stood in front of Buckingham Palace. However, it had not been designed on a monumental enough scale to allow for the easy passage of carriages through its portal. Therefore, in 1851 it was re-erected as an entrance to Hyde Park. In 1908 a roadway was cut to the south and west of it, leaving it on a traffic island.

Only senior members of the royal family and the King's Troop Royal Horse Artillery may officially pass through Marble Arch.

Royal Salutes

The Queen's Birthday is marked in Hyde Park each 22nd April by a 41-gun salute by the guns of the King's Troop Royal Horse Artillery. The first 21 firings signify that it is the Sovereign's birthday which is being saluted and the 20 after indicate that the salute is being carried out in a royal park.

With the outbreak of the Second World War in 1939 the Horse Artillery Batteries were mechanised, the internal combustion engine being better fitted for modern warfare than the horse. After the war King George VI (1895-1952) expressed a desire that something of the old, equine tradition should be maintained. As the result of the monarch's wish, a permanent saluting battery unit was established. The following year the Troop received its name after a visit made by the king to its St.John Wood's barracks.

When the regiment is on parade with its guns, it takes precedence over all other regiments and occupies the place of honour on the right of the line.

Tyburn

Tyburn is on the crossroad of two Roman roads. It probably became a place of execution because it was an important junction, on one of the busiest roads into

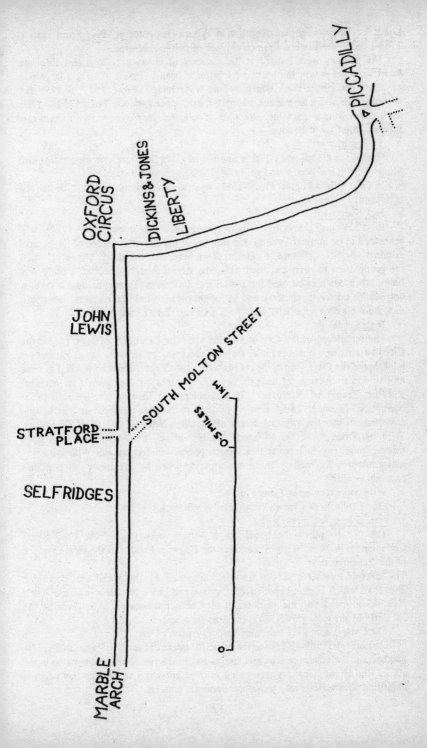

PICCADILLY

OXFORD
CIRCUS

DICKINS & JONES

LIBERTY

JOHN
LEWIS

SOUTH MOLTON STREET

STRATFORD
PLACE

SELFRIDGES

1KM

0·5 MILES

MARBLE
ARCH

London. The first recorded execution at Tyburn took place in 1196. From 1388 to 1783 Tyburn was London's principal place of public execution.

The gallows were located at the junction of Bayswater Road and Edgware Road, on what is now the Marble Arch traffic island. Down to 1571 a large elm provided the gibbet from which people were hung. From 1571 to 1759 the 'Tyburn Tree' was a permanent, triangular, man-made gallows. From 1759 to 1783 the gallows were a temporary structure. Thereafter, they were moved to Newgate Prison in the City of London.

Tyburn Martyrs

During the C16th and C17th a number of Catholics were executed at Tyburn. Many of them had been found guilty of plotting against the state.

In 1681 Oliver Plunket (1629-1681) was the last Catholic martyr to be hanged at Tyburn.

Jack Sheppard

In 1724 the charismatic highwayman Jack Sheppard (1702-1724) was sentenced to be hung at Tyburn. On the day of his execution, some of Sheppard's criminal associates planned to cut him down before he was dead. However, when the group tried to carry out their plan, the crowd thought Sheppard's body was being taken down to be used for anatomical dissection (Tyburn being a source of corpses for doctors to dissect), and so fought off his would-be rescuers. Sheppard died from his own popularity with those who had come to watch him die.

Jonathan Wild

The rebuilding of the City of London after the Great Fire of 1666 placed the City Corporation's finances under extreme pressure. In 1694 an Act of Parliament bankrupted the City. One of the means which the Corporation then utilised to raise money was to auction off the principal civic offices, including the City Marshal and the Keeper of Newgate. This development fostered an atmosphere of corruption, in which the definition of legality became blurred. It was in this environment that the criminal career of Jonathan Wild (c1682-1725) flourished. Wild purported to act as an agent through whom individuals, who had been robbed, might try to recover their stolen goods. In fact, it was Wild who was masterminding the thefts. There was a period when he effectively ran London's criminal world.

Wild was executed at Tyburn in 1725.

(The City offices were all eventually bought back.)

Cato Street Conspirators

The last people to be beheaded at Tyburn were five of the Cato Street Conspirators in 1820. (Cato Street, near the Edgware Road, was the meeting-place of the conspirators.)

The conspirators were people who felt displaced by the social and economic upheavals which Britain experienced after the end of the Napoleonic Wars. Their plan was to murder all the members of the Cabinet at a dinner to be given by the 1st Earl of Harrowby (1762-1847) in Grosvenor Square.

The conspirators were beheaded with a surgeon's knife.

Castlereagh (1769-1822) was the principal target of the conspiracy. In 1815 he had become the government's chief spokesman in the House of Commons on home affairs (the Home Secretary then being in the Lords) and as such he had become identified with various very unpopular domestic policies.

Castlereagh committed suicide in 1822 by cutting his carotid artery.

The Death Penalty & The House of Commons

Since 1965 the death penalty has been limited to a number of acts such as high treason and piracy upon the high seas.

In the general population there is clear support for the hanging of murderers, especially in instances of murders committed as part of terrorist atrocities. However, Parliament has repeatedly chosen to ignore the wishes of that majority.

Periodically, the House of Commons votes on whether or not to restore hanging. The question is usually put in such a way that it is far from being a blanket restitution but such a restitution as is proposed in the Parliamentary motion would almost certainly prove be the thin end of a wedge.

The Commons is always allowed a free vote on the matter. There is near total opposition to restitution from the Labour and Liberal parties and there are always enough liberal Conservatives to insure that the death penalty is not restored. Support for the death penalty within Parliament peaked in the late 1980s and is now in decline. October 1993, after the shooting of an unarmed policeman in Clapham, was the last time there was a division on the matter and the majority was such that it is unlikely that there will be another one for some years.

Speaker's Corner

Right of Assembly

In 1855 there was a mass rally held in the north-east corner of Hyde Park to protest at Lord Robert Grosvenor's (1801-1893) Sunday Trading Bill. At the time there was no legal right of assembly.

In 1866 large demonstrations took place in Hyde Park. These were part of a popular movement which was demanding a broadening of the electoral franchise. (The Second Reform Act of 1867 was passed as a response to a general desire for the right to vote to be extended within the population.)

As a result of the demonstrations Park Lane was widened, the railings being set back within what was then the park's perimeter to make room for the broadened road.

In 1872 Parliament passed the legislation which granted the right of public assembly. As a result, Speaker's Corner was established in the north-east corner of Hyde Park. The Corner has no immunity from any of the laws respecting slander or incitement to cause a breach of the peace.

Donald Soper

Donald Soper is the most famous Methodist minister in Britain. For many years Soper conducted his religious and social work from the West London Mission. He has spoken regularly at Hyde Park Corner since 1926. He worked actively with the homeless and prostitutes. In 1965 he was made a life peer.

Direction

Re-enter the Marble Arch subway system using Exit 4. Resurface at either Exit 1 or Exit 2. Head east along Oxford Street.

Oxford Street

Ermine Street was the Roman road which formed the basis of Oxford Street and the Bayswater Road. It gave the east-west axis to the West End and determined the northern edge of Hyde Park.

Department Stores

A number of factors combined to assist the development of the department store in London during the second half of the C19th. Foremost among these were the opening of Bon Marche store in Paris and the example of the Great Exhibition of 1851, which had shown how a vast array of goods could be displayed within a single building. In addition, advances in glass and gas technology meant that goods could be displayed more attractively than had previously been the case and that shops could be better lit.

For the most part, the department stores developed out of drapery shops.

The Oxford Street department stores, notably Selfridges, are sited in the section of the street to the west of Oxford Circus. (There were others to the east of the Circus but they have closed.)

Dixons

On the right, at Nos. 491-497 Oxford Street, is Dixons the electrical goods retailer.

In 1948 Stanley Kalms joined his father's one shop photographic equipment retailing business in Enfield, north London. Kalms proved a highly adept salesman. Not only that but he also proved skilled at sourcing goods, he was a pioneer of importing items which had been manufactured in the Far East. Through the 1950s and into the early 1960s, as Britain enjoyed a new level of material prosperity, the market for photographic goods expanded rapidly. Dixons prospered in this environment.

In 1967 the company began retailing electrical goods for which it is now best known. The British are very partial to such goods. They have among the highest per head ownership rates in the world of items such as video recorders and home computers. (This may have something to do with the long winter evenings.)

Marks & Spencer - M&S

On the left, at No. 458 Oxford Street, is the flagship store of Marks & Spencer. The company is perceived principally as a clothes retailer. However, its food sections are highly regarded.

The business was founded by Michael Marks (1859-1907) as a stall in Leeds's Kirkgate market in 1884. Marks's first great innovation was to put a sign on his stall which read "Don't ask the price, it's a penny". This stemmed from his being unable to speak English at the time, having only recently arrived from Slonim in Russia. However, the notice also proved a highly successful retailing strategy.

Thomas Spencer was a cashier for Isaac Dewhirst, the wholesaler who was Marks's first business contact. In 1894 Spencer bought a half share in Marks's business for £300. M&S opened its first `Penny Bazaar' at Cheetham, Manchester, in September 1894.

Marks was an innovative retailer. He allowed customers to handle the stock rather than forcing them to be served over a counter by an assistant. The company was the first to have self-service outlets.

Marks & Spencer was built up into a national institution by Marks's son Simon Marks Lord Marks (1888-1964). He built up a chain of fixed-price bazaar stores. His great colleague was Israel Sieff Lord Sieff (1889-1972), whom he met while studying at Manchester Grammar School. Each man married the other's sister.

Marks & Spencer opened its first branch in London in the Edgware Road in 1912; within a couple of years the company was established London-wide.

After the First World War Simon Marks began his own innovations as a retailer. He abandoned the fixed-price format although he retained initially a price ceiling of five shillings. Marks & Spencer adopted the use of the St.Michael brand in the 1920s. The `Michael' was taken from Michael Marks. Simon Marks developed `specification buying', using the company's purchasing power to oblige manufacturers to follow exactly its instructions as to quality. The company lay down rigorous standards which its suppliers had to meet. Failure to do so led to loss of favour, success in doing so meant that the manufacturer entered a haven of profitablity which even the largest manufacturers sought to enter.

It was in the early 1950s that clothing began to establish itself as Marks & Spencer's principal section. All its other sections, with the exception of food, were eased out, to allow clothes an ever greater share of sales space.

In 1968 Marks & Spencer overtook Woolworths as the Britain's leading retailer.

In 1970 the company established its national chilled food distribution network. This turned it into the leading chilled, high-quality convenience food retailer.

Laura Ashley

On the right, on the south-east corner of Oxford Street and North Audley Street, is an outlet of Laura Ashley the clothes retailing company.

Laura Ashley (1925-1985) and her husband (later Sir) Bernard Ashley founded the company Laura Ashley in 1958. The Ashleys opened their first shop within the premises of Annacat, a dress company that pioneered the frilly Victorian look. The business developed into a national and international retailer under the direction of Sir Bernard Ashley.

In the late 1980s the company was badly caught out by the development of power dressing. Its soft, flowing image was at odds with the trend. In March 1997 the company launched a campaign in the United States which included the phrase "Laura Ashley - say it without flowers".

Selfridges

On the left, at No. 400 Oxford Street, is Selfridges the department store.

Harry Gordon Selfridge (1858-1947) was an American (although subsequently he became a British citizen) who made his reputation as the general manager of Marshall Field's retail department in Chicago.

Selfridge believed that the British knew how to make goods but not how to sell them, he arrived in London in 1906 planning to build the finest store ever seen in Britain. Sam Waring (1860-1940), of Waring & Gillow the furniture store, backed Selfridge on condition that Selfridges would not sell any furniture.

In 1909 Selfridges the department store opened in Oxford Street. The store revolutionised Britain's shopping, with its credit scheme, a bargain basement, annual sales, innovative window displays, and departments with their goods in full view so that the public could inspect them at their own leisure. The 1920s were the store's golden era. (In 1928 the store made the world's first sale of a televison.)

While Selfridge's wife Rose (d.1918) was alive his personal conduct had been orderly and conventional. After her death he cultivated an exotic private life and spent money freely. Selfridge found himself unable to operate so effectively in the economic downturn of the 1930s. In 1939 the company's board forced him to resign. His final years were spent living in straitened circumstances in Putney.

Direction
On the north side of Oxford Street, cross St.James Street. After three shops turn left in Gees Court, the entrance to St.Christopher's Place.

St.Christopher's Place
St.Christopher's Place is a pedestrianised Victorian shopping street off Oxford Street. Its C19th appearance has acquired an overlay of outdoor cafes and restaurants.

Direction
Go back to Oxford Street. Turn left into Oxford Street.

Stratford Place
On the left is Stratford Place, a cul-de-sac.
Stratford Place was built on the site of Stratford House which had itself been built up on the site of the Lord Mayor's Banqueting House.
The Lord Mayor's Banqueting House
In 1439 the City of London was granted a water supply from the springs at Bayswater by Westminster Abbey. The Banqueting House was used by the Lord Mayor of London and City dignitaries after they had made an official visit to inspect the springs.

Browns
To the south of Stratford Place both South Molton Street and Davies Street join Oxford Street. South Molton Street runs north-west to south-east. On the right, at Nos. 23-27 South Molton Street, is Browns the fashion clothes retailer.
Browns is owned by the Burstein family. The Bursteins have played an important role in developing British design talent.

HMV
On the right is one of the Oxford Street stores of HMV the music retail company, which is owned by EMI the record company.
HMV takes its name from `His Master's Voice', a painting by Francis Barraud of a Jack Russell dog listening to a gramophone. The painting was bought by William Owen, an American businessman who built up the Gramophone Company, one of EMI's predecessor companies.

Debenhams
On the left, at Nos. 334-348 Oxford Street, is Debenhams the department store.
Debenhams grew out of a drapery shop which was established in Marylebone in the C18th. In 1813 William Debenham joined the partnership. In 1926 the Debenham family allowed their controlling interest to be bought out.
In the post-1945 era Debenhams was by far the largest owner of provincial department stores in Britain.

Burtons the menswear retailer acquired Debenhams in 1985.

Tesco

On the right, at No. 311 Oxford Street, is a branch of Tesco the supermarket chain.

In 1919 Jack Cohen (1898-1979) set up a grocery stall in a London street market. Cohen soon had a chain of stalls and moved into wholesaling. In 1931 he opened his first Tesco store in Burnt Oak, north London. The company was a dry groceries goods retailer with a `pile it high, sell it cheap' policy. Tesco reputedly took its name from one of Cohen's early tea suppliers - T.E.Stockwell of Terring & Stockwell of Mincing Lane. (Tea companies were at the forefront of the international movement of food stuffs. A number of them were involved in the establishment of early British supermarket chains.)

In 1935 Cohen visited the United States and returned with the intention of bringing self-service supermarkets to Britain. He was prevented from implementing his vision by the outbreak of the Second World War. However, in 1947 the company opened its first self-service store at St.Albans.

Tesco's expansion beyond food stuffs into clothing was due in large part to the influence of Sir Leslie Porter, a son-in-law of Cohen, who joined the business in 1959.

The company expanded through acquisition. However, by the mid-1970s it had begun to acquire an image problem, it being perceived as a business which valued quantity over quality. From the late 1970s on Tesco undertook a large-scale modernisation programme which markedly improved its image.

In the early 1980s Tesco became bigger than Sainsbury's. Since then the two companies have rivalled one another as to which is the country's leading grocer.

Tesco pioneered the Metro format - supermarkets in town centres with relatively small floor sizes (it is arguable that this is what Marks & Spencer food departments have been doing for years). It opened its first Tesco Metro in Covent Garden in 1993, which was followed by others in Hammersmith and Oxford Street.

John Lewis's

On the left, between Old Cavendish Street and Holles Street, is the John Lewis department store.

John Lewis (1836-1928) worked as a buyer in Peter Robinson's store in Chelsea's Sloane Square before setting up on his own as a retailer. In 1864 he opened his first shop at No. 132 Oxford Street (on what is now part of the site of the company's flagship store). Using retained profits, he built the shop up into one of the street's principal department stores.

In 1897 Lewis acquired Cavendish Buildings in Cavendish Square with the intention of extending his shop through them so that it ran through from Oxford Street to Cavendish Square. Other property owners opposed his plan because they felt it would commercialise the square's character. The matter went to law and when Lewis defied a court injunction on the matter it led to his spending a brief spell in Brixton Prison. Ultimately, Lewis obtained his wish and extended his store through to the square.

While he lived, Peter Jones (d.1905), Lewis's former employer, was one of his principal rivals. In 1906 Lewis bought Jones's company. Without Jones the

Sloane Square store began to decline. To reverse this state of affairs, Lewis made over the Chelsea business to his own eldest son John Spedan Lewis (1885-1963). However, Lewis senior insisted that his son should first work a full day at the Oxford Street store before attending to the affairs of its Sloane Square sister.

John Spedan Lewis had his own ideas about retailing. He used his new opportunity to implement them. As a result, father and son fell out. John Spedan Lewis went to work at Peter Jones full-time. Subsequently, John Lewis visited the Peter Jones store and was favourably struck by what he saw there. The two were reconciled after both their businesses were hit by the downturn in trade in the early 1920s, John Lewis's surviving the better in the adverse conditions.

John Spedan Lewis's ideas extended to business ownership. After his father's death he established the John Lewis Partnership which owns the John Lewis department store chain along with other businesses. The Partnership allows its workforces to benefit from its success.

Holles Street

On the left is Holles Street, which used to contain the first of London's Blue Plaques. (It was in fact brown, blue being adopted subsequently.)

A Blue Plaque is placed on a building to commemorate someone of note who has lived there. The person who is being commemorated needs to have been dead for at least a couple decades.

The Blue Plaque scheme was set up by the Royal Society of Arts. The Holles Street plaque was put up to commemorate the birthplace of the poet Lord Byron (1788-1824). (The building was pulled down as part of the street's redevelopment).

In 1901 the London County Council assumed responsibility for the scheme, the matter passing on to the Greater London Council on the Council's creation in 1965. With the Greater London Council's abolition in 1986 administration of the scheme passed to English Heritage.

About a dozen or so plaques are put up each year.

The London College of Fashion

On the left, above the shops on the northern side of Oxford Street between Holles Street and John Princes Street, is the London College of Fashion. The College is part of the London Institute.

The College's entrance is in John Princes Street.

Oxford Circus

For many years Stanley Green (1915-1994) stood around Oxford Circus wearing a sandwich board. Written on the board was the accusation that protein was the root of lust. Mr. Green's board now resides in The Museum of London.

Direction

At Oxford Circus turn right into Regent Street.

Regent Street

Prior to the construction of Regent Street, Swallow Street was the principal avenue linking Oxford Street and Piccadilly.

In the late C18th the officials of the Crown Estate appreciated that in 1811 the 500-acre Marylebone Park would revert to the crown. The officials considered not only developing the park itself but also creating a great avenue through the West End which would both act as an approach to the Park and as a means of improving the areas through which it ran. (If the areas were improved, higher rents could then be charged.) Ultimately, Regent's Park, as it became known, was only lightly developed.

Initially, the project was led by John Fordyce (1735-1809), the Surveyor-General to the Department of Woods & Forests, and after his death by the architect John Nash (1752-1835).

In view of Regent Street's standing as one of the great examples of C19th European planning, the road's course is somewhat eccentric. Its first section runs north from Pall Mall until it reaches Piccadilly Circus. From there it exits, at almost a right-angle, and proceeds to go into a rightward curve until it rights itself again on a northern path parallel, if further to the west, to that which would have been its course had it continued along its initial projection.

The street has this shape because to buy up the property to the due north of the lower section of Regent Street would have been too expensive for the overall project to have remained viable.

The street crosses Oxford Street without wavering but as soon as it reaches Langham Place it jumps to another parallel northern path, again to the west, and changes its name to Portland Place. In this guise it bifurcates just below the Marylebone Road, pulling itself together on the northern side in order to assume the altogether more innocent identity of a park avenue. In this guise it successfully crosses Regent's Park before giving up the ghost on the druidic altar of Primrose Hill.

Regent Street encouraged demarcation of the older confusion to the east from the more planned districts of Mayfair and St.James's to the west.

Clientele and The Growth of Big Stores

In the late C19th Regent Street's clientele shifted from being predominantly the aristocractic residents of the West End to being the middle classes of the new suburbs and the Home Counties beyond them. The resulting lower profit margins forced businesses to expand in order to maintain their profitability. Larger businesses required larger premises.

Street Decorations

The first Regent Street decorations were put up in 1951 as part of the Festival of Britain. They were devised by Jill Greenwood (1910-1995), a shop designer for Jaeger the clothes retailer. (Greenwood was the wife of Tony Greenwood, a Labour politician. The Festival was commissioned by a Labour government.)

In 1954 Greenwood designed Regent Street's first Christmas lights and in 1959 Oxford Street's first ones.

Dickins & Jones

On the left, at Nos. 224-244 Regent Street, is Dickins & Jones the department store.

The House of Fraser department store company was founded in Glasgow in the middle of the C19th. In 1959 the company bought Harrods.

In 1994 the House of Fraser department store business was split off from Harrods and floated off on the Stock Exchange. The Regent Street branch of Dickins & Jones was groomed to act as the chain's flagship store.

House of Fraser owns Army & Navy Stores, Arnotts, Barkers of Kensington, Binns, Cavendish House of Cheltenham, Dickins & Jones, Dingles, D.H.Evans, David Evans, Frasers of Glasgow, Hammonds of Hull, Howells of Cardiff, Jollys of Bath, Kendals of Manchester, Rackhams of Birmingham, and Schofields. The roots of some of the individual businesses, such as Jollys and Cavendish House, go back to the C18th.

Some of these businesses were already chains in their own right before being drawn into the House of Fraser's orbit. Attempts at rebranding provincial department stores have run into difficulty with local particularism.

Liberty & Company
On the left is Liberty & Company. (This is covered in the Soho walk.)

Jaeger
On the left, at Nos. 204-206 Regent Street, is Jaeger the clothes retailer.

In 1880 Lewis Tomalin picked up the theory of the German zoologist Dr. Gustav Jaeger that people were best off being clothed in garments made from wool and other animal hairs. Jaeger licensed the use of his name to Tomalin, who, in order to promote the idea, opened the first Jaeger shop in 1884. The business soon metamorphosed into a conventional clothes retaling company. In the early 1920s Humphrey Tomalin gave the business a fashion-oriented image.

Hamleys
On the left, at No. 188-196 Regent Street, is Hamleys the toy store.
William Hamley opened his first toy shop in High Holborn in 1760.
Teddy Bears
English teddy bears tend to be slightly more expressive than their German counterparts; English bears' eyes and ears tend to be marginally larger.

Burberrys
On the right, at No. 165 Regent Street, is a branch of Burberrys.

In 1856 Thomas Burberry set himself up as a fabric manufacturer in Basingstoke, Hampshire. Mr. Burberry was inspired by the quality of Hampshire smocks to develop a fabric which was both weatherproof and untearable, while also being comfortable and cool for the wearer.

In 1899 he moved his business to London.

In 1924 the company devised the renowned Burberry check. The check came to the fore during the 1960s. It is featured on numerous products.

Garrard
On the left, at No. 112 Regent Street, is Garrard the jewellers, the crown jewellers since 1843.

In 1735 the goldsmith George Wickes opened a shop on the corner of Haymarket and Panton Street. In 1792 Robert Garrard joined the business.

Austin Reed

On the right, at Nos. 103-113 Regent Street, is the flagship store of Austin Reed the clothes retailer.

The Reed family's tailoring and outfitting business was based in Reading, Berkshire. In 1888 Austin Reed (1873-1954) joined the firm. Towards the end of the C19th he made a trip to the United States in order to observe the developments in retailing which had taken place there. In 1900 he opened a store in Fenchurch Street in the City of London. The City was full of potential customers whose taste's were not subject to the whims of fashion. The company built a straightforward image aimed at attracting custom from business people.

The Veeraswamy Restaurant

On the right at Nos. 99-101 Regent Street is The Veeraswamy Restaurant, one of London's first Indian restaurants.

Aquascutum

On the left, at No. 100 Regent Street, is Aquascutum.

John Emary founded Aquascutum in 1851 in order to exploit his patent for shower-proofing woollen fabric; the name aquascutum was formed through a conjunction of the Latin words for `water' and `shield'. The product was a beneficiary of the First World War; officers were issued with Aquascutum coats, thus giving the product social cachet while demonstrating its durability.

Cafe Royal

On the left, at No. 68 Regent Street, is Cafe Royal, a five-storey restaurant and banqueting complex.

In 1865 Daniel Nicols, a bankrupt French wine merchant, opened the Cafe Restaurant Nichols in Glasshouse Street. In 1867 he moved to No. 68 Regent Street where the Cafe Royal remains today.

The fin-de-siecle era of the 1890s made the Cafe Royal famous. Artists and writers flocked there to enjoy one of the finest wine cellars in Europe. In the 1930s the Cafe still had a Bohemian reputation.

After the Second World War, the Cafe Royal went into something of a decline until it was acquired by Charles Forte (later Lord Forte).

To Finish

Go to Piccadilly Circus underground station, which is on the Piccadilly and Bakerloo Lines.

To Continue

Walk back up Regent Street and turn left into Vigo Street. Vigo Street is on the western side of the juncture of the straight and curved sections of Regent Street.

9. Mayfair

To Start

Go to Piccadilly Circus underground station. Leave the station by the exit which is on the western side of the Regent Street. Walk up Regent Street and turn left into Vigo Street. Vigo Street is on the western side of the juncture of the straight and curved sections of Regent Street.

Gieves & Hawkes

On the right, at No. 1 Savile Row, is Gieves & Hawkes the tailors, a business formed through the merger of an army uniform tailor with a tailor of naval uniforms.

In 1771 the Hawkes tailoring business was founded. Its customers included the Duke of Wellington (1769-1852).

In 1785 Melchizedeck Meredith established a tailoring business in Portsmouth. The Meredith firm made uniforms for the naval hero Lord Nelson (1758-1805). In 1852 James Gieve joined the business.

Ozwald Boateng

On the left, at No. 9 Vigo Street, is Ozwald Boateng, Bespoke Couture.

Penguin Books

On the left, at No. 8 Vigo Street, is where Penguin Books was started in 1935.

In the early 1930s Allen Lane (1902-1970) was the managing director of Bodley Head the publishing house. The company's financial predicament led him to publish paperbacks on his own account. The idea was not an original one (von Tauchnitz had done it in Leipzig in the 1840s), what was original was the way in which it was executed - the books were produced as proper books rather than as disposable items. Lane succeeded in getting the scheme off the ground when the publisher Jonathan Cape (1879-1960) allowed him to reprint ten Cape authors. Penguin was launched in 1935. In 1937 Lane resigned from Bodley Head so as to be better able to concentrate his energies on Penguin.

Lane was a good enough publisher to let others expand the business for him, moving Penguin from being a reprint house into also acting as an original publisher. During the Second World War the company flourished. It used its paper ration for printing authors new to its list rather than to maintain its back catalogue.

In 1978 Peter Mayer was appointed chief executive of Penguin Worldwide. He attracted considerable attention by putting a lurid cover on M.M.Kaye's novel `The Far Pavillions' (1979); it was the sort of sales approach with which Penguin had not previously been associated. The book became a bestseller. Mayer achieved notoriety by axing several titles from the backlist. (Subsequently, he allowed the backlist to grow back to the point where it was longer than when he took over.)

Penguin owns a number of hardback houses. This is to ensure that, in an age when most publishers have integrated hardback/paperback publishing rights, it has a proper supply of titles.

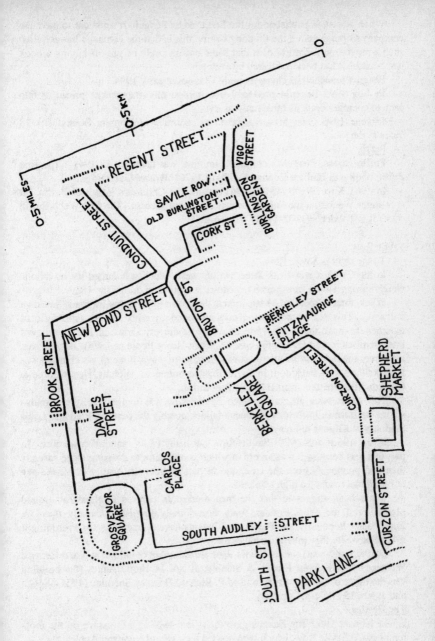

When a book is published for the first time by Penguin it tends not to have the company's orange spine; the thinking behind this is that the company has acquired such a reputation for worthiness that some buyers might be put off buying a book just because it has been published by Penguin.

Penguin launched its cheap Penguin Classics in early 1994.

In July 1995 Penguin produced five million mini-paperbacks priced at 60p each to commemorate its 60th anniversary.

In June 1996 Peter Mayer resigned as chairman of Penguin Books after 18 years in the job.

Puffin

Puffin Books, Penguin's children's imprint, was launched in 1941. The first Puffin book was Barbara Euphan Todd's (d.1976) `Worzel Gummidge'.

In 1961 Kaye Webb (1914-1996) became the Children's Editor of Puffin. It was under Webb that the imprint became a roaring success. The first Webb Puffin was J.R.R.Tolkien's (1892-1973) `The Hobbit'.

Savile Row

To the right is Savile Row.

In the C18th it was Cork Street (to the west) which was famed for its tailors. Neighbouring Savile Row began to acquire is reputation during the 1850s.

When James Poole (d.1846) joined the Volunteers Corps he made his own uniform. This led to him being commissioned by some of his fellow Corps members to make theirs. In 1806 he opened a drapery shop. In 1823 he moved into premises in Old Burlington Street. When Henry Poole (d.1876), James's son, took over the business he altered it in a number of ways. One of his changes was to make the shop's back door in Savile Row its entrance. Thereby, Henry Poole & Company became the original Savile Row tailor.

The 1920s were an era in which Savile Row was invigorated, the stimulus stemming from an in-flow of European tailors, notably the brothers Fred and Louis Stanbury at Kilgour & French.

In the 1960s and 1970s Savile Row lost many of its `natural' customers. In part this was because it was an era in which people took to dressing more casually than had previously been the case, and in part because the quality of off-the-peg tailoring had reached a high standard.

It has been suggested that the men dressed in tailored Englishwear around Mayfair and the West End are only occasionally English. Usually they are Europeans. Reputedly, the French and Italians have a reputation for overdoing it to a point where they give themselves away.

On the right (east) side of Savile Row are a number ot tailors: at No. 8 Bernard Weatherill and Kilgour French & Stanley; at No. 14 Hardy Amies (the building was the home of the playwright and M.P. Richard Brinsley Sheridan (1751-1816)); and at No. 15 Poole & Company.

The Beatles

In January 1969 The Beatles gave their final public performance on the roof-top of No. 3 Savile Row, which then housed their record company Apple.

Classical Greece in Britain

No. 12 Savile Row was the home of George Grote M.P. (1794-1871) the historian of Classical Greece.

In the late C17th and early C18th Britain obtained a domestic political harmony this gave its admirals the resources to capture the world's trade routes which its merchants were able to profitably exploit. As a result, British society found itself going through commercial and social upheavals. The C18th passion for the Classics was in part a response to those changes. Britons saw the rapid improvement in their material well-being being like that of the Athenians in the C5th BC and that of the Romans in the C1st BC. The Classical imagery and symbolism used by writers, artists and architects was easily decipherable to an educated public whose schooling left them with a thorough knowledge of the ancient Greek and Latin authors.

The first general history of ancient Greece, `The History of Greece' (1786), was written by John Gillies (1747-1836). His purpose in writing the work was to vindicate the conduct of his hero the martial autocrat Frederick the Great of Prussia.

The next notable history, also `The History of Greece' (1784-1810), was by William Mitford of Beaulieu (1744-1827), an M.P. and a friend of Edward Gibbon (1737-1794), the author of `The Decline and Fall of the Roman Empire'. Mitford was inclined to look favourably on the despots and to look down upon the Athenian democrats.

George Grote was a banker and M.P. who believed that democracy, as exemplified by the Athenians, benefitted everyone both rich and poor. As an M.P., Grote represented the City of London. He wrote `The History of Greece' (1846-56).

Direction
    Walk along Burlington Gardens.

Cornwallis
    On the right is Old Burlington Street. On the left, at No. 29 Old Burlington Street, lived the general the 1st Marquis of Cornwallis (1738-1805).

    Cornwallis was the commander of the British force which surrendered at Yorktown in 1781, a defeat which spelt the beginning of the end of the American War of Independence.

    Culford Hall in Suffolk was the Cornwallis family's country seat. The iron bridge (1803) on the lake at Culford is believed to have been made from cannons captured during Lord Cornwallis's years (1786-93) as Commander-in-Chief in India. For many years the bridge was `lost' because the grounds of the Hall, which is now used as a school, became unkempt. With the passage of time, there was no longer anyone around who knew that there was a bridge there.

The Museum of Mankind
    On the left (south) side of Burlington Gardens is the Museum of Mankind, the Ethnographic Department of the British Museum. Since 1970 the Museum of Mankind has resided in Burlington Gardens.

The University of London
    The statues on the building's front are all of people but are not connected with the Museum. They were put there as part of the building's original decoration, it having been built as a home for the University of London.

The University of London was established much later than the oldest universities in the other great European capitals. It was constituted by royal charter in 1836 as an organisation, to which a number of colleges and schools were federated. In 1838 the University held its first examinations.

Initially, the University was housed in rooms in Somerset House. Its first Chancellor was the 2nd Earl of Burlington (later 7th Duke of Devonshire) (1808-1891).

In 1853 the University moved to rooms in Burlington House. In 1858 certificates of studentship for those who wished to sit its examinations were done away with (except in the medical faculty); this meant that anyone could take a degree.

In 1866 the University moved to Burlington Gardens.

In 1878 the University of London became the first university in Britain to admit women as candidates for degrees, on equal terms with men. In 1912 the University made its first appointment of a woman to a professorial chair.

In 1911 the University decided that it should be accommodated in buildings which matched its standing. A site was acquired in Bloomsbury. In 1936 the University moved to Senate House in Bloomsbury.

The Burlington Arcade

Just beyond the end of the Museum is the northern entrance to The Burlington Arcade.

Direction

Turn right into Cork Street.

Hancocks

On the left, at No. 1 Burlington Gardens, is Hancocks the jeweller.

Hancocks utilises metal from a cannon captured during the Crimean War of 1854-6 for rather a different use from building bridges, the firm makes Victoria Crosses (V.C.s), the highest British military gallantry medal.

The Victoria Cross

The Victoria Cross was established by Queen Victoria (1819-1901) in 1856. The medal has always been given to all ranks of all the services. The Queen handed out the first Victoria Crosses at an investiture ceremony held in Hyde Park in 1857.

Tradition had it that the cannon was a Russian cannon captured during the course of the war. However, in the 1970s the metallurgist Peter Burke discovered that the metal was from a cannon of Chinese origin and not one of Russian manufacture. Even so, it is almost certain that the Russian-cannon-of-Chinese-origin was brought back from The Crimea.

Cork Street

On the left, at Nos. 11-12 Cork Street, are the Waddington Galleries.

The principal art dealing season is from May through to October. On the whole, Britons are not big buyers of art and dealers make their money from London being one of the great international cities. European buyers and conservative English critics have a fairly small overlap in their tastes.

Leslie Waddington

Cork Street is the centre of the Waddington empire.

Leslie Waddington is the leading contemporary art dealer in Britain.

Waddington was born into the trade, his father ran a gallery in Dublin. The first of Waddington's Cork Street galleries opened in 1957.

Waddington has represented artists such Patrick Heron, Peter Blake, and Patrick Caulfield. In the British art business, if Waddington shivers other dealers worry about catching colds. His April 1994 announcement that he was scaling down the size of his British operations and opening a new gallery in Paris caused consternation in the art world. This seems to have been a partial redeployment of his resources in response to the increasing internationalisation of the European art market in the wake of the abolition of internal customs barriers in 1992.

Direction

Turn left into Clifford Street. Walk to the end of Clifford Street and, at the junction with New Bond Street, look to the left.

New Bond Street

To the left is the bottom section of New Bond Street. This is dominated by jewellers. (By Burlington Gardens, New Bond Street turns into Old Bond Street.)

New Bond Street and Regent Street have rivalled one another over the years. Bond Street is now the more upmarket of the two.

Asprey

On the western (right) side of New Bond Street, on the corner of Grafton Street, is Asprey the jewellers.

The Asprey family had been Huguenot craftsmen in Britain for several generations, before they founded the Asprey jewellery business in 1781 in the then Surrey village of Mitcham (which is now a south London suburb). The company moved to Bond Street in 1848.

In November 1995 Asprey was bought by Prince Jefri Bolkiah, a younger brother of the Sultan of Brunei. At the time of the sale, the company was 52%-owned by the Asprey family.

Direction

Turn right into New Bond Street. Turn left into Bruton Street.

The Time & Life Building

On the left, on the south-western corner of New Bond Street and Bruton Street, is The Time & Life Building (No. 1 Bruton Street) (1952).

In 1953 Time-Life, the American magazine company, commissioned a number of works from the sculptor Henry Moore (1898-1986), which it installed in its New Bond Street building, notably a screen which was mounted on the building's exterior. In 1993 Time-Life's lease on the building expired. The company removed from the premises those Moore sculptures which it regarded as its own chattels and left those which it regarded as fixtures of the building. Westminster City Council ordered the company to restore to the building those sculptures which it had removed, Time-Life refused to do so and the matter went to litigation. In January 1995 there was a judicial ruling in the company's favour.

Direction
Turn left into Bruton Street.

Holland & Holland
On the right, at Nos. 31-33 Bruton Street, is Holland & Holland the gunsmiths. The firm have been making guns since 1830.

In 1989 it was bought by the Wertheimers, the French family who control Chanel.

Camper & Nicolson
On the right, at No. 25 Bruton Street, is the shop of Camper & Nicolson the Gosport-based yacht builders, which has been in business since 1782.

No. 17 Bruton Street
On the left, at No. 17 Bruton Street, is a plaque which commemorates the birth (21 April 1926) of the present Queen in a house on the site.

Direction
Bruton Street runs into Berkeley Square.

Lansdowne House
Dominating the southern side of Berkeley Square is the site which until 1985 was occupied by Lansdowne House (1768), one of the great aristocratic town houses of London.

W.C.s
Lansdowne House contained one of the first water closets to be installed in the C18th.

The water closet is supposed to have been invented in 1596 by Sir John Harington (1561-1612). The beneficiary of his inventiveness was his godmother Queen Elizabeth I (1533-1603), for whom he constructed one in (the now disappeared) Richmond Palace. Because few houses had supplies of running water and those that had had highly irregular water pressure, the device remained essentially a curiosity. In addition there was no drainage system to accommodate their general adoption.

In 1778 Joseph Bramah (1748-1814) devised a ballcock-regulated cistern, an improved version of Alexander Cunningham's S-trap water-closet. The device was introduced in the great London town houses, and like numerous other consumable items it was soon copied by those lower down the social order. London's large middle-classes were a market that could make a manufacturer wealthy. So not only were more w.c.s made but better ones were designed in the manufacturers' hopes of securing competitive advantage over their rivals.

Thomas Cook

Running due south from Berkeley Square's south-eastern corner is Berkeley Street. On the right, at No. 45 Berkeley Street, is the headquarters of Thomas Cook the travel company.

In 1841 Thomas Cook (1808-1892) used a railway to transport people from his native Leicester to a temperance rally at nearby Loughborough. In 1845 Cook organised a tour to Liverpool. His business was given a considerable fillip by the Great Exhibition of 1851 to which he organised numerous excursions. The first Thomas Cook group tour to Europe took place in 1855.

In 1862 the International Exhibition was held in London. By then the railway companies had become more skilled in handling tours. As a result, Cook found himself frozen out of tour arranging and so was forced to focus on arranging hotel accommodation, thus broadening his company's expertise. In 1865 he moved his business from Leicester to London. The firm was helped to develop by Cook's son John Mason Cook (1834-1900) who proved to be a very able businessman. In 1871 the firm became Thomas Cook & Son. In 1878 Thomas Cook retired.

In the 1920s Thomas Cook the company was almost ruined itself by the expense of building a palatial headquarters in Mayfair. In 1928 the business was bought by Compagnie des Wagons-Lits et des Grands Express Europeens of Belgium, which was then chaired by the British financier Lord Dalziel (1852-1928). After the Second World War the company was bought by a consortium of British railway companies. In 1948 the British railway industry was nationalised, thereby taking Thomas Cook into state ownership. In 1974 the business was bought from the government by the Midland Bank.

In 1992 the Midland Bank sold Thomas Cook to LTU of Germany, a travel company, and Westdeutsche Landesbank of Germany, a bank. In May 1995 Westdeutsche turned Thomas Cook into a wholly-owned subsidiary.

Cadbury Schweppes

At the eastern end of the northern side of the square, at No. 25 Berkeley Square, is the group headquarters of Cadbury Schweppes.

The Cadbury part of the company makes confectionery and the Schweppes part manufactures soft drinks. The two sides of the business balance one another. When the weather is hot people do not eat as much confectionery but do they drink more soft drinks and when it is cold people do not drink as many soft drinks but they do eat more chocolate.

The Corporatisation of Mayfair

Before the First World War Mayfair was primarily a residential area. After the war domestic help became increasingly hard to hire and consequently the great town houses of the district became increasingly expensive to run.

During the Second World War the City of London was heavily bombed and this meant that there was more pressure for office space. Thus the trend towards Mayfair's depopulation and commercialisation was continued.

Direction

Cross to Berkeley Square's central island. Cross the island's park and leave it by the central exit in the middle of the western side.

Use the zebra crossing to cross over to the square's western side.

Turn left and walk south.

The Clermont Club
On the left, at No. 44 Berkeley Square (1745), is the casino The Clermont Club.

John Aspinall
In 1961 legislation was passed to allow casinos to open after John Aspinall exploited a loophole in the previous Gaming Acts to operate de facto casinos using private houses as venues for gambling evenings.

In 1962 Aspinall opened The Clermont Club, a legal casino.

A quarter of a century later he and the financier and businessman Sir James Goldsmith sold The Curzon Club for £90m.

Aspinall has used much of the wealth he has derived from casino-ownership to underwrite his two private zoos in Kent.

Annabel's
Beneath The Clermont Club, at No. 44 Berkeley Square, is Annabel's the nightclub.

In 1963 Mark Birley opened Annabel's. The club was named after Mrs. Birley, who subsequently became Lady Goldsmith.

Bel Finch
No. 44 Berkeley Square was built by the architect William Kent (1684-1748) for the courtier Lady Isabella Finch (d.1771). Even at the time of its building, No. 44 was regarded as rather a grand house for a spinster.

Maggs Bros
Further down the west side of Berkeley Square, at No. 50 Berkeley Square, is Maggs Bros. Ltd., the dealers in rare books, manuscripts, and autographs.

Direction
Leave Berkeley Square by Fitzmaurice Place, which runs due south of the square's south-western corner.

At the southern end of Fitzmaurice Place, turn right into Curzon Street.

Shepherd Market
On the left, at No. 47 Curzon Street, is the entrance to the north-east corner of Shepherd Market, a group of streets lined with shops, pubs, and restaurants. The district takes its name from the builder Edward Shepherd who developed the area in the mid-C18th.

The May Fair
The May Fair which gave Mayfair its name took place during the first half of May. Originally, the fair took place in the Haymarket but in the mid-1680s it was moved to the site which Shepherd Market and Curzon Street now cover. The fair started as a cattle market in 1686 but soon became general in character. In 1764 it was suppressed.

Direction
The district's southern artery is Shepherd Street.

From Shepherd Street turn right into Hertford Street. Hertford Street joins Curzon Street

Crewe House

Opposite Hertford Street is Crewe House (c1730), which was built as a home for Edward Shepherd. In 1985 the building was bought by the Saudi government for use as its London embassy.

Direction

Turn left into Curzon Street.

Chesterfield House

On the right is South Audley Street. On the right (east) side of South Audley Street, opposite Stanhope Gate, is the site of what was once Chesterfield House (1749).

The 4th Earl of Chesterfield's (1694-1773) was a leading politician of his day. He spent most of his political career in opposition. The earl was forced to retire into private life because he went deaf. He is now best remembered as a man of letters, his most famous work being `Letters to His Son' (1774), which is an epistolary book on manners and how to achieve worldly success. Chesterfield assisted his own worldly success by not wedding the mother of the son to whom the letters were addressed but instead marrying Melusina Countess of Walsingham (d.1778), a bastard daughter of King George I (1660-1727).

No.2 South Audley Street

On the right, to the north of the site of Chesterfield House, is No. 2 South Audley House, a brick house with a wonderfully decorated exterior.

Direction

Continue along Curzon Street until it joins Park Lane.

No. 45 Park Lane

On the right is No. 45 Park Lane (1965), the former premises of The Playboy Club.

Walter Gropius, the founder of the Bauhaus movement, was involved in the building's design. Unfortunately, he was not given a free hand.

The building is now owned by a younger brother of the Sultan of Brunei.

The Playboy Club

Because of the rise in oil prices in the late 1970s the amount of money being gambled in London casinos skyrocketed. The growing profits accentuated rivalries between some of the casino heads; the fiercest conflict was between Cyril Stein of Ladbroke and Victor Lownes of Playboy. Ladbroke ran an operation to attract gamblers to Ladbroke-owned clubs which broke with the spirit of the 1968 Gaming Act. People within the company did this by using information obtained in a dubious manner to identify potential customers, whom were then approached. The company was raided and the police objected to the renewal of the clubs' licences; the licences were not renewed.

Playboy, under Lownes, had sought to portray itself as the virtuous company in the matter. However, in 1981 it was discovered that the company had committed some minor, technical offences of the Act. The Playboy management in the United States panicked and sacked Lownes. The sacking indicated that the company was controlled - as opposed to owned - from outside Britain. This was a far greater infringement of the Act than any of the technical offences which had been hanging over the company. The company lost its licence and therefore was obliged to sell its casino interests. (In the late 1970s it had been the profits from the London casino operation which had kept the Playboy empire afloat.)

Park Lane

The London Hilton

To your left is The London Hilton hotel (1963), which was built on site of Londonderry House, a town house which was long one of the most notable features of Park Lane.

The Park Lane Achilles

On the far side of Park Lane, lurking in the south-east corner of Hyde Park, is the Park Lane Achilles (1822).

The Richard Westmacott (1775-1856) sculpted statue was erected to honour the Duke of Wellington (1769-1852), the victor of Waterloo, who lived in Apsley House to its south. The statue was made from captured French guns which were melted down. It was one of the first nude public statues to be erected in England, and, upon its unveiling, the work rather dismayed the group who had commissioned it.

Direction

Turn right and walk (north) along Park Lane.

The Dorchester

North of Deanery Street is The Dorchester (1930), a renowned hotel, which took the name of an aristocratic town house which stood on the same site. The original Dorchester House derived its name from the Earls of Dorchester, who were Dorset landowners. The money to buy the Earls' estates was earned from moneylending during the English civil wars.

The McLaren Showroom

On the south-eastern corner of the junction of Park Lane and South Street is the showroom of McLaren, the Surrey-based Formula 1 team. McLaren is closely associated with Ron Dennis. The company started development of the TAG McLaren road car in 1988. In 1994 it delivered its first finished version of the vehicle.

Direction

Turn right into South Street.
Turn left into South Audley Street.

No. 38 South Street

On the right, across South Audley Street, in the eastern continuation of South Street, is No. 38 South Street (1922), the last great town house to be built in Mayfair. It was constructed for the lawyer and industrialist Henry McLaren (later Lord Aberconway) (1879-1953).

(By the look of the exterior of No. 38, one could imagine that the reason why no more Mayfair town houses were built was not so much socio-economic in character as aesthetic.)

Direction

Continue north along South Audley Street.

The Grosvenor Chapel

On the right is the Grosvenor Chapel (1730), which was built in mid-C18th to help meet the religious needs of the Anglicans in the growing population of the Grosvenors' Mayfair estate.

Spies

On the left, at No. 59 South Audley Street, is The Spy Shop. Also on the left, at No. 62 South Audley Street, is The Counter Spy Shop.

J.Purdey & Son

On the left, at No. 57 South Audley Street, on the junction with Mount Street, is J.Purdey & Son the gunsmiths.

The company was founded in 1814 by James Purdey (d.1863), a blacksmith. During the 1930s the Purdey family ceased to be involved with the business, which is now controlled by Vendome, the company which owns of the Cartier and Dunhill luxury goods brands. Such is the company's waiting-list that anyone wishing to buy a set of Purdey sporting guns new will have to wait well over a year for them to be constructed. A Purdey shot-gun costs over £30 000.

Grosvenor Square

South Audley Street runs into the western end of the southern side of Grosvenor Square (1731).

The Grosvenor family built the square as the centre-piece of their Mayfair estate.

Mayfair and The Grosvenors

In 1677 Sir Thomas Grosvenor (1656-1700) married the 12-year-old Mary Davies (1665-1730). She was the heiress of her father Alexander Davies (1636-1665), who had been the heir of his uncle Sir Hugh Audley (c1577-1662). Audley had created an estate which consisted of 100 acres of modern Mayfair and 400 acres of what became Pimlico and Belgravia.

In 1720 Mayfair began to be developed. By that time Mayfair's landlords were able to draw on the lessons of several decades of London's western growth. They were thus able to make precise stipulations on matters such as lay out and building use and so have the leverage with which to guard against the social deterioration of the district. (As Mayfair began to prove attractive, and so drew the wealthy to live there, so the landlords to the east found the social character of their estates going into decline.)

It was only in the 1820s that Park Lane, on Mayfair's western edge, became a fashionable address. This followed the improvements carried out to Hyde Park which included iron railings replacing the previous brick wall and the erection of the Decimus Burton (1800-1881) designed Hyde Park Corner Screen (1825). An additional factor may have been the arrival of the Grosvenors, the ground landlords, whose previous house at Pimlico had been demolished to provide a site for the Millbank Penitentiary.

After the First World War, domestic help became increasingly expensive to hire and thus the great town houses of the West End became increasingly costly to run. Even the 2nd Duke of Westminster (1879-1953) moved out of Grosvenor House in Park Lane. The House was the first of the grand Mayfair town houses to be demolished. The Grosvenor House Hotel (1928) was built on its site. The British version of the board game Monopoly was first sold during the 1930s. For the game's first British players, the inclusion of Park Lane had a particular resonance as it touched upon what was happening in contemporary Park Lane.

The United States Embassy
The United States (1959) Embassy takes up the western side of Grosvenor Square.

The United States government is believed to have tried to buy the freehold (the full ownership) of its embassy in Grosvenor Square. Eventually, the Grosvenor Estate agreed to the sale but with one condition that the Grosvenors' property which was taken from the family by the United States government at the time of the American Revolution should be restored in full. The Grosvenor Estate still owns the freehold of the building.

Direction
Turn right and walk along the southern side of the Grosvenor Square.

The Connaught Hotel
On the right is Carlos Place. At No. 1 Carlos Place is The Connaught Hotel (1896).

In 1896 Auguste Scorrier rebuilt the Carlos Place hotel and renamed it The Coburg Hotel. During the First World War, because of anti-German sentiment, the hotel was renamed The Connaught Hotel.

Direction
Cross to the Grosvenor Square's eastern side.

The Canadian High Commission
At the southern end of the square's eastern side is the Canadian High Commission. (Commonwealth countries' embassies in one another's countries are known as High Commissions.)

The Canadians have never asked for their freehold. The Grosvenors are active investors in Canadian real estate.

Direction
Walk up the eastern side of the Grosvenor Square and turn right into Brook Street.

The Savile Club
On the right, at No. 69 Brook Street, is The Savile Club, which was founded in 1868. Originally, it was known as The New Club.

Gimpels Fils Gallery
On the right is the southern section of Davies Street. On the left, at No. 32 Davies Street, is the Gimpel Fils Gallery.

The brothers Charles (d.1973) and Peter Gimpel founded their London art gallery in 1946. They were the sons of the art dealer Rene Gimpel and nephews of the art dealer and public benefactor Lord Duveen (1869-1939).

The Grosvenor Estate Office
To the left is the northern section of Davies Street. On the left, at No. 53 Davies Street, is the Grosvenor Estate Office.

The survival of the Grosvenor Estate was largely the work of Hugh `Bend'Or' Grosvenor the 2nd Duke of Westminster (1879-1953) and his two successive chief agents Major Basil Kerr and George Ridley (1909-1996). Bend'Or created a trust in favour of his one-year-old kinsman the present and 6th Duke.

Following the death of the 2nd Duke, the Grosvenors faced a £19m death duties bill. After taking the best professional advice to be had, they mortgaged their property to raise immediate cash and then sought to extract the maximum income from the estate that they could so as to be able to repay the mortgage. It took sixteen years for the estate and the tax authorities to negotiate an agreed settlement. In the years between the 2nd Duke's death and the reaching of the settlement the estate benefitted from the effect of inflation.

It was the success of this strategy that enabled the 6th Duke to become Britain's wealthiest individual. However, the strategy could have misfired and the estate would have then been destroyed under the weight of the mortgage.

Claridges
On the right, at No. 57 Brook Street, is Claridges (1899). William Claridge was a former butler who established himself as a hotelier. The hotel acquired a very good reputation. In 1895 it was bought by the Savoy Hotel's owners.
Because of the number of foreign royalty who stayed at Claridges, it became known as the `Annex of Buckingham Palace'. There is a story that a caller once asked to speak to the king and the receptionist replied, "Certainly, sir. With which king would you like to speak?"

Bruce Oldfield
On the right, at No. 31 Brook Street, is the showroom of the haute couture designer Bruce Oldfield.

Direction
Turn right into New Bond Street.

Fenwicks

On the left, on the south-eastern corner of the junction of Brook Street and New Bond Street, is Fenwicks.

In 1882 John Fenwick (1846-1905) set himself up as a draper in Newcastle. The Bond Street store was opened in 1891. In 1897 Fenwick's became a limited company. The Fenwick family are still involved in the business.

Sotheby's

On the left, at Nos. 34-35 New Bond Street, is Sotheby's the auction house.

Sotheby's was founded by Samuel Baker (c1711-1778). Baker held his first sale in March 1745, it was a book auction. He entered the first rank of contemporary auction houses when he sold the library of the art patron and physician Dr. Richard Mead (1673-1754).

For many years the business was focussed on the book trade. The firm handled the sales of the libraries of Napoleon and Talleyrand.

The individual who shaped the modern rivalry between Sotheby's and Christie's was Sir Anderson Montague-Barlow M.P. (1868-1951). Until Montague-Barlow's arrival as a partner in Sotheby's, the two auction houses had kept off one another's territory. In 1917 Sotheby's moved to Bond Street. Thereafter it began to challenge Christie's for the fine art business.

In 1983 Alfred Taubman the American mall millionaire bought control of Sotheby's.

French Trousers

Tim Clarke (1913-1995) spent most of his working life as a ceramics specialist at Sotheby's. During the Second World War, part of his life when he was not working in the auction house, Mr. Clarke won an M.B.E. (a medal) for removing a Frenchman's trousers. After the fall of France, the political situation in Middle East became fluid and it was uncertain as to whether the French in the region would ally themselves to the Free French or to Vichy France. Clarke's military duties in Syria brought him into contact with a French officer whose loyalties were unclear. Clarke felt that the situation was of sufficient seriousness to warrant his detaining the man. He did this by debagging the Frenchman. When General de Gaulle heard of the incident he wanted Clarke court-martialled. However, at that particular juncture, Winston Churchill was finding the French general rather irksome and so responded by having Clarke gonged.

Savory & Moore

On the right, at No. 143 New Bond Street, is a building formerly occupied by Savory & Moore the chemists. The shop has a very fine period front.

Wildenstein Gallery

On the right, at No. 147 New Bond Street, is the Wildenstein Gallery, which Georges Wildenstein (1892-1963) opened in 1937. For many years the Wildenstein Gallery specialised in Old Masters.

The Fine Art Society

On the right, at No. 148 New Bond Street, is the Fine Art Society, which was founded in Bond Street in 1876.

Tessiers

On the left, at No. 126 New Bond Street, is Tessiers the gold and silversmiths, which Lewis de Tessier founded in 1811.

Direction

Turn left into Conduit Street.

The Westbury

On the rights, at Nos. 39-41 Conduit Street, is The Westbury, a hotel, which, when it opened in 1955, was the first hotel in Britain to be run by an American company.

Vivienne Westwood

On the right, at No. 43 Conduit Street, is the showroom of the clothes designer Vivienne Westwood.

To Finish

Walk to the eastern end of Conduit Street and turn left into Regent Street. At the juncture with Oxford Street descend into Oxford Circus underground station, which is on the Central, Victoria and Bakerloo Lines.

To Continue

Walk to the eastern end of Conduit Street, cross Regent Street and turn left. Walk northwards up Regent Street and turn left into Great Marlborough Street.

10. Soho

To Start

Go to Oxford Circus underground station, which is on the Central, Bakerloo and Victoria Lines. Leave the station by the exit which is on the southern side of the juncture of Oxford Street and Regent Street. Walk south along the eastern side of Regent Street. Turn left into Marlborough Street.

Carnaby Street

On the right is the northern end of Carnaby Street.

John Stephen

The designer and retailer John Stephen, a Glaswegian, was at the heart of Carnaby Street's flowering. He was the progenitor of the male fashion boutique.

In 1959 Stephen and some partners opened the first men's boutique on the street, going on to run several shops along it concurrently. He went on to have nearly one hundred shops and a number of international licensing deals. Over the years he has scaled down his operations but is still active as a designer and retailer.

The Monster Raving Loony Party

David Sutch initially found fame as a rock singer. He first ran for Parliament as the candidate of the National Teenage Party in the 1963 Stratford-upon-Avon by-election caused by the Profumo Scandal; his manifesto included the pedestrianisation of Carnaby Street (something which was to come about, along with his call for the lowering of the voting age from 21 to 18). Subsequently, he set up the Monster Raving Loony Party, which has become an ornament of the British electoral system.

Sutch changed his name to Screamin' Lord Sutch by deed poll.

In May 1991 Stuart Hughes became the Monster Raving Loony Party's first elected representative when he was returned for Sidmouth's Woolbrook Ward to East Devon District Council. Mr. Hughes was a local hotelier. (The West Country has a long tradition of being independently inclined in politics.)

Inderwicks

Inderwick's the smokers' requisites business, which resides on the west side of Carnaby Street, was founded in Wardour Street in 1797. It was John Inderwick who started the fashion for Meerschaum pipes. The business is now Britain's oldest tobacconist.

Liberty & Company

On the left, on the south side of Great Marlborough Street, is Liberty & Company the department store.

Arthur Lasenby Liberty (1843-1917) started his retail career as a sales assistant in a Regent Street store. In 1862 he visited the International Exhibition in South Kensington and was struck by the scope that East Asian, and particularly Japanese, products might have as retail items. He was proven right but his employers refused to make him a partner. In 1875 Liberty set up in business for himself and was soon taken up by the fashionable world. He made stylistic innovations such as encouraging the use of pastel colours.

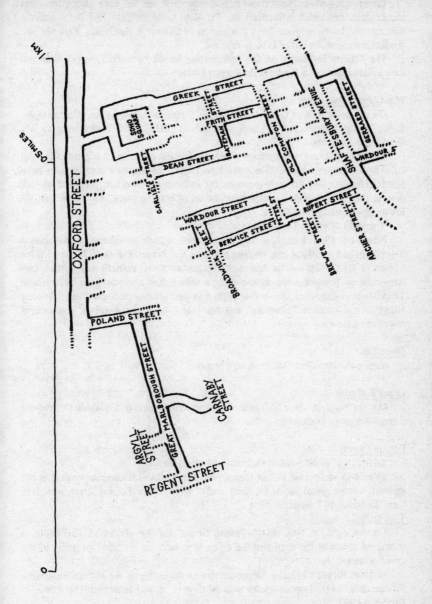

Liberty played an important impressario role in the era's decorative arts movements, his tastes influenced the Pre-Raphaelite painters and the Aesthetic Movement. In the original 1881 production of Gilbert & Sullivan's `Patience' the costumes were made out of Liberty fabrics.

The Liberty buildings are the compromise struck between Liberty's flair and the conservatism of its landlord the Crown Estate.

The London Palladium

On the north side of Great Marlborough Street, is Argyll Street. On the right, at No. 7 Argyll Street, is The London Palladium (1910). The theatre hosts variety shows and musicals.

To play the London Palladium is regarded as the pinnacle of a career for most British variety performers. Since the late 1960s, the theatre's management have hired it out for one-off performances by individuals who are prepared to risk several thousand pounds to fulfil their dream of playing there, e.g. Brian Lee, an Elvis impersonator from Essex.

`Saturday Night at The Palladium'

From its 1956 inception the commercial television company Associated Television had theatrical impressarios, such as Val Parnell (1894-1972) and Prince Littler (1901-1973), on its board. Figures such as Parnell and Littler saw television as being a boon to the theatre rather than something to be resisted. Television would whet viewers' appetites to see artistes perform live. `Sunday Night at the London Palladium' was for many years the jewel in commercial television's crown.

Direction

Turn right into Great Marlborough Street.

Grant & Cutler

On the right, at No. 56 Great Marlborough Street, is Grant & Cutler, the foreign language booksellers.

Poland Street

To the right is the southern section of Poland Street.

The 1683 victory of Polish forces over the Turks was commemorated in the name of a (now gone) pub at the north end of what is now Poland Street, which, in turn, the street took its name from.

The Oldie

On the right, at Nos. 45-46 Poland Street, are the offices of The Oldie, a magazine aimed at the aged and the aging who have no intention of going to the grave quietly.

In 1986 Richard Ingrams stepped down as the editor of the satirical magazine Private Eye. Mr. Ingrams, who was getting on a bit, launched The Oldie in February 1992.

Direction

Turn left into Poland Street.

The King's Arms
On the right, at No. 23 Poland Street, is The King's Arms pub.
Historic Druids
The Ancient Order of the Druids is reputed to have been founded at a meeting held in The King's Arms in 1781.

In the early C20th Druidism was openly associated with the progressive strands of the Labour movement. In the 1920s it shrank from public scrutiny. However, it continued to be active, with meetings at places such as Clapham Common.
Modern Druids
There are at least ten different Orders of Druids in Britain.

Druids regularly provide a subject for news agency photographers at the spring and autumn equinoxes which make the national newspapers if there are few hard news stories circulating at the time.

In January 1994 King Arthur, a Druid, lost his legal battle not to pay poll tax (a local tax). He was withholding payment on the grounds that as a Druid he was a member of a religious order and therefore was not legally obliged to pay.

Direction
Poland Street runs into Oxford Street. Turn right into Oxford Street.

The Plaza
Bourne & Hollingsworth
On the left, on the north side of Oxford Street, between Wells Street and Berners Street, is The Plaza shopping centre. The Plaza occupies what was formerly the Bourne & Hollingsworth department store (1928). It is still possible to make out B.s and H.s on the building's exterior.

All of Oxford Street's present-day department stores are to the west of Oxford Circus.

The 100 Club
The 100 Club is in the basement of Century House, No. 100 Oxford Street.

The Feldman Swing Club opened there in October 1942. The Club was founded by the clarinettist (and pattern-cutter) Robert Feldman (d.1992); it became a leading jazz venue and subsequently went on to host performances of just about every type of popular music.

Direction
Turn right into Soho Street.

The Radha Krishna Temple
Members of Radha Krishna are sometimes to be seen making their way along Oxford Street singing `Hare Krishna, Hare Krishna'. A by now traditional rejoinder to this runs `Harry Worth, Harry Worth, Harry Secombe, Harry Secombe, Harry H. Corbett, Harry H. Corbett'.

Soho Square
Soho Square was built in the 1680s, it was one of the first London squares to be layed out. The square's original inhabitants were aristocrats. After the middle

of the C18th its social standing declined as addresses to the west became more fashionable.

No. 13 Soho Square has a fine convex shop front.

The Statue of King Charles II

King Charles II (1630-1685) is represented by a statue in the park in the centre of Soho Square.

Direction

Turn left into Soho Square and then turn right and walk down the square's eastern side.

St.Patrick's Church

On the southern side of the junction of Soho Square and Sutton Row is St.Patrick's Church, one the oldest Catholic churches in London. It opened in 1793.

The church has a pleasant brick exterior which dates from 1893.

William Beckford

Down from St.Patrick's, on the eastern side of the square, is No. 22 Soho Square.

The wealthy West Indian merchant William Beckford (1709-1770), the Lord Mayor of the City of London in both 1762 and 1769, lived at No. 22 Soho Square from 1751 to 1770. That Beckford's home should be in the West End, rather than in the City, can be read as an early indicator of how the City would become depopulated, becoming a business district with very few residents.

Direction

Leave Soho Square by Greek Street, which runs into the eastern end of the square's southern side.

Greek Street

There is a theory that Greek Street may have taken its name from a late C17th community of Greek refugees from Melros who, having escaped from Turkish rule, established themselves in London. There was a Greek Orthodox Church built for them on what is now part of the site of St.Martins School of Art. (There is an alternative theory that Greek Street took its name from Gregory `Grig' King who developed the street in the early 1680s.)

(Charlotte Street, to the north of Oxford Street, used to be a Greek quarter.)

The House of St.Barnabas

On the left, at No. 1 Greek Street, is the House of St.Barnabas in Soho, which provides accommodation for homeless women.

No.1 Greek Street is one of the finest examples of 1750s English rococo. The house was the home of Alderman Richard Beckford (1712-1756).

The House of Charity was founded in 1846. In 1861 it bought No. 1 Greek Street.

The Gay Hussar

On the left, at No. 2 Greek Street, is The Gay Hussar, a restaurant which has a reputation of being associated with the lunching left. Despite holding opposing political opinions the Labour spindoctor Brian Murphy (1929-1995) and the tory spindoctor Sir Tim Bell were good friends. If they lunched at The Gay Hussar Murphy would pick up the bill and if at Claridges then Bell would pay.

Milroys

On the left, at No. 3 Greek Street, is Milroys the whisky retailer.

Wallace Milroy is the author `Malt Whisky Alamanac'.

Whisky

The word `Whisky' is descended from `Uisge Beatha', the Gaelic for `water of life'.

Whisky is reputed to have been invented by the Scottish Friar John Cor at the end of the C15th. Whether or not this was the case, 500 years of Scottish whisky making were celebrated in 1994.

Malts are made from malted barley. Grain whisky is made from unmalted grain. Blends are blends of malt and grain.

Blended Whiskies

Blended whiskies were first sold in the middle of the C19th. The timing was fortunate, until then brandy had been the Englishman's favourite tipple. At the time the French brandy industry was on it knees as the result of an epidemic of the phylloxera vine disease, which brought the European wine making industry to the verge of collapse.

Malt Whiskies

Before the 1960s malts were only ever bottled in short, occasional runs. During that decade there was a wave of consolidation among the major blending distilleries. For the malt producers, this raised the prospect that they might not have a future role in the industry. In response, the malt producers started bottling their produce themselves and selling it. Glenfiddich was the first to enter the field. Its success encouraged others to follow.

The Angel's Share

Whisky has to be distilled. Then, it has to be stored for at least three years. During maturation, approximately 2% of the volume evaporates each year, this is known as `the angels' share'. (The evaporation takes place because the sherry barrels, in which the whisky is stored, are made of oak which is porous.)

L'Escargot

On the right, at No. 47 Greek Street, is L'Escargot restaurant, which was opened by Georges Gaudin at the start of the C20th. The restaurant's motto is `Slow but sure'. Its decorations feature the image of Gaudin riding a snail.

The Establishment

On the right, at No. 18 Greek Street, are the former premises of The Establishment, Peter Cook's (1937-1995) nightclub.

Peter Cook

Beyond The Fringe

In 1959 John Bassent instigated the `Beyond the Fringe' revue by bringing together a number of experienced university revue performers - Dudley Moore and Alan Bennett from Oxford University and Peter Cook and Jonathan Miller from Cambridge University. The revue was a sensational hit at the following year's Edinburgh Festival. In 1961 it opened at The Fortune Theatre in London's West End. In 1964, after a run on Broadway, Miller and Bennett went their own separate ways, while Cook and Moore continued to work together, making four series of the television show `Not Only...But Also' (1965-71). The show featured them as two cloth-capped idiots called Pete'n'Dud.

As a solo performer, Cook's leading character was E.L.Wisty, a megalomaniac who was held back from dominating the world only by his inability to summon up the effort to get up off the park bench to which he was eternally rooted.

The Establishment

Peter Cook's other activities included opening `The Establishment' with Nicholas Luard. The Establishment was a nightclub, and as such was able to circumvent the then existing official censorship of the Lord Chamberlain's Office. Lenny Bruce and Edna Everage were among the performers who appeared at the club. (Cook also became the principal shareholder in Private Eye the satirical magazine.)

Lenny Bruce

In April 1962 the American comic Lenny Bruce performed at The Establishment. A year later he was deported from Britain. A theory has been expounded that to a large extent Bruce, who as a foreigner who could be treated in such a way, was bearing the brunt of the Conservative Home Secretary Henry Brooke's (1903-1984) ire at not being able to touch British people who were involved in the satire boom.

Barry Humphries

Barry Humphries is an Australian who has worked in Britain as an actor and revue artiste since 1959. His character Edna Everage made her first British appearance at The Establishment. She did not meet with any notable success at the time. Subsequently, Dame Edna's career developed until the Housewife Superstar was given her own West End revue in 1976. Others followed `A Night With Dame Edna' and `An Evening's Intercourse'. Since the early 1980s she has been a staple of mainstream television as well.

The Coach & Horses

On the left, at No. 29 Greek Street, is The Coach & Horses pub.

The Coach & Horses's renowned landlord is Norman Balon. Mr. Balon's rather free use of short words of Anglo-Saxon origin has been interpreted as being a means of helping him express himself.

Kettner's

On the right, at No. 29 Romilly Street, is Kettner's restaurant, which was established in 1868 by Auguste Kettner who had been chef to Napoleon III.

The restaurant is now owned by Peter Boizot, who founded Pizza Express.

Direction

At the junction of Greek Street and Shaftesbury Avenue turn right into Shaftesbury Avenue.

Cross the Avenue and turn left into Gerrard Place. Turn right into Gerrard Street.

Gerrard Street

The first Chinese immigrants to come to England are believed to have arrived in the late C18th on board East India Company ships. By the late C19th, Limehouse in the East End was catering to the needs of a transient population of Chinese seamen. Pennyfields, off the West India Docks Road, was the centre of the Chinese quarter.

In 1908 Chung Koon (d.1957), a former cook's chef on the Red Star Line, opened Maxim's in Soho. Maxim's was London's first Chinese restaurant. Others followed, notably Koon's Cathay Restaurant.

After the Second World War London's Chinese restaurants found a market not only among former servicemen who had served in East Asia but also among American military personnel who were stationed in Britain.

By the mid-1960s the sex industry had taken Soho down market. It had the effect of deflating rents and gave a window of opportunity for some Chinese entrepreneurs to start up restaurants in the heart of London's West End.

In the 1970s the Gerrard Street district became the commercial, cultural and social centre for London's Chinese community.

In Chinatown the colour red is very evident because Chinese people traditionally associate it with good fortune.

The Chinatown street signs contain Chinese characters. Quite why there should be a Chinese character for Macclesfield, as in Macclesfield Street, is a mystery.

Chinese businesses have spread onto Shaftesbury Avenue and are starting to spread to the north of it.

British Chinese Take Away Food

Britain's first Chinese takeaway was opened in Bayswater by Chung Koon's son John Koon (1926-1997).

In the 1950s and 1960s there was a wave of immigration into Britain of Chinese people from the New Territories. Initially, men arrived by themselves. Subsequently, they were joined by their families. Soon after this wave of immigration Chinese restaurants began springing up all over Britain.

British Chinese take away food consists principally of easy-to-prepare southern Chinese dishes which Britons are happy to eat. However, there are also some non-southern Chinese elements in British Chinese take away food. Originally, the spring roll was a snack from northern China brought to Britain by pre-1939 immigrants. Chop suey was reputedly devised in America as the Chinese labourers' counterpart to Irish stew, it being based on the same ingredients.

The Wag Club

At the end of the street is The Wag Club, a nightclub.

In the 1930s The Wag's Wardour Street site was occupied by The Shim-Sham Club, a legendary jazz venue.

The Wag opened in April 1984. It was established by Chris Sullivan, a former St.Martins School of Art student. The club was the archetypal hip club of the mid-to-late-1980s. It was a venue where the worlds of fashion and pop music were able to mingle fruitfully.

Direction

At the western end of Gerrard Street, turn right into the southern section of Wardour Street. Cross over Shaftesbury Avenue and turn left. Walk down Shaftesbury Avenue and turn right into Rupert Street.

The Gielgud

On the right, on the corner of Shaftesbury Avenue and Rupert Street, is The Gielgud theatre, which was formerly known as The Globe Theatre.

The actor Sir John Gielgud appeared in numerous H.M.Tennent productions.

H.M.Tennent Limited

The theatrical agents `Binkie' Beaumont (1908-1973) and H.M.Tennent (d.1941) met while working for the production-managers Howard & Wyndham. In 1936 Beaumont and Tennent broke away and set up their own agency H.M.Tennent Limited. `The Firm', as it became known, was based at The Globe Theatre.

The reclusive Harry Tennent died in 1941. From the 1940s to the 1960s `The Firm' dominated British commercial theatre. The company did not exert its influence through contracts. Rather, its positive influence was exerted through the very considerable charm of Beaumont and its negative influence through its refusal to have anything to do with anyone who ran foul of him.

Beaumont disliked publicity. He believed his influence was the greater for being exercised behind the scenes. He regarded money spent on advertising a hit as being wasted and money spent on advertising a failure as being counterproductive to its subsequent sweeping under the carpet.

Beaumont's influence may have begun to wane from the 1950s but he was still by far the largest player in British commercial theatre up to the time of his death.

In 1980 the film producer Harry Saltzman (1915-1994) bought a controlling interest in H.M.Tennent. His influence failed to revitalise the company and in 1991 it ceased to be active.

Theatre Cats

Most West End theatres have a theatre cat. One of the better known ones was Beerbohm (d.1995) of The Globe Theatre. From time to time, he made impromptu guest appearances during stage performances.

Archer Street

On the left is Archer Street, which in the 1940s Archer Street was where musicians used to hang out between gigs.

Brewer Street

Rupert Street runs into Brewer Street.

In the south-west corner of Soho there are a number of streets which take their names from the trades with which they were once associated, e.g. Great Windmill Street and Brewer Street.

Glasshouse Street in Soho probably took its name from a glass factory. The location would have been useful in terms of the glassmakers availing themselves of London's night-soil as a source of saltpeter for their glass-making.

Direction
Cross Brewer Street and continue northwards through Walker's Court, which links Brewer Street to Berwick Street.

The Raymond Revuebar
On the left of Walker's Court is The Raymond Revuebar, which Paul Raymond opened in 1958.

Since the late 1950s Mr. Raymond has been able to utilise the profits of his pornography and entertainments businesses to buy property. He is believed to own nearly 400 properties in Soho.

Sex Shops
In the late 1970s and early 1980s Covent Garden underwent a renaissance. In the mid-1980s Covent Garden's fashionability spread west over the Charing Cross Road into Soho. Westminster City Council made licensing stricter to reduce the number of licences granted to sex shops; in 1984 there were over 300, by the start of 1992 there were six. As the area grewer more fashionable so the rents went up. Ironically, he businesses that proved best able to pay the rents were sex shops and so the trade was to some extent resurrected.

Peter Street
On the right is Peter Street, which probably derives its name from a C17th saltpeter works which stood between it and Brewer Street.

Soho Prostitution
The Messina brothers arrived in England in the 1930s from Malta by way of Italy and Egypt. The Messinas established a thriving vice business in Soho. Their operations suffered somewhat during the Second World War when there was greater promiscuity. In 1950 the brothers were the subject of a sustained campaign by the journalist Duncan Webb, who wrote for `The People' newspaper. The police, now the subject of public interest, pursued the family relentlessly.

In the Messinas' wake two more Maltese - Bernie Silver and Frank Mifsud - established themselves as Soho's vice kings. For many years they were able to insulate themselves from prosecution by systematically corrupting police officers.

In the 1970s, with the end of organised police corruption, the criminal control of prostitution in Soho was shattered.

Berwick Street Market
Berwick Street Market is a street market which takes place six days a week.

The King of Corsica
On the left, at No. 91 Berwick Street, is The King of Corsica pub.

The British tradition of offering a haven to those people who are suffering persecution in their own lands was, in part, born out of a wish to antagonise the

French and the Spanish and to thwart their imperial activities. In the C18th Corsican patriots were a favoured cause.

In 1752 Theodore King of Corsica (d.1756) was imprisoned for debt. Four years later, he was buried in the graveyard of St.Anne Soho.

General Pasquale Paoli (1725-1807) was buried in St.Pancras Old Church burial ground. In 1889 his body was returned to Corsica.

Direction
Walk along Berwick Street until the junction with Broadwick Street.

Dr. John Snow
Dr. John Snow (1813-1858) is commemorated by The John Snow pub on the south (left) side of Broadwick Street.

In 1831 London suffered its first outbreak of cholera. It took over a decade for the connection to begin to be made between the state of London's drains and its water supply and the state of public health in the city. Contemporary medical wisdom believed that cholera was carried in an invisible cloud floating in their air.

In 1845 a cholera epidemic ravaged the population of Soho. Dr. Snow mapped out the incidences of the disease and observed that a water pump was the probable source of the outbreak of the disease. Using his research Snow was able to persuade the parish elders to remove the pump's handle. The epidemic subsided. Snow's methodology, which was carried out without a knowledge of the existence of cholera bacteria, gave birth to epidemiology. A red granite kerbstone marks the spot where the pump once stood.

(Dr. Snow's initial distinction lay in his being the first British physician to study anaesthesia in a scientific manner (which has a degree of irony in it, in view of his arguing that cholera was not carried by invisible clouds). In 1853 Snow administered chloroform to Queen Victoria (1819-1901) during the birth of Prince Leopold (1853-1884).)

The Long-Term Effect of Cholera on Soho
There are quite a large number of three-storey houses which can be seen from the junction. These buildings are low for their location at the centre of a major capital. This stems in large part from the district having gone into a steep social decline during the mid-C19th.

The cholera outbreaks of the 1840s drove away Soho's more affluent inhabitants. Workshops and shops were built over the gardens of their former homes, thus ending the likelihood of the area again becoming attractive to the middle classes as a place in which to live.

Direction
Turn right into the eastern section of Broadwick Street.

Agent Provacateur
On the left, at No. 14 Broadwick Street, is Agent Provacateur, a lingerie shop where haute couture almost meets the sex shop trade.

The shop opened in December 1994. The business is run by Joe Corre and Serena Rees. Mr. Corre is the son of Vivienne Westwood and Malcolm McLaren.

Direction

Turn right into Wardour Street. Walk southwards down Wardour Street.

Wardour Street

Wardour Street is a street name which is synonymous with the movie trade.

Mezzo

On the left, at No. 94 Wardour Street, is Mezzo, part of the Conran restaurant empire.

Meard Street

On the left is Meard Street. The passage's berailinged house fronts seem misplaced in contemporary Soho. It is as though a street from a quiet, cathedral city has come up to London for the day in order to engage in a spot of malfeasance.

The Intrepid Fox

On the right, at No. 97 Wardour Street, is The Intrepid Fox, a pub which acquired its name during the hotly contested Westminster election of 1784. The Whig politician Charles James Fox (1749-1806) was one of the candidates who sought to be returned to Parliament for the borough of Westminster.

The seat was a highly prestigious one to sit for because of the way in which the House of Commons, through its being dominated by the aristocracy, had become highly unrepresentative of popular opinion. Westminster had one of the largest electorates (12 000) of any Parliamentary borough. Therefore, those M.P.s who were returned for it could be regarded as having the weight of popular opinion behind such views as they cared to give forth of in the House, in a way which M.P.s who were aristocratic nominees sitting for rotten boroughs could never pretend to.

Fox was elected.

Anne Summers

On the right, at No. 83 Wardour Street, is an Anne Summers shop.

The Gold family has been highly successful in converting a business which was once perceived by some as a Soho sex shop into a veritable pillar of suburbia. Much of this success can be attributed to the business skills of Jacqueline Gold who took over the company in 1981 when she was aged 21. Ms. Gold oversaw the development of Anne Summers Parties through which the company sells it wears directly to the public in private homes.

St.Anne Soho

Further down Wardour Street, on the left, is the tower (1717) of what was the Church of St.Anne Soho (1686). St.Anne's was destroyed by aerial bombing in 1940.

The church's garden, formerly its graveyard, is several feet above street level because many thousands of parishioners have been buried in it since the church was built in the late C17th.

The detective fiction writer Dorothy L. Sayers (1893-1957) was a churchwarden of St.Anne's. Sayers was cremated and her ashes were scattered in the churchyard.

Centrepoint

The original Centrepoint occupies the crypt of St.Anne Soho. The organisation provides temporary accommodation for 350 young people each night. It was founded in 1969 by Father Kenneth Leech, the church's curate. Centrepoint has expanded into a series of hostels, flats and bedsits which are all to aid the homeless young.

Direction

Turn left into Old Compton Street.

Old Compton Street

Old Compton Street was largely built in the 1670s. It was named after Henry Compton Bishop of London (1632-1713).

The West End gay area is centred on Old Compton Street. The district was gentrified to a certain extent as the sex trade was curtailed. However, with the recession of the early 1990s the heterosexual leisure pound was hit harder than the gay one, with the result that gay businesses had a better chance of survival.

Compton's of Soho

On the right is Compton's of Soho, Bass the brewer's flagship gay pub.

The pink pound is important to those companies involved in the leisure, drinks and catering industries. The income from gay food and drink outlets tends to be higher and steadier than it is from other outlets.

The Grey Matter

Dr. David Hope is a prominent Anglo-Catholic Anglican bishop. Dr. Hope was vicar of All Saints in Margaret Street, `the Anglo-Catholic cathedral'. In 1985 he was appointed Bishop of Wakefield. He opposed the ordination of women. In 1991 he was appointed Bishop of London.

In March 1995 Bishop Hope felt it necessary to make a public declaration both that his sexuality was `greyer' than that of most people and that he was celibate. He felt moved to make the declaration because of pressure which was being brought upon him by Outrage, the gay lobbying group.

In April 1995 it was announced that Dr. Hope would succeed Dr. John Habgood as Archbishop of York.

Hope's nickname is reputed to be Ena the Terrible.

The Two I.s

On the right, at No. 59 Old Compton Street, is the site of what was The Two I.s coffee bar, which in the 1950s was one of the birthplaces of British rock'n'roll. The singers Cliff Richard and Tommy Steele were among those who were discovered in The Two I.s.

Peter Grant

Peter Grant (1935-1995), the future manger of Led Zeppelin, was employed at the Two I.s. He had a number of jobs before finding his vocation - including wrestling as His Highness Count Bruno Alassio of Milan (he was 6ft. 5in.).

Working at The Two I.s led him into becoming a road manager for American acts visiting Britain and then a manager for British acts.

In 1968 Grant was managing The Yardbirds when they broke up. Jimmy Page, a member of the band, invited Grant to manage his next group - this was Led Zeppelin. Under Grant's instinctive management the band refused to follow the traditional promotional activities of releasing singles and making television appearances. Instead, Led Zeppelin carved out its own enormously lucrative career in the music business. Among the services which Grant performed for the band, and rock musicians as a whole, was increasing share of concert grosses received by performers.

There is a story that once, after members of Led Zeppelin and their entourage had trashed their hotel rooms, Grant was settling up with a hotel manager, when the manager remarked that he had always wanted to throw a television set out of a hotel window room to see what it was like. Grant peeled off a $500 bill from his wad which he proffered to the manager and said "Have one on me".

The French Pub

On the right is the southern section of Dean Street. On the left, at No. 49 Dean Street, is The York Minster, popularly known as The French Pub. In 1914 Monsieur Berlemont became its landlord. For 45 years it was run by Berlemont's son Gaston Berlemont.

The pub's clientele has included the likes of General de Gaulle.

The Groucho Club

On the left is the northern section of Dean Street. On the right, at No. 45 Dean Street, is the media watering hole The Groucho Club. On its front, the Club has brackets for its members to park their bicycles in.

The Club was founded in 1985. It came into being because a number of influential figures in the publishing and media worlds wished to have somewhere convenient to entertain their clients and one another. The Groucho took its name from Groucho Marx, the American comedian and wit, who once remarked that he would not join any club that would have him as a member.

Tony Mackintosh, The Groucho's chairman, has acquired something of a reputation as a weather vane as to which parts of London are trendy. In the 1970s he ran Dingwalls in Camden, in the 1980s The Zanzibar in Covent Garden, and in the 1990s The Groucho Club in Soho.

A small cluster of imitator establishments have sprung up around it.

The Colony Room

Further up on the right, at No. 41 Dean Street, is the entrance to The Colony Room, a private drinking club, which Muriel Belcher (d.1979) opened in December 1948. Its niche was to allow people to circumvent the licensing laws and drink between afternoon closing time and evening opening (all day drinking in English and Welsh pubs only became legal in 1988). The Club's initial clientele were City types, however, matters changed when Ms. Belcher hired the painter Francis Bacon (1909-1992) as a `hostess'. The Room developed into one of the principal homes of Bohemian London.

On her death, Ms. Belcher left the Room to her barman Ian Board (1929-1994), who continued to run the facility in the Belcher fashion.

Laurie Lee

As an aspriting poet Laurie Lee (1914-1997), the future author of 'Cider with Rosie', drank in The Colony Room and became famed for his tight-fistedness when it came to buying other people drinks. The journalist Jeffrey Bernard used to measure time relative to him - "that was three years after Laurie Lee last bought a drink". (With the publication of 'Cider' in 1959, Lee made his fame and his fortune and moved back to the Gloucestershire village of Slad where he had been born - there he "was careful not to buy anyone a drink for two years".)

Direction

Continue along Old Compton Street. Turn left into Frith Street.

The Bar Italia

On the right, at No. 22 Frith Street, is The Bar Italia coffee bar, which has been run by the Polledri family since the late 1940s.

John Logie Baird

Above the Bar Italia is a plaque which commemorates how No. 22 Frith Street was where television was first demonstrated by John Logie Baird (1888-1946) in 1926. Two years later Selfridges the department store made the first ever sale of a television set.

Ronnie Scott's

On the left, at No. 46 Frith Street, is Ronnie Scott's, the jazz club.

Originally, the tenor saxophonist Ronnie Scott (1927-1996) worked in dance bands. In 1959 Scott and his fellow saxophonist Peter King opened Britain's first six-nights-a-week jazz club in a basement in Gerrard Street. Peter King gave up playing to become the club's business manager. Scott continued to perform with his own quartet. In 1964 the club moved to premises in Frith Street.

Ronnie Scott, who had a somewhat sardonic manner, often acted as the club's master of ceremonies. He was infamous for his appalling jokes, many of which he received requests for. Examples of Scott's humour are "His mother was a titled lady - she was Southern Area Light Heavyweight Champion" and, if the Club was not full, "Let's join hands and try to make contact with the living".

Direction

Turn left into Bateman Street and then turn right into Dean Street.

Karl Marx

On the right, at No. 28 Dean Street, is the Quo Vadis Restaurant. A former resident of the building was Karl Marx (1818-1883) the political and economic theorist.

The Marx Memorial

In Britain the place most strongly associated with Marx is his grave in Highgate Cemetry. Marx was originally buried with his wife. However, in 1954 his body was moved to a site where his admirers could pay their respects more conveniently.

The Red Fort
On the left, at No. 77 Dean Street, is The Red Fort, which was one of a generation of Indian restaurants which emerged in London in the mid-1980s and took Indian cuisine upmarket.

Private Eye
To the left, in the western section of Carlisle Street, at No. 6 Carlisle Street, are the editorial offices of Private Eye the satirical magazine.

Private Eye was founded by four men who had been contemporaries at Shrewsbury the public school - Christopher Booker, Paul Foot, Richard Ingrams, and Willie Rushton (1937-1996). The magazine's first edition was published in October 1961. Booker was the first editor, however, Ingrams staged a successful coup and took over the chair.

At the magazine's foundation Andrew Osmond was its main shareholder. In 1962 the comedian Peter Cook (1937-1995) bought Osmond's equity. It was Cook who devised the magazine's speech bubble cover. He was responsible for introducing Barry Humphries and Nick Garland to the magazine.

The magazine's `Street of Shame' column is where much of Fleet Street dirty linen gets washed.

In 1986 Ingrams stepped down as editor of the Eye. He was succeeded by Ian Hislop.

Gnomes
Lord Gnome, the magazine's supposed proprietor, had his origin in a remark that the Labour politician Harold Wilson made in the Commons about Swiss bankers - `the little gnomes of Zurich'. (Robin Cook the racing tipster and Labour politician is generally held to look rather gnome-like.)

Pizza Express
On the north-eastern corner of Dean Street and Carlisle Street is Pizza Express.

In 1965 Peter Boizot opened Britain's first pizzeria at the southern end of Wardour Street, Soho. The chain's hallmark is its use of live music, primarily jazz (one of Mr. Boizot's passions (another is hockey but you don't have to watch it being played while you eat)). The company has a strong young-affluent aspect to its customer profile.

Direction
Turn right into Carlisle Street.

Bloomsbury
On the corner of Bloomsbury Square and Soho Square, at No. 38 Carlisle Street, is Bloomsbury the publishing house, which was set up in 1986.

Direction
Turn left into Soho Square.

MPL Communications
On the left, on the northern section of the western side of Soho Square, is MPL.

Paul McCartney, the former Beatle, is a force within the music publishing industry. McCartney's solo material and the copyrights he has acquired are held through MPL Communications. However, McCartney does not control The Beatles catalogue, which is owned by Michael Jackson the American pop star.

Paul McCartney was awarded a knighthood in the 1997 New Year's honours list.

Eglise Protestante Francaise de Londre

Towards the western end of the square's northern side is the Eglise Protestante Francaise de Londre, a French Protestant church.

The Settlement of Huguenots

The tradition of Huguenot residence in Britain was well-established before the Revocation of the Edict of Nantes in 1685, which led to a wave of emigration from France.

Some Huguenot surnames have become so much part of the fabric of British life, that it takes a stretch of the imagination to think of them as being French in origin.

John Courage was an Aberdonian of Huguenot descent who moved to London, where he founded the Courage brewing business.

The Dollonds of Dollond & Aitchison the opticians were a Huguenot family. In 1750 John Dollond (1706-1761) established an optical workshop in Vine Street, Spitalfields.

Asprey, Cazenove and Courtauld are other examples.

Direction

Turn left into Soho Street. Turn right into Oxford Street.

Virgin

On the left, at Nos. 14-16 Oxford Street, is the Virgin Megastore, the flagship of Richard Branson's Virgin music retail business.

Richard Branson established `Student' magazine when he was 16. In 1969 fixed retail prices for records were abolished and he entered the market as a mail-order record business.

In 1971 there was a prolonged postal strike. Branson's response to this was to open a record shop. He then went on to start up a record label in 1973. Virgin Records was put on a solid financial footing by the success of Mike Oldfield's `Tubular Bells' (1973) album. In the late 1970s the business was expanded through signing up many of the acts that appeared in the wake of punk, notably the Boy George-fronted Culture Club.

(Branson is reputed to have very little interest in music; when he was the guest on the popular Radio 4 record-selection show `Desert Island Discs', he is meant to have had someone else pick for him his `personal' choice of records.)

In spring 1984 the lawyer Randolph Fields (1952-1997) introduced Branson to the idea of starting up an airline. The inaugural flight of Virgin Atlantic Airways took place in June 1984.

In 1988 W.H.Smith bought most of Virgin's smaller record stores, leaving Virgin free to concentrate on its megastore format (which possesses greater international potential).   In September 1991 Branson took W.H.Smith's into partnership.

In 1992 Virgin Music the record company was sold to Thorn-EMI for £560m.

In November 1993 the Virgin Games Stores were sold off to Rhino Group.

In October 1994 Virgin Vodka was launched.   The triple-distilled vodka is produced in partnership with Wm. Grants & Sons the whisky distiller.

In November 1994 Virgin launched Virgin Cola.   The soft drink is manufactured by the Virgin Cola Company, which is a joint venture between the Virgin Trading Company and Cott, the Canadian soft drinks company.

In December 1994 Virgin announced that - in partnership with Norwich Union - it was launching Virgin Direct Personal Financial Services.   Virgin Direct will sell cut-price insurance, p.e.p.s (personal equity plans), and pensions.

In February 1996 Virgin was part of the London & Continental Railways consortium which won the contract to build the Channel Tunnel rail link.

In March 1996 Richard Branson hired Jeremy Pearce, the former managing director of Sony's European music licence division, to head V2, the new Virgin label.

To Finish

Continue eastwards along Oxford Street and descend into Tottenham Court Road underground station, which is on the northern and Central Lines.

To Continue

Continue eastwards along Oxford Street to the juncture with Charing Cross Road. Turn right into Charing Cross Road.

11. Charing Cross Road and Trafalgar Square

To Start

Go to Tottenham Court Road underground station, which is on the Northern and Central Lines. Leave the station by the exit which is on the south side of Oxford Street. Turn right and then turn right again into Charing Cross Road.

Denmark Street

On the left is Denmark Street, which is colloquially known as Tin Pan Alley. Until the early 1960s Denmark Street was the centre of the popular music industry. There are still a number of instrument shops on it and on Charing Cross Road.

Waterstones

On the right, at No. 121 Charing Cross Road, is a branch of Waterstones the bookstore chain.

In the 1980s Tim Waterstone imported the American concept of user-friendly bookstores into the Britain - large stocks, knowledgeable assistants, and late opening hours. He opened the first Waterstone bookstore in September 1982. In 1989 he sold the chain to W.H.Smith.

Foyles

On the right, at Nos. 113-117 Charing Cross Road, is London's largest bookshop - Foyles, which was founded in 1906 by the brothers William (1885-1963) and Gilbert Foyle (1886-1971). The brothers tried to enter the civil service by competitive examination, but neither succeeded. As a result, they had no occupation but they did have the textbooks they had used. They sold their books and decided that their vocation might be bookselling. They first set up in Islington, and then moved to sunny Peckham before establishing themselves on Charing Cross Road.

Foyles Literary Luncheons

Foyles has long hosted Literary Luncheons. The poet Sir Stephen Spender (1909-1995) regularly attended Foyles luncheons. On one occasion he took exception to a remark about the obscurity of modern poetry and stormed out of the room in which the meal was being served, only to discover that he had stormed into the kitchen and so had to go back into the main room and make a second, somewhat less dramatic exit.

The Phoenix Theatre

On the left, at No. 112 Charing Cross Road, is The Phoenix Theatre (1930).

Theodore Komisarjevsky

The 1920s and 1930s saw the building of a large number of cinemas. These pleasure domes were produced in a wide range of fantastical styles. The foremost cinema architect of the period was Theodore Komisarjevsky (1882-1954).

DENMARK
STREET

CHARING

CROSS ROAD

SHAFTESBURY
AVENUE

O

WILLIAM IV
STREET

TRAFALGAR
SQUARE

STRAND

YORK PLACE

VILLIERS STREET

NORTHUMBERLAND
AVENUE

0.5 MILES

EMBANKMENT
TUBE STATION

1 KM

The interior decorations of The Phoenix Theatre are an example of Komisarjevsky's work. The theatre was built for the Bernsteins, who owned the Granada cinema chain.

Komisarjevsky designed The Granada Cinema (1931) in Tooting in a Venetian-Gothic style. In its prime the building was London's most spectacular picture-palace. In 1973 it was closed as a cinema.

Central St.Martins

On the right, at Nos. 107-111 Charing Cross Road, is a branch of Central St.Martins the art college. Originally, the Charing Cross Road building was an independent institution called the College for the Distributive Trades.

The London Institute

Central St.Martins is part of the London Institute, a federation of art and design colleges. The Institute was created by the Inner London Education Authority in 1986 in response to the then governmental policy of cutting back higher education in art and design. The measure is regarded as having been a broad success.

Blackwell's

On the left, at No. 100 Charing Cross Road, is the London branch of Blackwell's the Oxford bookstore.

(The Norrington Room in the basement of the Blackwell's bookshop in Broad Street, Oxford, is something which every bibliophile should experience at least once. And if you want to know why, go there and find out.)

Sports Pages

On the left is Caxton Walk. On the right of Caxton Walk, at Nos. 3-5 Caxton Walk, is the Sports Pages sports books bookshop. The business was founded in 1985 by John Gaustad, a New Zealander.

No. 84 Charing Cross Road

On the left is No. 84 Charing Cross Road, the former premises of the booksellers Marks & Co. (Co. stood for Cohen).

In 1949 the New York author Helene Hanff (1916-1997) wrote to Marks & Co., in response to a magazine advertisement, asking them to find her some books. This led to a correspondence with Frank Doel the shop's manager, which was published as a book `84 Charing Cross Road' (1971). The book was made into a movie.

Miss Hanff and Mr. Doel never met.

Cambridge Circus

Cambridge Circus is at the junction of Charing Cross Road (1887) and Shaftesbury Avenue (1886).

New Oxford Street (1847) was the first of the great West End roads which were made in the C19th. Before these streets were created the squares must have exercised a far greater influence on people's experience of the West End. There were few alternative focusses. (In 1905 Kingsway became the last of the great central roads to be cut.)

Charing Cross Road and Shaftesbury Avenue were, for the purposes of economy, largely constructed by widening existing roads.

Charing Cross Road established itself as the principal location for bookshops in London. The secondhand trade and specialist booksellers tend to be located in the section of the road to the south of Cambridge Circus. To the north of it are shops which tend to sell new books.

Shaftesbury Avenue was named after the social reformer the 7th Earl of Shaftesbury (1801-1885). In 1888 theatres began to open on Shaftesbury Avenue.

Slum Clearances

During the C19th cutting a road through a district was perceived as a good means of slum clearance. The clearances did nothing to solve the slum problem but they were good at shifting it into someone else's court. In the C19th the East End's slums became as notorious as they did in large part because the City of London and the West End had gotten rid of theirs.

The Palace Theatre

On the right, on the west side of Cambridge Circus, is The Palace Theatre (1890). The theatre has been owned by the Really Useful Group since 1983.

The Really Useful Group

The Really Useful Company was formed by Andrew Lloyd Webber the musical composer in 1977. Really Useful's primary activity is producing musicals and live entertainment.

Andrew Lloyd Webber

Andrew Lloyd Webber has been a public supporter of the Conservative Party. In 1997 Lloyd Webber was made a life peer. He chose Lord Lloyd-Webber (please note the hyphen) as his title.

Musicals & The West End Theatres

The tourist boom of the mid-1980s boosted West End theatre attendances. Foreign tourists are now essential to the health and vitality of West End theatre.

Angels & Bermans

Running into Cambridge Circus from the left (north-east) is Shaftesbury Avenue. On the left, at No. 119 Shaftesbury Avenue, is Angels & Bermans, the theatrical dress suppliers.

The Marquis of Granby

On the right, on the corner of Earlham Street and West Street, is The Marquis of Granby pub, which took its name from the general the Marquis of Granby (1721-1770), the eldest son of the 3rd Duke of Rutland. The Marquis was of the habit of helping his former non-commissioned officers set up in business. A number of the ex-N.C.O.s became publicans and in gratitude named their pubs after the Marquis. There are several Marquises of Granby in London and it is a pub name to be found elsewhere in England.

The Marquis himself enjoyed a drink.

(Some of the Marquises have changed their names. The Paxton's Head in Knightsbridge used to be a The Marquis of Granby. Nearby Rutland Gate was built on the site of what was Rutland House. (Sir Joseph Paxton (1801-1865) was the designer of the Crystal Palace, which was erected in Hyde Park to house the Great Exhibition of 1851.))

Direction
Cross over Cambridge Circus and continue along Charing Cross Road.

The Limelight
On the right is The Limelight, a nightclub housed in what used to be a Welsh Presbyterian church.

Zwemmer
On the left, at No. 80 Charing Cross Road, is the Zwemmer Media Arts Shop. (The Zwemmer Art Bookshop is on the northern side of Litchfield Street at No. 24 Litchfield Street.)

Wyndham's Theatre
On the left, bookended by St.Martin's Court, is Wyndham's Theatre (1899).

The actor Sir Charles Wyndham (1837-1919) played characters which re-inforced the social attitudes of his audience. Thus he acquired a (not altogether deserved) reputation for respectability. When a developer approached the 3rd Marquis of Salisbury (1830-1903) with a request to develop part of the Marquis's estate to the east of Charing Cross Road, the peer replied that if a theatre was to be built on the land it could only be built for Wyndham. The New Theatre (now The Albery) (1903), behind Wyndham's on St.Martin's Lane, was also associated with Wyndham.

Direction
Follow Charing Cross Road as it curves to the left and runs into St.Martin's Place.

The Statue of Sir Henry Irving
On the right, at the southern end of Charing Cross Road, is a statue of the actor Sir Henry Irving (1838-1905).

The Old Curiosity Shop
The shop which inspired Charles Dickens's (1812-1870) novel `The Old Curiosity Shop' (1841) was on the site of Irving's statue.

The National Portrait Gallery
On the right, in St.Martin's Place, is the National Portrait Gallery (1895). The Gallery was founded at the prompting of the historian the 5th Earl Stanhope (1805-1875). In 1859 it opened in Great George Street. Its present building was paid for by William Henry Alexander, the site having been provided by the government.

Its galleries are chronological in order and can be seen progressively while descending through the building.

Pitcher & Piano

Running east of the north-east corner of St.Martin's Place is William IV Street. On the north (left) side of William IV Street, at Nos. 40-42, is a Pitcher & Piano pub.

The Pitcher & Piano chain was founded by Crispin Tweddel. The business opened its first pub in 1986. The atmosphere seems to be aimed at young, upwardly mobile, white collar workers. The chain has the practice of allowing beer to be bought by the pitcher which is rare in Britain.

Direction

Cross over to the steps of the Church of St.Martin-in-the-Fields.

St.Martin-in-the-Fields

The Church of St.Martin-in-the-Fields was rebuilt (1726) by the architect James Gibbs (1682-1754). Gibbs's combination of a steeple and classical portico - the former rising unprecedentedly out of the roof of the latter - was highly controversial at the time (although it subsequently became a commonplace in ecclesiastical architecture). King George I's (1660-1727) happy response to the innovative design was to become one of St.Martin's churchwardens.

Royal births are recorded in the register of St.Martin-in-the-Fields.

On the north side of the chancel was the Royal Box while the Lords of the Admiralty sat on the south side of the chancel.

In 1829 the churchyard was cleared to make way for Duncannon Street. Among those who were buried at St.Martin's were the orange seller and royal mistress Nell Gwynne (1650-1687), the highwayman Jack Sheppard (1702-1724), the painters William Hogarth (1697-1764) and Sir Joshua Reynolds (1723-1792), and the furniture maker Thomas Chippendale (d.1779).

Trafalgar Square

The Royal Mews

Most of what is now Trafalgar Square was once occupied by a stabling complex which was known as the Royal Mews.

The word `mews' is descended from the Latin `mutare'. Originally. a mews was a building where hunting hawks were kept while they were moulting their feathers. Horses were stabled in the royal mews at Charing Cross and so the horse associated aspect of the word developed.

Modern Mewses

Mewses are now small streets in fashionable areas which are made of buildings which used to be the stables of the large period houses behind them.

Trafalgar Square

The architect John Nash (1752-1835) drew up the Charing Cross Improvement Scheme which created Trafalgar Square. In 1830 the Royal Mews main stable block (1732) designed by William Kent (1684-1748) was demolished. Nash died before he could see his plan put into effect.

The Trafalgar Square Christmas Tree

Each Christmas since 1947 the Norwegian government has donated a spruce tree which is erected in Trafalgar Square. The tree is given as thanks for Britain's part in assisting Norway during the course of the Second World War.

(One feature of Britain which is reputed to be of particular interest to Norwegian tourists is the canal system. This may have something to do with the latent Viking within them.)

New Year's Eve

The Square acts as the venue for people in London to celebrate New Year's Eve.

Nelson's Column

Nelson's Column (1849) is in the centre of Trafalgar Square.

The naval hero Lord Nelson (1758-1805) won the Battle of Trafalgar in 1805, destroying the combined French and Spanish fleets and so giving Britain and her allies the initiative in their struggle against Napoleon.

The victory was widely celebrated at the time in Britain. However, Nelson's column was not raised until nearly forty years after the battle. That a column was ever erected at all owed something to inter-service rivalry and the erection of the Army-funded Duke of York's Column (1834). Nelson's naval admirers were able to exploit the prior completion of the Duke's Column by building the decidedly taller of the two.

At over seventeen feet tall the statue can not be held to be a lifesize representation of Nelson, whose actual height was nearer to five feet than six.

The four lions were added in 1867. (Sea-lions would have had a more nautical, if less formal, air to them.)

Pigeons

Pigeons were originally a coastal bird. The species extended its range inland, London's buildings providing substitutes for cliffs.

In March 1996 it was reported that the police were investigating the mysterious disappearance of hundreds of pigeons from Trafalgar Square. A possible cause was a man whom passers-by had seen trapping the birds in baited boxes. It was speculated that he might have been selling the pigeons' carcasses to restaurants.

One theory forwarded at the time was that the warmth of the previous summer and autumn had led to a larger crop of berries and nuts than usual. This meant that wood pigeons were able to feed themselves in woodland, therefore, they did not need to break cover to feed in the fields, therefore, they were less likely to be shot, thus, creating a rise in prices that restaurants were prepared to pay, and therefore, creating an incentive for a bit of urban poaching.

Squeaky Pigeons

Those pigeons which have not been oiled correctly tend to squeak a bit when they take flight.

Trafalgar Square Statues

The Statue of King George IV

King George IV (1762-1830) commissioned a statue (1834) of himself which was to be placed on top of Marble Arch, which then stood in front of Buckingham Palace. However, the king died before the statue had been finished. It was felt that the statue might perhaps best be placed somewhere else. However, there was no obvious site which suggested itself and so the statue was `temporarily' erected in the north-eastern corner of Trafalgar Square. It is still there.

The Empty Plinth

The plinth in the square's north-western corner was for many years empty. In July 1996 the Royal Society for the Arts announced that over the following five years five statues would each spend a year on the vacant plinth.

The National Gallery Statues

Taking up the square's northern side is the National Gallery.

The statue in front of the eastern part of the Gallery is of George Washington. The statue in front of the western part of the Gallery is of King James II (1633-1701).

The presence of King James II owes more to the craft which Grinling Gibbons (1648-1720) exercised in executing his image rather than to any popular partiality to a king who in 1688 fled his own realm.

James is kept company by a statue of George Washington the first President of the United States. Washington played a role in depriving Britain of some of its remoter provinces.

The National Gallery

The National Gallery (1838) houses the nation's collection of Western Art.

After making a Grand Tour of Europe in the 1780s Sir John Leicester (later Lord de Tabley) (1762-1827) decided to collect contemporary British art. In 1823 he offered his collection to the government as the nucleus for a national gallery. The then Prime Minister Lord Liverpool (1770-1828) declined the offer.

In 1823 John Julius Angerstein (1735-1823) the insurance tycoon and art collector died. The idea of establishing a national gallery by buying Angerstein's collection was promoted by both King George IV (1762-1830) and the art patron Sir George Beaumont (1753-1827). In 1824 the government acceded.

The National Gallery effectively came into being when the House of Commons voted money for the purchase of 38 paintings from the estate. Beaumont added some paintings from his own collection. From 1824 to 1834 the paintings were housed in a building in Pall Mall on the site of what is now the Reform Club.

The Gallery was eventually accommodated in its present home. Initially, it shared the building with the Royal Academy of Arts.

In 1837 John Constable's (1776-1837) `The Cornfield' (1826) became the first work by a living British artist to enter the National Gallery collection. The painting was bought for the Gallery by a subscription.

In 1854 the government bought Burlington House in Piccadilly to house the Royal Academy of Art and a number of learned societies. This gave the Gallery considerably more space in which to display its collection.

The following year Parliament made its first grant to the Gallery of money for purchases.

With the opening of the Tate in 1897 much of the National Gallery's British collection was transferred there.

In 1985 the offer of the brothers Sir John, Simon and Timothy Sainsbury, members of the supermarket family, to finance an extension was accepted by the Gallery. The Sainsbury Wing (1991) was designed by the American architectural practice of Venturi Scott Brown. The Wing houses the Gallery's Early Renaissance collection.

John Julius Angerstein

John Julius Angerstein (1735-1823) arrived in London from Russia at the age of 15 and was apprenticed in the Russian merchant house of Thomson & Peters.

On coming of age, Angerstein became an insurance underwriter at Lloyd's of London. He went on to dominate the Lloyd's in the late C18th, creating much of the institution's character according to his own will.

Angerstein's rural retreat still exists. It is at No. 90 Mycenae Road, Greenwich. Appropriately enough, the building is used as a local art gallery. (Angerstein had a hypochondriac streak to his character. One of the house's rooms was fitted with air flutes so that its temperature could be maintained at a constant.)

Samuel Courtauld

In the 1920s the textiles manufacturer and public benefactor Samuel Courtauld (1876-1947) made a number of purchases with the National Gallery Fund's money without consulting the Gallery itself. Gallery officials are reputed to have marked down Vincent Van Gogh's `Chair' (1889) for resale. The painting, like Courtauld's other acquisitions for the Fund, forms part of the core of the National Gallery's modern holdings. Courtauld's choice of paintings for the Gallery was like that for his own private collection - informed and essentially conservative.

Dame Myra Hess

During the bleak days of the Second World War the pianist Dame Myra Hess (1890-1965) organised a series of daily lunchtime concerts in the National Gallery. These took on a deep signficance - they epitomised that, beyond the dire daily grind of combatting the awfulness of war, there were cultural values worth struggling for. The concerts had an uplifting effect on morale. They were so popular that they were continued until April 1946.

South Africa House

On the east side of Trafalgar Square is South Africa House (1935), the South African embassy.

For many years a continuous 24-hour a day, 365 days a year anti-Apartheid demonstration was mounted outside the building. Many passers-by were probably more aware of the protest than they were of the fact that the building was an embassy.

Direction

Walk down the eastern side of Trafalgar Square. Cross over the Strand to the corner of the Strand and Northumberland Avenue.

Charing Cross
The Equestrian King Charles I

On the right, standing between Trafalgar Square and the top of Whitehall, is an equestrian statue (1633) of King Charles I (1600-1649).

It is the oldest of the royal statues which stand in the West End. It was sculpted by Hubert Le Sueur (c1595-c1650), although it was not initially erected. In terms of scale, the statue flatters the king, making him out to be taller man than he in fact was. (He was 4ft. 7in. (1.4m.) tall.)

With Parliament's victory in the Civil War and the execution of Charles in 1649, Oliver Cromwell (1599-1658) ordered that the statue be sold for scrap. The brazier John Rivett acquired it and was soon carrying on a lively trade in selling objects cast from the statue's metal.

With the Restoration of the monarchy in 1660, it emerged that Rivett had in fact carried out a deception and that he had buried the statue in his garden from where it was unearthed and restored to the crown. King Charles II (1630-1685) (who was 6ft. (1.83m.) tall) had the statue re-erected (1675) on the site of the original Charing Cross, which had been used for the 1660 executions of those of the regicides (his father's judicial murderers), who were not dead or in exile.

It is to be wondered whether any of the purchasers of the objects supposedly cast from the statue asked for a refund.

Each 30th January there is a ceremony of laying a wreath at the foot of the statue. The ceremony's purpose is to commemorate Charles I's execution. It is followed by a High Mass held at the Church of St.Mary-le-Strand.

Charing Crosses

In 1290 Queen Eleanor of Castille (1246-1290), King Edward I's (1239-1307) consort, died at Harby in Nottinghamshire. Her body was carried back to London to be interred in Westminster Abbey.

The Queen had been immensely popular with the ordinary English people. Therefore, each night of the journey, while her body was lain in state, large crowds paid their respects. (The fact that your average medieval peasant does not get the chance to gawp at a dead queen every day may have played a part in her `popularity' in death.) The following year, King Edward commemorated his wife by commissioning the erection of a stone cross at each of the thirteen sites where her body had been lain overnight. The night before Queen Eleanor's body was interred in Westminster Abbey, the procession rested at Charing Cross. Edward erected a memorial cross on the site.

The cross fell victim to Civil War and was destroyed by the puritans in 1647. In 1675 the equestrian statue of King Charles I (1633) was erected on its site.

The Centre of London

If you ask someone where the centre of London is they will probably hesitate before giving you an answer. That answer will probably be `Trafalgar Square'. The reason for the hesitation is that the City of London is decidedly older than the West End and that within the West End there are many sections which are older than Trafalgar Square, which is itself on the periphery of the West End.

If the Square has a claim to being the centre of London it is one that it has purloined from its neighbour Charing Cross. In the ground by the equestrian statue of King Charles I, there is a small bronze plaque. This is the point from which mileage is measured from London to elsewhere in the country. It was placed there in 1955.

Direction

Turn left into Northumberland Avenue.

Northumberland Avenue

Northumberland House, the town house of the Percy Dukes of Northumberland, was built in 1605. Despite the building's great beauty and the opposition of the Percies, the building was pulled down in 1874 and replaced by

Northumberland Avenue. The Avenue was intended to provide access for a bridge across the Thames - the bridge was never built.

Syon House

Syon House is the Percy family's Middlesex country seat in what is now suburban west London.

The nuns who occupied the house prior to the Dissolution of the Monasteries (1535-40) moved to Europe, eventually finding a home in Portugal. There their convent was visited by a Duke of Northumberland. He presented them with a silver model of the house. "We still hold the keys," said the abbess. "I dare say," replied the Duke, "but we have altered the locks since then!"

The Sherlock Holmes

On the left, at No. 11 Northumberland Street, is The Sherlock Holmes pub, which has a collection of items associated with the writer Arthur Conan Doyle (1859-1930) and his most popular literary creation. The collection is reputed to be a vestige of the 1951 Festival of Britain. (The pub's original name was The Northumberland Arms.)

In 1891 Arthur Conan Doyle was practising as a physician at No. 2 Devonshire Place. As a newcomer to the district he had relatively few patients. He used the time between appointments to write the first of the Sherlock Holmes stories.

Conan Doyle based Sherlock Holmes in part upon the person Dr. Joseph Bell, who had taught him medicine at Edinburgh University, and in part upon the character C. Auguste Dupin, the French detective whom Edgar Allen Poe had created in the story `The Murders in the Rue Morgue' (1841).

(No. 221b Baker Street was the supposed residence of Sherlock Holmes. The Abbey National bank, which occupies No. 221 Baker Street, is reputed to employ someone to reply to the detective's correspondence.)

(Marylebone Library in Marylebone Street has a collection of Sherlock Holmes memorabilia.)

Direction

Craven Passage is to the left (south-east) of The Sherlock Holmes pub. Turn left into Craven Passage. Cross Craven Street.

Ben Franklin

To the left, at No. 36 Craven Street, is the former London home of Ben Franklin, one of the Founding Fathers of the United States of America.

Direction

Descend the steps into Charing Cross Arches. Above the Arches is Charing Cross Railway Station.

The Players Theatre

On the right is The Players Theatre, which specialises in putting on music hall shows.

The building started its life as The Hungerford Music Hall. It metamorphosed into The Forum cinema in the 1920s, and became the home of The Players Theatre in 1946.

The Players company's original home was No. 43 King Street in Covent Garden. In the Victorian era No. 43 King Street had been renowned as Evans Music & Supper Rooms.

Sandy Wilson

The early 1950s saw a spate of American musicals succeed in the West End `South Pacific', `Kiss Me Kate', `Guys and Dolls', and `The King and I'.

Sandy Wilson's `The Boyfriend' was the first successful British musical written in response to the American invasion. It was first staged at The Players Theatre in April 1953. The show moved onto Wyndham's in the West End where it played for five years. `The Boyfriend' is a nostalgia pastiche of 1920s musical comedy.

Heaven

On the left is Heaven, the gay nightclub.

In the late 1970s Jeremy Norman spent time in New York where he was impressed by the city's gay nightlife culture. Norman sought to introduce some of it to London when he opened the Émbassy Club in Bond Street in 1978. In December 1979 he opened Heaven in the arches under Charing Cross Railway Station. The club's 2000-person capacity far exceeded in size any previous regular gay venue in London. In 1981 Norman sold the club to Richard Branson.

Charing Cross Station

A number of railway stations which serve south London and the counties beyond are located to the north of the Thames - Cannon Street, Charing Cross, and Victoria.

Many of the stations were erected on plots of land which had long been in unitary ownership: the original Charing Cross Station (1863) was built on what had been Hungerford Market.

Originally, Cannon Street was the hub of the continental rail traffic. After the formation of the Southern Railway this traffic was shifted first to Charing Cross and then to Victoria.

The present station and its accompanying office building, Embankment Place, were designed by Terry Farrell. (Other buildings by Farrell include the overseas intelligence service MI6's Vauxhall Cross headquarters, and the TV-am Building in Camden.)

Monopoly

None of London's great southern railway stations are included in the British version of the board game Monopoly. This was because the game's streets were selected by the Leeds printer Victor Watson (1878-1943) and his secretary Marjorie Phillips. Watson felt that Londoners were often unduly rude about the North of England and so selected stations which were northern-oriented. (Watson had been born in Brixton in south London but his family had moved to Leeds while he was still a child.)

The only south London street name in the British version of monopoly is the Old Kent Road. It is the first property on the board and thus the cheapest.

Direction

Turn right into Villiers Street. Walk through Embankment underground station and look out onto the Thames.

The Embankments

Until the late C19th the Thames was a broader, shallower river. The street name Strand has its origin in the Anglo-Saxon word for beach or shore. The street the Strand is not only several yards above the river's current high-water mark it is also a couple of hundred metres to the north-west of the river's original low water mark.

Pre-1857 Authority over the River

In 1197 King Richard I the Lionheart (1157-1199) granted the City of London the Conservancy of the Thames in return for a large contribution to his crusading funds. During the late Middles Ages the City of London used its economic strength to build up control over the Thames from upriver at Staines to far out into the estuary to the mouth of the River Medway.

Quite what the exact nature of the City's authority was unclear. Other parties frequently litigated against the City about it. The matter was only finally resolved when the Corporation found itself in direct confrontation with the crown. This came about after it was seriously proposed to embank the river, therefore, who had the right to do what to which part of the river meant who had the right to profit from such, therefore, who owned the river became a hotly contested matter. Ultimately, in 1857, the Corporation caved in to the crown's claim that the City had only ever exercised stewardship and that the crown had always been the owner.

Sir Joseph Bazalgette & The Embankment

The Metropolitan Board of Works charged Joseph Bazalgette (1819-1891) with building the Thames Embankment.

The Embankment was built to confine the river within a particular course. The intention was to manage the river by making it narrower and faster. (One of the effects of speeding the river was to discourage any tendencies towards freezing that remained after the early 1830s rebuilding of London Bridge.)

The Embankment has a number of different sections. On the north bank the Victoria Embankment (between Westminster Bridge and Blackfriars Bridge) was built during the years 1864-70. The Chelsea Embankment (1871-4) is a westward continuation of the Victoria Embankment, there being a gap between them which is solidly filled by the Palace of Westminster which nestles behind its own solid flood defences. On the south side the Albert Embankment (between Vauxhall Station and Lambeth Bridge) was constructed over the years 1866-70.

Secondary features of the process were the building of the District Line tube along the Victoria Embankment and of sewage drains.

The process of embanking swept away scores of riverside quays, houses and workshops. Something of the riverside's old character is probably preserved at Strand-on-the-Green (south of Gunnersbury, several miles to the west on the District Line).

Bazalgette is commemorated by a bust on Victoria Embankment.

London's Sewage

The hot summer and low rainfall of 1858 led to the Great Stink. The Stink prompted the authorities not only to embank the river but also to deal with London's sewage problem.

The Metropolitan Board of Works also charged Bazalgette with building a system of sewers which ran east-to-west across London.

Bazalgette's drainage system was completed in 1875. In the northern arm, sewage was pumped to Beckton in east London. In the southern arm, sewage was pumped out to Crossness in Kent. Originally, the sewage was discharged raw into the river at the outfall station. In 1887 a decision was made to treat the sewage chemically at the outfall stations, after which the effluent was then allowed to enter the river, while the sludge was dumped at sea at a site known as the Black Deep.

The Growth of East London

Joseph Bazalgette's sewage system made East London what it is today. The south-western corner of Essex, the part which lies to the immediate east of the River Lea before in enters the Thames, was, until well into the C19th, occupied by the mansion houses of wealthy City of London merchants and their descendants.

The construction of the Metropolitan Main Drainage System's Northern Main Sewer had been intended to relieve the City and East End but, in conjunction with the advent of cheap railway travel, its very building provided landowners and builders along its course with a valuable opportunity for speculative development which they were quick to exploit.

The opening of the sewer allowed urbanisation to take place without the district's new-comers being buried in their own filth. The district's wealthy inhabitants moved on. The change is illustrated by West Ham Park which is now a public amenity. Previously it was a private garden. (West Ham Park is London's leading botanical garden after Kew Gardens.)

Direction

Walk back through Embankment underground station and then start to walk up Villiers Street

Look into Victoria Embankment Gardens which is on the right. To the left is York House's Watergate.

Watergates

The watergate was remodelled in the early C17th for the royal favourite George Villiers Duke of Buckingham (1592-1628).

The Thames's old breadth and the river's importance as a highway can still be traced both by the survival of old watergates and the names of a number of streets. Often the watergates are set twenty or thirty metres inland of the present embankment.

Most of the surviving watergates are on the stretch of river to the south of the West End. They tended to serve either royal palaces or the palatial London residences of the aristocracy and the princes of the church, a fact which reflects the courtly character of London's early westward development.

(A late C17th watergate is to be found in the riverside garden of the Ministry of Defence Building, it used to lead to Whitehall Palace. Another example is at Somerset House. When, in the late C18th, Somerset House was rebuilt, in order to serve as government offices, it was equipped with an impressive watergate, the large central arch which now towers over the Victoria Embankment.)

Direction

Retrace your way back up Villiers Street. Pass the Arches and continue towards the Strand.

Of Alley

On the right is York Place, formerly known as Of Alley.

The Alley was built as part of a development, the five street names of which commemorated George Villiers Duke of Buckingham whose riverside mansion once occupied the site.

George Villiers Duke of Buckingham

The Duke of Buckingham achieved the remarkable feat of being both the favourite of King James I (1566-1625) and of James's son King Charles I (1600-1649) (royal favourites usually came acropper with the accession of a new monarch). Buckingham rose from being the younger son of a Leicestershire gentleman to being the de facto first minister and a leading European statesman. His ascent stemmed from his good looks, his charming personality and the workings of court politics. His relationship with James I may have had a homosexual element to it. However, what is quite without doubt is that he was genuinely popular with the rest of the Stuart family including James's wife, Anne of Denmark (1574-1619).

Buckingham's meteoric career was brought to a violent and bloody end by John Felton (c1595-1628), a privately inspired assassin.

The Charing Cross Monument

On the left are the Charing Cross Hotel (1887) and the Charing Cross Monument, which were erected at the same time. Both were designed by E.M.Barry (1830-1880).

To Finish

Descend into the Villiers Street entrance of Charing Cross underground station. The station is on the Jubilee, Bakerloo and Northern Lines.

To Continue

Continue along Villiers Street to its juncture with the Strand.

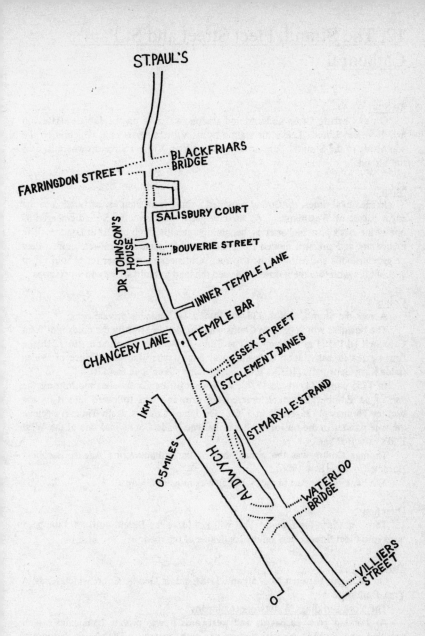

12. The Strand, Fleet Street and St.Paul's Cathedral

To Start
Go to Charing Cross underground station, which is on the Jubilee, Bakerloo and Northern Lines. Leave the station by its Villiers Street exit, which is on the south side of the Strand. Turn around and walk up Villiers Street to where it joins the Strand.

Strand
In medieval times, the Strand provided a route from the City of London to the royal palace of Westminster. As the city grew westwards the Strand emerged as one of the city's principal arteries, becoming a retailing hub of C18th London. The aristocrats and prelates moved from the riverside palaces to newer, more select neighbourhoods and allowed their former residences to be either let or sold off to speculators who tore them down and used the land to build shops and workshops.

Coutts
Across the Strand, at Nos. 438-440 Strand, is Coutts the private bank.

The business which became Coutts was founded in 1692 by the goldsmith John Campbell (d.1712) at the sign of The Three Crowns in the Strand. In 1716 the firm started its association with the royal family when the then Prince of Wales (later King George II) (1683-1760) bought some silver plate from it.

In 1755 James Coutts (d.1778), a kinsman of the Campbells, and himself the son of an Edinburgh banker, entered the firm and was followed into it by his brother Thomas (1735-1822) in 1760. On James Coutts's death Thomas became the sole partner in the business. It was he who made Coutts into one of the West End's principal banks.

Thomas Coutts was the grandfather of the philanthropist Angela Baroness Burdett-Coutts (1814-1906).

The bank is now part of the National Westminster Group.

Direction
Turn right into the Strand. You will not leave the Strand until after the road turns into Fleet Street. Stay on the south side of the road.

York Buildings
On the right, between Nos. 50 and 51 Strand, is George Court which leads to York Buildings.

The York Buildings Waterworks Company
As London grew eastwards and westwards it was private companies which supplied the newly urbanised districts with water. The York Buildings Waterworks was set up in York Buildings in 1675. The Waterworks supplied much of the West End with water.

In 1712 the company installed a very early steam engine to pump water. (James Watt (1736-1819) did not invent the steam engine. What he did was to improve it to the point where its widescale adoption became commercially viable.)

For most of the C18th the York Buildings Waterworks Company was engaged in a range of speculations which were unrelated with its original activity. In the early 1720s the company involved itself in ventures such as insurance and land speculation in estates which had been declared forfeit following the Jacobite Rebellion of 1715 (the company sold the last of its Jacobite estates in 1783). This led it into a precarious and highly litigious phase of its existence.

In 1818 the Company was bought by the New River Company, a rival water company.

The Royal Society of Arts

On the right is Durham House Street which leads to the home of the Royal Society of Arts.

In 1754 William Shipley (1714-1803), a drawing master from Northamptonshire, founded the Society for the Encouragement of Arts, Manufactures & Commerce. In 1760 the Society held the first organised art exhibition in England.

In 1774 the Society moved into its home, a Robert Adam (1728-1792) designed building which was part of the Adelphi development (see below). The Society's hall contains a mural painted by James Barry (1741-1806) during 1777-83. When Barry started on the work he seemed about to put his stamp on the London art world. When he finished it he was a spent force.

In 1847 the Society received its royal charter. The Society played an important part in organising the Great Exhibition of 1851, as it did with the Great Exhibition of 1862, the series of Exhibitions which took place in South Kensington during the mid-1880s, and the Festival of Britain in 1951.

In 1852 the Society organised the first photographic exhibition. In 1854 it held the first educational exhibition. In 1856 the Society started holding educational examinations; this led to the establishment of the R.S.A. Examinations Board.

In 1864 the Society awarded its first Albert Medal to Rowland Hill (1795-1879) the postal reformer. (It was as a result of Hill's pioneering work in organising the United Kingdom's postal system that Britain became the only country the name of which is not borne on its own stamps.)

In 1867 the Society erected London's first blue plaque - to the poet Lord Byron (1788-1824) in Holles Street. Blue plaquing was passed on to the London County Council and eventually on to English Heritage.

In 1908 the Society received permission to term itself the Royal Academy of Arts.

The Adelphi Theatre

On the left is The Adelphi Theatre.

The original Adelphi Theatre opened in 1806.

At the end of the C19th the Strand had the role, which Shaftesbury Avenue now occupies, as London's principal theatrical district. Now only The Adelphi, The Savoy, and The Vaudeville theatres remain.

The Adelphi Development

On the right is Adam Street, in which some of the surviving buildings of the Adams' Adelphi development still stand.

The project was developed by the four Adams brothers (hence the the name The Adelphi, the ancient Greek word for `brothers'). The most famous of the four was the architect Robert Adam (1728-1792).

In 1768 the Adelphi was planned as a residential area on land which had formerly been covered by a slum. The enterprise ran into financial difficulties. (One of the factors which may have discouraged potential residents was the Adams' plan to rent a cellar complex beneath the development to the government as a gunpowder store.) In 1773 a lottery was authorised by Parliament to rescue the enterprise from the financial straits into which it had fallen.

By the 1870s the area began to be redeveloped anew.

Stanley Gibbons

On the left, at Nos. 399-401 Strand, is the Stanley Gibbons stamp dealing business.

Stanley Gibbons (1840-1913) started dealing in stamps while working in his family's pharmacy in the coastal town of Plymouth. On the death of his father, Gibbons disposed of the business's pharmaceutical aspect and became solely a stamp dealer. In 1865 he published his monthly price list, this was to grow into the Gibbons Catalogue. In 1874 Gibbon moved his business to London.

Shell-Mex

On the right, between Nos. 81 and 82 Strand, is the entrance to Shell-Mex House (1931), part of Shell the oil multinational.

The Cecil Hotel

Shell-Mex House's site was once occupied by The Cecil Hotel (1886). When the 800-room hotel opened it was the largest hotel in Europe. It closed in 1930.

The Savoy

On the right is The Savoy Hotel (1889), which takes its name from a palace which used to occupy the site.

The Savoy Palace

The Savoy Palace dated from the mid-C13th. King Henry III (1207-1272) had a tricky relationship with his barons. Needing all the allies he could make, Henry gave the palace to Peter Earl of Richmond & Savoy (d.1268), a kinsman of his wife.

After having passed through various hands, the palace returned to the crown at the end of the C14th. A century later, King Henry VII (1457-1509) endowed it as a hospital.

The Savoy Chapel is the last remnant of the hospital. The present building was erected after a fire in 1864.

The Savoy Theatre

The Savoy Theatre (1881) was developed by the impressario Richard D'Oyly Carte (1844-1901). The Theatre was where most of the operas of W.S.Gilbert (1836-1911) and Arthur Sullivan (1842-1900) were produced. It was the first public building in London to have electric lighting.

The Savoy Hotel

The Savoy Group hotel company is the leading upmarket hotel operator in London. The company owns The Savoy, The Berkeley, Claridges, and The Connaught.

Richard D'Oyly Carte opened the Savoy Theatre in 1881. After a trip to the United States, on which D'Oyly Carte was impressed by the material comfort of the hotels in which he had stayed, he decided to utilise The Savoy Theatre's profits to build the best hotel in London.

In 1889 the Savoy Hotel opened. The Savoy was the first hotel in Britain to have fitted electric lights and to have so many private bathrooms.

Escoffier

The great French chef Auguste Escoffier (d.1935) was its first maitre chef des cuisines. Escoffier improved kitchen working conditions, forged the modern image of the chef, and set the tone for modern cooking with his maxim `Faites simples'. In addition, he and Cesar Ritz the hotel's manager were sacked sacked by The Savoy after admitting to having engaged in systematic fraud at its expense.

The Savoy Grill

The Savoy Grill is known as `The Canteen'. The Grill is one of the most exclusive restaurants in London and is most uncanteenlike in character.

A Little Piece of Europe

The British drive on the left hand side of the road.

Reputedly, the only place in London where it is possible to drive on the right hand side of the road is the small section of road in front of the Savoy Hotel and The Savoy Theatre.

Simpson's-in-the-Strand

On the right, at No. 100 Strand, is Simpson's-in-the-Strand, a restaurant now principally famed for its roast beef.

Simpson's was founded in 1828 by a Mr. Reiss as an establishment which sought to provide a congenial atmosphere for playing chess. John Simpson (c1802-1866), a caterer, joined the business in 1848. It was he who turned it into the eaterie that it is largely to this day.

The original Simpson's was demolished in order to accommodate the widening of the Strand. In 1904 the restaurant re-opened under the wing of the Savoy Hotel.

Direction

Cross Lancaster Place, the road which leads to Waterloo Bridge.

The Lyceum

Having crossed Lancaster Place, you should look across the Strand. There you will see The Wellington pub. To the right of The Wellington is The Lyceum theatre.

The Lyceum did not metamorphose into a theatre until late into the C19th. Previously, for over a century, it had been a place of entertainment of various forms, ranging from opera to waxworks. (Prior to a fire in 1830, it was located slightly to the east of its present site).

Sir Henry Irving

The Shakespearean actor Sir Henry Irving (1838-1905) is the individual who is most strongly associated with the Lyceum theatre. For many years his manager was Bram Stoker (1847-1912), the author of the novel `Dracula' (1897). The characterisation of the Transylvanian count is supposed to have been based in large part upon the personality of Irving.

Somerset House

On the right is Somerset House (1786), which was once the site of one of the great princely mansions which spread out westward from the City of London along the Thames's northern shore. In the mid-C16th its owner was the 1st Duke of Somerset (c1506-1552), Lord Protector and uncle of the young King Edward VI (1537-1553) (King Henry VIII's only son). In 1552 the House passed into the crown's possession.

That Somerset House was never used as the Sovereign's residence may have stemmed from its being too close to the City for comfort. Instead, it became a place where royal wives and widows were housed. (Nearby Portugal Street was named in honour of Queen Catherine of Braganza (1638-1705), the wife of King Charles II.)

Queen Charlotte (1744-1818) was the last royal consort to reside there. In 1775 King George III (1738-1820) gave her Buckingham House (now Buckingham Palace) and she moved out of Somerset House.

The palace was rebuilt (1776-86) so as to provide accommodation for various departments of state. It was the first purpose-built set of government offices in Britain. The building also accommodated a number of learned societies.

The two wings are C19th additions.

The Inland Revenue

The Board of Inland Revenue was inaugurated in 1849. It deals with taxes, death duties, and stamp duties. For many years the Board was the principal occupant of Somerset House. (That such a humdrum body should occupy such a grand building was the cause of some perplexity.)

The Courtauld Collection

Since 1990 the Courtauld Collection has been housed in the north wing of Somerset House, having been accommodated previously in Woburn Square. The Collection was born out of a visit made in 1922 by the textiles magnate Samuel Courtauld (1876-1947) to an exhibition at the Burlington Fine Arts Club.

The Courtauld Institute is part of the University of London. The Institute was founded by Courtauld in 1931. The Courtauld was the first academic body in Britain to teach art history as a discipline in its own right.

Courtauld gave the Institute part of his personal collection during his own lifetime and left it much of the rest at his death. The Collection is particularly strong in the fields of the French Impressionists and the Post-Impressionists. Courtauld was the leading British collector in these markets.

Courtauld's personal collection bore the hallmarks of the systematic, caution of an experienced businessman; it has been opined that the collection reveals little of the man. He bought according to informed advice. He made no spectacular purchases - never spotting an underrated artist - but then he made no major blunders - the collection did not have any weak paintings or weak artists represented. He bought art from the previous century in a mature market.

The Collection has acted as a magnate for other bequests to the University.

Roger Fry

The collection of the painter and critic Roger Fry (1866-1934) hangs in the Courtauld Galleries.

A number of specific exhibitions have had a profound effect on British artistic sensibilities. Roger Fry organised the 1910-1 `Manet and Post-Impressionists' exhibition at The Grafton Galleries. It was not the first exhibition in England to show paintings by Cezanne, Gaughin, Manet, and Van Gogh, but it was the first to show so many of their best works and to term the artists Post-Impressionists. Further exhibitions of their works were held in 1912 and 1913.

Fry was an interpreter to the English of modern art. His limitation as a critic stemmed from his having trained as a painter. Through his artistic education he found himself bound to a particular technical and aesthetic outlook. He could go as far as Post-Impressionism but his training stopped him going further.

St.Mary-le-Strand

On the left, in the centre of the Strand, is the Church of St.Mary-le-Strand (1717).

A church first stood on the site in 1147. The Church of the Nativity of Our Lady & The Innocents was pulled down by Protector Somerset (c1506-1552), its stone being used to help build Somerset House. The church's parishioners were allowed to use the Savoy Chapel.

St.Mary-le-Strand was the first church to be built under the Fifty New Churches Act of 1711; its architect was James Gibbs (1682-1754), whose first public building it was. (Gibbs was a Catholic but kept quiet about the fact.)

Bonnie Prince Charlie

It is said by some that Bonnie Prince Charlie (1720-1788), the Catholic-born Stuart heir, was received into the Anglican Church at St.Mary-le-Strand during a secret visit he made to London in 1750.

The Strand Maypole

The Strand Maypole stood in front of St.Mary-le-Strand. It was pulled down by the puritans in 1644. It was replaced by another maypole following the Restoration of the monarchy in 1660. In 1718 the replacement was taken down, ending its days as a support for a telescope in Wanstead, which was used for astronomical observations - superstition giving way to the rational.

King's College

On the right is King's College, which was established in 1828 following a public meeting which was called as a response to the establishment of University College on Gower Street. University College operated clearly outside the fold of the Church of England, which had until then monopolised higher education in England. King's College was opened in 1831.

In 1849 the College started mounting evening classes. Among those who attended them was the writer Thomas Hardy (1840-1928).

In 1908 King's College became a college of the University of London.

Aldwych Underground Station

On the right is the former Aldwych Underground Station, which was opened in 1907 to serve theatre-goers. However, the focus of London's theatreland subsequently shifted westwards to Shaftesbury Avenue. In October 1994 the station was closed.

Surrey Street and Arundel Street

On the right are Surrey Street and Arundel Street. The streets were built on the site of what had once been Arundel House, the town house of the Howard Dukes of Norfoik.

Thomas Howard Earl of Arundel (1585-1646) amassed the first large art collection in England. His grandson Thomas Henry Howard 6th Duke of Norfolk (1628-1684) was also a great collector. Arundel House was pulled down in 1678. The Howard family and some of their titles are commemorated in the street names - Arundel, Howard, Norfolk, and Surrey.

St.Clement Danes

On the right, in the centre of the Strand, is the Church of St.Clement Danes (1680). The church was designed by Sir Christopher Wren (1632-1723). The tower (1720) is by James Gibbs.

Danes

`Aldwic' means old colony. The Aldwych was an area which King Alfred (849-901) gave to the Danes near London after he had vanquished them in battle. (The Vikings were great traders as well as warriors.)

(The older City churches, particularly those from the era of the Danish settlement, were often known by a patron's name. An example of this is St.Mary Woolnoth in Lombard Street (i.e. the church dedicated to St.Mary which was built by Wulfnoth).

Rugby

Among the rectors of St.Clement Danes was William Webb Ellis, who invented rugby football in 1823 while a schoolboy at Rugby public school. That his sporting innovation should have been turned into a game, which spread both nationally and internationally, stemmed from the climate that enthused the school after his departure.

Thomas Arnold (1795-1842) was the headmaster of Rugby from 1827 to 1841. Arnold's ideas on education had a major impact on the subsequent development of English public schools and universities. He sought to induce the boys to educate one another with the social skills and outlook which Victorian society believed they needed. Their childish games, such as rugby, were no longer to be suppressed, on the contrary, Arnold believed they should be encouraged.

The Royal Air Force

From 1919 to 1955 the Royal Air Force's principal office was in Television House on the corner of Kingsway. St.Clement Danes was severely damaged by bombing during the Second World War. The church was reconstructed in 1958. The R.A.F. contributed £150 000 towards the church's rebuilding costs. The R.A.F. holds commemoration services in the church, which often hosts the weddings of its officers.

Essex Street
On the right is Essex Street.
Essex House
At the bottom of Essex Street are a brick arch and a set of steps, which were formerly the watergate to Essex House.

For a while Robert Devereux 2nd Earl of Essex (1566-1601) was a great favourite of Queen Elizabeth I (1533-1603). However, Essex eventually fell from grace. In 1601 he tried to raise the City of London in revolt against the crown. His attempt failed and he and his supporters were surrounded in Essex House. He was taken prisoner, tried for treason, and executed.
Essex Hall
Essex Hall in Essex Street is the head church of the Unitarian movement. The first Unitarian church was established on the site in 1774. (In the United States the first Unitarians tended to come from a Congregationalist background, whereas in Britain they tended to be from a Presbyterian one.)
Rev. Richard Price
The Rev. Richard Price (1723-1791) was the minister of a Unitarian chapel in Stoke Newington. Price attracted public attention through his support first of the American Revolutionaries and then of the French ones.

The Royal Courts of Justice
On the left are the Royal Courts of Justice (1882).

Originally, the superior courts sat in Westminster Hall during legal terms. They sat at a variety of other places out of term. The Law Courts were built to provide permanent year-round accommodation. The complex, designed by G.E.Street (1824-1881), was paid for with Chancery funds which had gone unclaimed.

In 1880 the pressure imposed by building the Courts contributed to the death of Street. (That his death was premature is indicated by his being the only architect who is buried in Westminster Abbey who had not been knighted.)

The building houses two of the three branches of the Supreme Court - the Court of Appeal and the High Court. The cases heard here are usually civil in character. The entrance to the building regularly serves as a backdrop for television news stories about major suits.
The Lord Mayor's Procession
Each November, the purpose of the Lord Mayor's procession from the Guildhall to the Law Courts is so that the Lord Chief Justice, the most senior judge in England and Wales, may swear the new Lord Mayor into office.
Badminton
On Wednesday nights, when the building is closed, its great Central Hall is used as a badminton court by some of the people who work here.
Thomas Holloway
No. 244 Strand, one of the houses which disappeared to provide the Royal Courts of Justice's site, was the headquarters of the pill manufacturer Thomas Holloway (1800-1883).

Holloway made his fortune from manufacturing patent medicines and then advertising them heavily; he is probably more important in the history of advertising than he is in the history of pharmacy. Through Holloway's financial generosity Royal Holloway College in Egham, Surrey, was founded. (Royal Holloway is part of the University of London.)

Twinings

On the right, at No. 216 Strand, housed in London's narrowest shop, is the tea retailer Twinings.

In 1706 Thomas Twining (1675-1741) acquired Tom's Coffee House in Devereux Court. The company acquired its premises at No. 216 Strand in 1717 and has used them continuously ever since. The present building dates from 1787.

The Royal Courts of Justice Lloyds

On the right, at Nos. 219-221 Strand, is the Royal Courts of Justice branch of Lloyds Bank. The bank's foyer is decorated with Doultonware ceramics.

The Doultons

In 1815 John Doulton bought a pottery in Lambeth. The Doulton family developed the business so that it provided much of the sanitary ware for the Victorians' efforts to improve hygiene and public health.

In the mid-1860s John Sparks, the principal of the Lambeth School of Art, persuaded Sir Henry Doulton (1820-1897) to employ some of the School's students. The designs which the students produced for the firm attracted considerable attention at exhibitions and, as a result, there developed a highly successful marriage of industry and art to which the bank's entrance bears testimony.

The Wig & Pen

On the right, at No. 229 Strand, is The Wig & Pen bar-restaurant, which occupies a building put up in 1625.

In September 1993 The Wig & Pen decided to open its doors to people other than its traditional closed clientele of lawyers and journalists - the two traditional Fleet Street occupations. The move was probably prompted in part by the fact very few journalists now physically work in or near Fleet Street.

The Temple Bar

In the middle of the Strand is the Temple Bar monument which marks the City of London's western edge.

The first known reference to Temple Bar dates from the late C13th. Originally, the Bar was a gate.

On state occasions the Sovereign asks the Lord Mayor of the City of London for permission to enter the City and then receives the Sword of State from the Mayor, which is in turn returned to her/him. The ceremony dates from 1588 when Queen Elizabeth I (1533-1603) went to St.Paul's Cathedral to give thanks for the defeat of the Spanish Armada.

The Temple Bar was designed by Sir Christopher Wren (1632-1723) and built in 1672. Wren's Bar, like the Monument, symbolised the City's rebirth after the Great Fire of 1666.

With time, the Bar became a barrier to the free flow of traffic and in 1878 it was dismantled and stored in a builder's yard. In 1889 it was bought by the brewer

Sir Henry Meux (d.1900), who re-erected it on his country estate at Theobalds, near Cheshunt in Hertfordshire.

The idea of the Temple Bar's return to London has been mooted from time to time. One possible site where it might be re-erected is to the north of St.Paul's Cathedral.

Traitors' Heads

In 1661 the custom of displaying the heads of executed traitors on London Bridge came to an end. From 1684 to 1746 the heads were displayed at Temple Bar.

(The heads were heavily salted to discourage birds from devouring them.)

Fleet Street

Until the 1970s newspaper printing was carried on in central London. It was possible for such large-scale industrial activity to be engaged in at the heart of a great metropolis because the principal movement of wares (paper rolls and printed newspapers) took place at night when the streets were deserted.

Banging Out

The newspaper industry emerged in Fleet Street at the start of the C18th from an already well-established printing tradition.

Printers still have their own long established rituals. When a printer finishes his apprenticeship he is `banged out' in a rite of passage. The former apprentice usually ends up being tied up, in a state of advanced undress, and covered in various vile and/or colourful substances.

Child & Company

On the right, at No. 1 Fleet Street, is Child & Company the private bank, which was founded in 1671. In 1729 it became the first bank to issue printed banknotes.

Following the 1923 death of the 8th Earl of Jersey (1873-1923), a descendant of the Child family, his executors sold Child's Bank to Glyn, Mills, Currie & Holt.

In 1939 the bank was acquired by the Royal Bank of Scotland. In 1987 the Royal Bank parent revitalised Child & Company, which had been run down to the point it was a single branch in Fleet Street, so that it could act as the its private banking division.

Direction

Turn left into Chancery Lane.

Serjeants' Inn

On the right, at No. 5 Chancery Lane, is the site which Serjeants' Inn occupied for the century and a half before its dissolution.

Originally, the serjeants-at-law had been the crown's servants (servientes ad legem). They became the barristers who had a monopoly on advocacy in the Court of Common Pleas. This monopoly survived down until 1846, and until 1875 only serjeants could be appointed judges in the superior courts. In 1877 the Society of Serjeants' Inn was dissolved.

Clifford's Inn

Just beyond, at No. 5 Chancery Lane, is the entrance to Clifford's Inn, the site of one of the now defunct Inns of Chancery.

The Inns of Chancery

In addition to the Inns of Court, there used to be the Inns of Chancery. These acted as preparation houses for the Inns of Court. Interest in a legal education declined from the late C17th to the early C19th. When the numbers of students wishing to study law began to fall off the Inns of Court used their seniority to ensure their own survival as institutions, sacrificing the Inns of Chancery. The Inns of Chancery became increasingly less involved in legal education. By the mid-C18th they were no longer possessed of a legal character. Their names, however, live on as place-names - Barnard's Inn, Clement's Inn, Clifford's Inn, Furnival's Inn, Staple's Inn, and Thavie's Inn.

The Public Record Office - The P.R.O.

To the north of the entrance to Clifford's Inn is the former home of the Public Record Office (1896).

Before 1838 official records were kept in about fifty different locations, including the Tower of London. The burning down of the old Palace of Westminster in 1834 acted as a stimulus for the government to construct a proper state archive. The P.R.O. received its first deposits in the 1860s. The Sir James Pennethorne (1801-1871) designed building was not finished until 1896.

The P.R.O.'s branch at Kew opened in 1977. In 1996 Chancery Lane's activities were moved to Kew.

The release of P.R.O. papers form a staple of British newspapers at the start of each year. In 1995 the focus of the newspaper articles switched from what Hitler and the Nazis were doing to what Stalin and the Soviets were thinking of doing.

The P.R.O. does allow some scholars access to some embargoed material if it is clear that their research will benefit from it and that they will be responsible in their use of it.

The Domesday Book

The Public Record Office contains the `Domesday Book' of 1086, a book which describes every settlement in England, listing all substantial property. (It was created for taxation purposes.)

The Casement Diaries

It was not until March 1994 that the explicitly homosexual `Black Diaries' of the British colonial administrator and Irish revolutionary Sir Roger Casement (1864-1916) were released. Originally, they had been regarded as being of so sensitive a charcter that a 100-year embargo had been placed upon them. The British government denied the diaries' existence until 1959 when the Paris-based Olympia Press published some extracts from them.

For much of the C20th Hyde Park was used by homosexuals for rendezvouses. The diaries record Casement's frequenting the park at night in search of sexual encounters.

There are still other papers relating to Casement which have yet to be released. Whether these are to do with his revolutionary tendencies or his homosexual ones is known but to a select few.

The Law Society

Oppposite the Public Record Office, on the left, at No. 113 Chancery Lane, is the Law Society.

The Law Institute was formed in 1825. The Institute received its first charter in 1831, becoming the Incorporated Law Society. The organisation's Chancery Lane premises opened in 1832. In 1903 it received another charter and became the Law Society.

The Law Society controls the solicitors' branch of the legal profession. The Society fulfils two separate functions, it is both the profession's trade union and its disciplinary body.

Direction

Turn around, walk back to Fleet Street, and turn left into it.

Hammicks Legal Bookshop

On the corner of Chancery Lane and Fleet Street, at Nos. 191-192 Fleet Street, is Hammicks Legal Bookshop.

The leading legal publishers in Britain include Butterworth, The Stationery Office, Longman, and Sweet & Maxwell.

The Inner Temple and The Middle Temple

Opposite Chancery Lane, between Nos. 16 and 17 Fleet Street, is an archway. This leads to two of the Inns of Court - the Inner Temple and the Middle Temple. There is a map of the two Temples on the left (east) side of the archway.

The `Temple' refers to the crusading Order of the Knights Templar, which was dissolved in 1312 (in a particularly unsavoury instance of Anglo-French co-operation). The `Inner' of the Inner Temple refers to its geographical relationship to the City of London, it being nearer to the City of London than the Middle Temple. (There was an Outer Temple which was developed for other uses before the end of the C16th. Essex Street now stands upon what was its site.)

In the mid-C14th another Order, the Knights Hospitallers, leased the property to some practioners of Common Law before themselves being suppressed in 1539 by King Henry VIII (1491-1547) as part of the Reformation.

In 1609 King James I (1566-1625) granted the Temple to the two Inns on condition that they maintain in perpetuity both the Temple Church and the house of the Master (the church's incumbent).

The Temple Church

The Temple Church, the Inner Temple, is one of only six surviving round churches in England. It was built by the Knights Templars in the C12th. They modelled it on the Dome of the Rock in Jerusalem.

Members of the two Temple Inns sit on separate sides of the church from one another.

The appointment of the Temple Church's chaplain, or Master, remains a royal peculiar, that is it lies within the prerogative of the Sovereign.

Sir Edward Coke

The most famous lawyer to emerge from the Inner Temple was Sir Edward Coke (1552-1634), the rather staid contemporary antithesis to Sir Francis Bacon (1561-1626). Coke helped develop the judiciary's independence of the crown by opposing royal policy whenever it was not good in law. In 1628 his researches led him to promote the Petition of Rights which sought to give Magna Carta a central position in the English constitution.

Coke's `Four Institutes' (1628-44) were the earliest textbooks on early modern Common Law.

It was Coke who stated that "a man's house is his castle".

The Influence of the Common Law

In terms of individuals avoiding being murdered England is the safest industrialised country in the world. In the early 1990s it had an annual murder rate of 1.1 per 100 000 of the population (in Scotland the rate is 5.5). England's safeness dates back to at least the C15th and in part stems both from the early abandonment of the blood feud and from the use of Common Law.

Prince Henry's Room

To the left of the archway to the Temples, at No. 17 Fleet Street, is Prince Henry's Room. The Room was the first place of historical interest that the London County Council bought and restored, using its powers under the London County Council (General Powers) Act of 1898. The Room was part of an inn which was probably rebuilt while King James I's (1566-1625) first-born son Henry (1594-1612) was Prince of Wales. To mark the alteration the inn seems to have changed its name to The Prince's Arms.

The Title of Prince of Wales

In 1284 the Welsh chieftans approached King Edward I (1239-1307) to choose a man born in Wales, who spoke no English, for their prince. The king presented them with his infant son (the future King Edward II) (1284-1327) as the first ever Prince of Wales. The future king had been born in Caernarvon Castle and could not yet speak.

St.Dunstan in the West

On the left is the Church of St.Dunstan in the West.

The poet the Rev. John Donne (1573-1631), as well as being Dean of St.Paul's Cathedral, was the rector of St.Dunstan in the West from 1624 to 1631. The Great Fire of 1666 came to within yards of the church. In 1671 the parishioners offered their thanks for the church's escape by erecting a clock.

When the church was rebuilt in 1833, the clock was bought by the 3rd Marquis of Hertford (1777-1842) who erected it on his Regent's Park villa. In 1935 the newspaper proprietor Lord Rothermere (1868-1940) restored the clock to St.Dunstan's.

The Dundee Courier

On the side wall of the building of No. 186 Fleet Street, next to St.Dunstan in the West, is a mural which bears the name of the Dundee Courier and a number of its sister papers.

The presence of provincial journalists did much to give Fleet Street its vibrance in its heyday.

Hoare & Company

On the right, at No. 37 Fleet Street, is the private bank Hoare & Company, which was founded in 1672 by Richard Hoare (1648-1718), a goldsmith (who was the son of a successful horse-dealer - the age's version of a secondhand car salesman). The bank's original premises were at The Golden Bottle in Cheapside. In 1692 the firm moved to No. 37 Fleet Street.

In 1929 the family partnership was converted into a private unlimited liablity company.

The bank is the only remaining independent private bank in London. It is a partnership in which members of the Hoare family still predominate.

El Vino's

On the right, at No. 47 Fleet Street, is the El Vino's Fleet Street wine bar.

The El Vino's business was founded in 1879 by Sir Alfred Bower (d.1948). In 1923 El Vino's acquired its Fleet Street premises. (In 1925 Bower served as the Lord Mayor of the City of London).

The Fleet Street wine bar was the haunt of generations of newspaper men. It has a reputation for being fussy about dress and used to be awkward about serving women. In 1982 the Court of Appeal obliged the firm to allow women, if they so chose, to stand at the bar and be served there.

Direction

Turn left into Johnson's Court, between Nos. 166 and 167 Fleet Street. Follow the signs to Dr. Johnson's House.

Dr. Samuel Johnson
No. 17 Gough Square

The cultural importance to the English speaking world of Dr. Samuel Johnson (1709-1784) lies in a melee of various literary activities. His most notable individual literary achievement was to compile a dictionary.

The earliest English dictionaries were essentially glossaries. Usually, they were focussed upon a single trade.

Johnson's Dictionary was superior to everything which had preceded it and it was not made redundant until the publication of the `Oxford English Dictionary' started towards the end of the C19th.

Johnson believed that the English language had been undergoing a decline since the end of the C16th. He saw the dictionary as a means of preserving English from decaying further, or at least slowing the rate of that decay. What Johnson did was to seek to deny the language's growth by trying to set it in the aspic of his dictionary's definitions. His work was done in an essentially conservative mentality.

Johnson lived in a number of residences in London. However, the only one of them which survives is No. 17 Gough Square to the north of the east end of Fleet Street. Gough Square was where he compiled his dictionary with the assistance of six clerks. He finished the final proofs in 1755.

The house was bought by Cecil Harmsworth Baron Harmsworth, a member of the Harmsworth newspaper dynasty, who gave it to a trust. The building was opened to the public in 1912. (The Johnson of Johnson's Court was not Samuel Johnson but rather a speculative builder who had the same surname.)

Biography

The Dictionary may have been Johnson's most notable achievement but it was by no means his only one. The novel and the biography were both very much fruits of the same tree. Both emerged in their modern form in the England of the 1740s and both were concerned with studying the conduct and motivation of people. The printer Samuel Richardson (1689-1761) wrote his novel `Pamela' in 1740 and Samuel Johnson his biography `Life of Savage' in 1744.

Johnson was himself the subject of a noted biography - James Boswell's (1740-1795) `Life of Johnson' (1790). (Sir John Hawkins (1719-1789) wrote a far less noted, and rather tedious, one which appeared in 1787. Hawkins's distinction was as a music historian.)

Direction

To return to Fleet Street via Hind Court, leave Dr. Johnson's House, then go right, left, right. Turn left into Fleet Street.

Bouverie Street

On the right, on the south side of Fleet Street, is Bouverie Street.

Bouverie-Pleydell is the family name of the Earls of Radnor. (The Pleydell-Bouveries are of Huguenot descent.) The family own a number of properties in the area, hence the street name.

The present Earl of Radnor is reputed to have remarked that he would not open his country house (Longford Castle in Wiltshire) to the public because "The people who come around here might be very nice, but you would n't want to see and hear them all the time. I am told that you can even smell them and eventually your house takes on an odour like a railway station". In large part, it was the income generated by the Pleydell-Bouveries' London estate which enabled the earl to afford to keep his stately home private. No doubt, many of those who work in Pleydell-Bouverie-owned properties use railway stations to help them to commute to and from work, thus enriching their landlords' coffers.

Freshfields

On the right, at No. 65 Fleet Street, is Freshfields the solicitors, one the City of London's largest law firms. Members of the Freshfield family have acted as Solicitors for the Bank of England from the early C18th on.

Whitefriars

On the right is Whitefriars.

Before the Dissolution of the Monasteries (1535-40), there was a Carmelite monastery on the site. The Carmelites wore a white mantle over their brown habits, hence the street name Whitefriars.

Alsatia

Alsatia was a district which lay between Fleet Street and the Thames, and Whitefriars Street and the Temple.

In medieval times ecclesiastical institutions were subject to Canon Law. Therefore, they had a right of privilege of being exempt from civil jurisdiction. It was possible for a person to take sanctuary on church precincts and remain immune from civil prosecution just so long as s/he was physically on that property.

From the Dissolution of the Monasteries (1535-40) until 1697 Alsatia remained outside of the City of London's jurisdiction. The area became a ghetto inhabited by outlaws and criminals. Even after the area's privileges had been abolished, it remained extremely lawless.

(Many people believe that the right of sanctuary still exists with respect to churches. It does not. It was abolished by King James I (1566-1625) in the early C17th.)

Ye Olde Cheshire Cheese

On the left, at No. 145 Fleet Street, is Ye Olde Cheshire Cheese pub, one of Dr. Johnson's favourite haunts.

Polly, a parrot, inhabited Ye Olde Cheshire Cheese. On the bird's 1926 death, aged 40, its obituary was carried in newspapers across the globe.

The Daily Telegraph

On the left, at No. 135 Fleet Street, is the 1928 building formerly occupied by the Daily Telegraph newspaper.

The Daily Telegraph was London's first daily penny paper. It was founded in 1855, after the prohibitive Stamp Duty on newspapers had been repealed.

Colonel A.B.Sleigh launched the Daily Telegraph & Courier as part of a vendetta which he was then waging against the then Prime Minister the 4th Earl of Aberdeen (1784-1860) and the Commander-in-Chief of the British Army the 2nd Duke of Cambridge (1819-1914). The expense of producing a newspaper soon outstripped Sleigh's means and ownership of it passed to the family of Joseph Levy (1811-1888), its printer.

In 1927 the newspaper was sold by Levy's descendants to the Berry brothers. The Berrys built it up into the country's leading broadsheet, a position which the paper still retains.

In 1985 the Berrys sold control of the business to the Canadian businessman Conrad Black.

In 1987 the Daily Telegraph moved to Peterborough Court, South Quay, Canary Wharf.

Reuters

On the right, at No. 85 Fleet Street, is Reuters the news agency.

In 1851 John Julius Reuter (1816-1899) founded the business by exploiting the absence of a unified Franco-German telegraph system. Financial information could not be traded directly between the Paris and Berlin bourses. Traders were dependent on trains traversing a distance of a hundred miles in order for information to be relayed from one system to the other. Reuter appreciated that a racing pigeon could be used to cross the distance in less time than it took for a train to do so. Reuter's plan worked but only for a year and then the two telegraph systems were connected to one another.

At the time London was already the largest and most dynamic city in Europe. In 1851 the Paris bourse and the London Stock Exchange became linked by telegraph. Reuter opened an office in London. He was able to exploit his knowledge of European exchanges to establish himself as a niche provider of international financial information.

In 1855 the Stamp Duty was removed from newspapers which as a consequence became cheaper and therefore were read by more people. This engendered competition among the newspaper proprietors who in their turn sought more news with which to fill their newspapers. Reuter was able to use his international financial information network as the basis for an international news network.

In 1865 Reuter turned his business into a company - Reuter's Telegram Company. The company transmitted private and commercial telegrams. This helped offset the high cost of gathering news.

The Reuters business became closely associated with the expansion of the British Empire. Colonial conflicts engendered news. In some instances, such as the Boer War of 1899-1902, there was a Reuters correspondent on the anti-British side of the conflict.

The company's telegram business was hit hard by the outbreak of the First World War in 1914. In addition, the amount of news, and the cost of collecting it, rose. In 1916 the company was turned into a private company in order to avoid a hostile takeover. The two leading figures in this development were Mark Napier and (later Sir) Roderick Jones (1877-1962). Napier died in 1919, leaving Jones the principal proprietor.

Roderick Jones made his journalistic name in South Africa by interviewing Dr. Jameson after the failed Jameson Raid of 1895-6. After this, Reuter had held him in ever growing esteem. On Reuter's death, Jones was called back to London, where he gradually assumed control of the company. Through the 1920s and the 1930s he viewed himself as being, and effectively was, Reuters.

Jones had a keen appreciation of the company's place in the British media. Therefore, he sought to involve the British press as shareholders, giving them an added reason to use its services. That the B.B.C. was to become in effect the 'voice of Britain' during the Second World War was a development that Jones did not foresee.

In 1941 Jones was ousted and the Reuters Trust established. A group of newspapers proprietors acquired a half-share of the company. After the war the proprietors kept their stakes in the business principally because Reuters was an asset which was too valuable to be allowed to fall into the hands of any one proprietor. However, they did not expect to see a profit from their holdings.

The company developed a unique corporate culture within the media world. It did this by hiring its employees straight from the Universities of Oxford and Cambridge and then sending them abroad as trainee reporters. Its management are nearly all drawn from the company's journalistic ranks.

In the public mind, Reuters was a news service, however, it always kept alive it original financial side. After 1945 Reuters began to expand its financial and economic services in order to keep the price of its news cheap for its owners. In 1963 Gerald Long became the company's managing editor. Long pressed the company into using computer-based information systems. Reuters invested heavily, always being prepared to spend in order to keep itself in the vanguard of technical developments.

In 1984 the company was taken to market. Its owners - six national newspaper companies - netted £100m each and walked away from the business as owners. They chose to plough their money into revitalising their own core businesses. In financial terms, this move by the papers was to prove short-sighted. The groundwork laid down in the 1970s began to pay off during the late 1980s, taking the company to the point where it is now one of the world's largest media businesses. The traditional newspaper aspects are dwarfed by the company's activities as a service provider for financial trading.

Direction
Retrace yours steps 15 metres back and turn left into Salisbury Court.

Salisbury Court
Samuel Richardson (1689-1761) set himself up as a printer in Salisbury Square c1724. Richardson wrote the novel `Pamela' (1740) which was a phenomenonal success across Europe. (Henry Fielding (1707-1754) responded with `Joseph Andrews' (1742), which was a parody of `Pamela'.)

Samuel Pepys
On the left is the birthplace of the diarist Samuel Pepys (1633-1703).

Direction
Turn left into St.Bride's Passage.

St.Bride Foundation Institute
At the end of St.Bride's Passage is St.Bride's Foundation Institute, which was created in 1891 as part of the amalgamation of a number of parishes and their moneys. The Foundation developed a library devoted to the subject of printing, starting with the purchase of the library of William Blades, a printer and historian of printing.

In 1922 the Institute's technical classes were moved to Stamford Street where they became known as the London School of Printing. In 1961 the School moved to the Elephant & Castle where it became the London College of Printing.

In 1966 the City of London took over administration of the Institute.

St.Bride's Church
To the left of St.Bride's Passage is St.Bride's Church.
Wedding Cakes
St.Bride's was designed by the architect Sir Christopher Wren (1632-1723). The church's steeple inspired William Rich (1755-1811), a local pastry cook, to devise the tiered wedding cake.

Direction
To the left of the St.Bride's Foundation Institute are some steps. Go down these steps. At the bottom of them turn right, then turn left into Bride Lane and go back up to Fleet Street. Turn right into Fleet Street.
Cross Ludgate Circus.

Ludgate Circus

The City of London's Ludgate gate was supposed to have been built by King Lud in 66 BC.

Ludgate was pulled down in 1760. The statues of King Lud and his sons, which were features of the gate, were moved to the Church of St.Dunstan in the West.

Ludgate Circus was built in 1875.

Farringdon Street

Farringdon Street (1737) runs into the north side of Ludgate Circus.

The Fleet River

It is possible to have a fleeting glimpse of the Fleet River on Hampstead Heath, where the river rises. Until the C19th the King's Cross area was known as Battlebridge after a bridge which crossed the Fleet (and a battle which was never fought). Holborn probably derives its name from the bourne (or stream) which flows through the hollow.

In 1733 the River Fleet was arched over between Holborn Bridge and Fleet Bridge. Farringdon Street was built over the Fleet's section north of Ludgate Hill in order to provide a venue where the Fleet Market could be held. The river has left its mark in terms of local street names - Turnagain Lane led to the river, Seacoal Lane recalls how ships from the coal mining region of north-east England could be brought upstream to unload their cargo, and Fleet Street itself.

New Bridge Street (1765) covers most of the Fleet's final stretch. The river's dark waters enter the Thames just upstream of Blackfriars Bridge.

The Fleet Prison

The Fleet Prison stood in Seacoal Lane on the City of London side of the Fleet. The prison was burned down both during the Great Fire of 1666 and during the Gordon Riots of 1780. It was demolished in 1846. The railway lines running into Holborn Viaduct Station cover part of what was the site. The prison acquired a particular notoriety through the practice of unlicenced Fleet marriages.

Fleet Marriages

The Fleet Prison was in the Liberties of the Fleet. Because of the Liberties' privileged status, couples could marry there without a licence. The service was often conducted by a clergyman who was himself imprisoned in the Fleet for debt. The first known Fleet marriage took place in 1613.

After Lord Hardwicke's (1690-1764) Marriage Act of 1753 ended the practice, the Scottish village of Gretna Green became a place where couples from south of the border ran away to to get married in haste under the unreformed marriage laws of Scotland.

Blackfriars

To the right is Blackfriars.

The district took its name from the Dominicans, who settled there in the C13th. In 1529 it was at Blackfriars Monastery that a decree of divorce was pronounced against Queen Catherine of Aragon (1485-1536).

The Black Friar

On the corner of New Bridge Street and Queen Street, at No. 174 Queen Street, is The Black Friar (1875), London's only Art Nouveau pub. It stands on the site of what was the Dominican monastery.

Direction

Ascend Ludgate Hill.

St.Paul's Cathedral

St.Paul's Cathedral stands at the top of Ludgate Hill.

The architect Sir Christopher Wren's (1632-1723) association with religious buildings started early, his father was the Dean of Windsor. In 1663 the Dean and Chapter of St.Paul's invited Wren to survey the Cathedral. He recommended that the building should be demolished and that a new cathedral built. His proposal met with opposition, however, the Great Fire of 1666 carried the argument for him.

Wren's building is the fifth cathedral to have been erected on the site.

Over the period 1666-1723 over £740 000 was raised from a tax on sea-borne coal entering London. This money was spent on the cathedral.

Wren's original design was for a building based on the form of a Greek cross. However, at the royal court, there was a party which desired the restoration of Catholicism to England and which therefore found Wren's proposal distasteful. The cathedral's plan became a matter for considerable politicking. In 1675 King Charles II (1630-1685) approved what has become known as the Warrant Design; the design is based on a Latin cross.

To avoid having to make further compromises, Wren started to build all of the ground plan and build upwards rather than starting at one end and working to the other. This meant that it was not possible to hold a service in the cathedral until 1697.

The dome of St.Paul's is not a single structure but rather two separate domes which have 60 feet of space separating them. The inner one, visible from within the cathedral, is made of brick. The outer one is made of a timber frame covered with lead.

Prior to the Second World War the cathedral had become crowded in by the buildings which had grown up around it. The aerial bombardment opened a series of vistas, some of which have survived.

Monuments

The figure of Rev. John Donne (1573-1631), the poet and Dean of St.Paul's, in the south aisle is the only monument which survived the Great Fire relatively undamaged. (This seems appropriate enough in view of the survival of St.Dunstan in the West in Fleet Street, where Donne was the rector.)

In the south transept is a statue (1795) of the prison reformer John Howard (1726-1790). This was the first monument to be admitted to Wren's St.Paul's.

Painter's Corner contains memorials to Van Dyck (1599-1641), Sir Joshua Reynolds (1723-1792), Benjamin West (1738-1820), Sir Thomas Lawrence (1769-1830), John Constable (1776-1837), J.M.W.Turner (1775-1851), Sir Edwin Landseer (1802-1873), Sir John Millais (1829-1896), Lord Leighton (1830-1896), and William Holman Hunt (1827-1910).

The Crypt

Wren was one of the first people to be buried in the cathedral's crypt. Its entrance is in the south transept.

In the west portion of the crypt, below the centre of the dome, is the burial place of the naval hero Lord Nelson (1758-1805). The sarcophagus was originally designed for Cardinal Wolsey (c1475-1530). Nelson's coffin was made from the mainmast of the French ship `L'Orient'. His body is preserved in spirit.

St.Stephen Walbrook

The Church of St.Stephen Walbrook can be viewed as Wren's forerunner for St.Paul's Cathedral. The two buildings combine a large central dome with a cross-in-square plan.

The Millenium Bridge

In December 1996 it was announced that a pedestrian bridge would be built across the Thames to link St.Paul's Cathedral to the new Tate Gallery at Bankside. The bridge's designer is Sir Norman Foster.

To Finish

Walk along the north side of St.Paul's. At the eastern end of St.Paul's Churchyard, turn left and descend into St.Paul's underground station which is on the Central Line.

To Continue

Walk along the north side of St.Paul's. At the eastern end of St.Paul's Churchyard, turn left and descend into St.Paul's underground station which is on the Central Line. Buy a ticket to Tower Hill. Take the eastbound Central Line service and change to the Circle Line at Liverpool Street. Go to Tower Hill underground station and use the subway to cross underneath Tower Hill. Walk westwards along the Tower of London's perimetre walkway to the Tower's entrance.

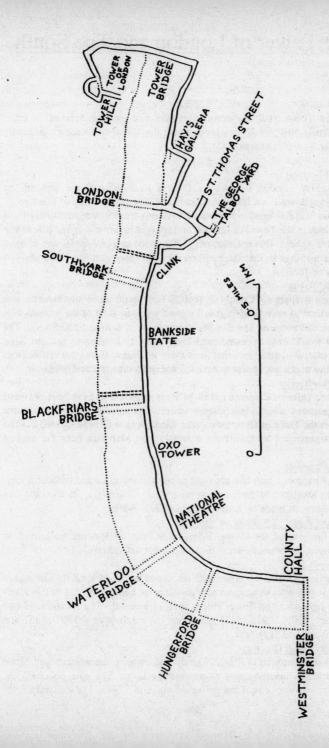

TOWER HILL
TOWER OF LONDON
TOWER BRIDGE
HAY'S GALLERIA
ST. THOMAS STREET
THE GEORGE TALBOT YARD
LONDON BRIDGE
SOUTHWARK BRIDGE
CLINK
BANKSIDE TATE
0·5 MILES / 1 KM
BLACKFRIARS BRIDGE
OXO TOWER
NATIONAL THEATRE
COUNTY HALL
WATERLOO BRIDGE
HUNGERFORD BRIDGE
WESTMINSTER BRIDGE

13.The Tower of London and The South Bank

To Start
Go to the Tower Hill underground station and use the subway to cross underneath Tower Hill. Walk westwards along the Tower of London's perimetre walkway to the Tower's entrance.

The Tower of London
The Tower of London has been a fortress since at least the time of the Normans. Lying down river, it both protected and menaced the City of London.

During the Middle Ages and the early modern period it was traditional for a monarch to sleep in the Tower of London on the night before his or her coronation in Westminster Abbey. Oliver Cromwell (1599-1658) stripped the Tower of most of its royal furnishings so that the tradition died out soon after the Restoration of the monarchy of 1660.

The White Tower
When King William the Conqueror (c1028-1087) built the White Tower it was the largest fortress to have been built in England since the time of the Romans (the Anglo-Saxons had not used stone in the construction of fortified buildings). The White Tower would have appeared particularly solid to Londoners because King William was careful to make sure that its wooden pitched roof was not visible from the ground, thus making it appear to have thicker walls than it actually had.

The Bowyer Tower
In 1478 the Duke of Clarence (1449-1478) is supposed to have been drowned in a butt of malmsey wine in the Bowyer Tower. The murder was ordered by the Duke's brother the Duke of Gloucester (later King Richard III) (1452-1485). (The malmsey was supposed to have been a rather good Malvasia from the east of Morea.)

The Star Chamber
The Star Chamber Court had the right to use torture and acted without a jury. The Court was abolished in the run-up to the English Civil Wars. Its abolition was a political concession made by King Charles I (1600-1649).

The Chapel Royal of St.Peter ad Vincula
Beneath the altar of the Chapel Royal of St.Peter ad Vincula are buried, in unmarked graves, the bones of many royal and noble individuals.

Tower Green
In Tower Green, there is a board with six names inscribed upon it. The names are those of people who were given the `privilege' of being executed in this semi-private place rather than on Tower Hill in front of a crowd. The six included two of King Henry VIII's (1491-1547) six wives - Anne Boleyn (c1507-1536) and Catherine Howard (d.1542).

The Western Wall Gateway
In 1239 King Henry III (1207-1272) built a gateway in the western wall of the Tower. The king's intention was to impress the City. The gate collapsed the following year. It was rebuilt but collapsed again in 1241. The collapses were

blamed on the vengeful ghost of St.Thomas a Becket (c1118-1170). There was no further attempt to rebuild it as a gate and, with the passage of time, its exact location was lost, its having existed being known only through a reference in a C13th chronicle.

In July 1995 it was announced that members of the Oxford Archaeological Unit had unearthed the first physical evidence of the gate.

The Moat

When the Waterloo Barracks were constructed in the 1840s the Tower's moat was drained.

Prisoners

The last time the Tower was attacked was in 1554. Its principal role since Tudor times has been as a state prison rather than as a fortress.

The explorer and adventurer Sir Walter Raleigh (c1552-1618) was for many years imprisoned in the Tower, his activities in the Caribbean having led him to run foul of the Spanish party at court. He was able to lead a reasonably congenial life, writing his `The History of The World' (1614).

Escapes

One of the most celebrated escapes from the Tower was that of the Jacobite rebel the 5th Earl of Nithsdale (1676-1744) from the Queen's House in 1716 on the eve of his intended execution. At the time, his lordship was dressed in women's clothing. He died nearly thirty years later.

The Crown Jewels

In 1303 the crown jewels were moved from Westminster Abbey to the Tower, being deposited in Wardrobe Tower.

During the English Republic of 1649-60 the regalia was either melted down or sold off. (The City of London had sided with Parliament against the king; the survival of large quantities of medieval Guild plate testifies to the efficacy of backing the right side during a war.)

By 1660, the year in which the monarchy was restored, the Annointing Spoon, the Ampulla and some individual jewels were all that survived of the crown jewels. The goldsmith Sir Robert Vyner (1631-1688) oversaw the preparation of the regalia used at the coronation of King Charles II (1630-1685) in April 1661.

In 1671 Captain Thomas Blood (c1618-1680) tried to steal the crown jewels. There is something of a mystery surrounding the attempted theft and Blood's subsequent pardon by King Charles. One possibility is that Charles, who was nearly always short of money, organised the attempt to steal his own property in order to sell it surreptitiously, there being no chance of his doing such publicly.

The present royal collection's jewels date largely from the end of the C19th after South Africa's mines began producing and Queen Victoria (1819-1901) had herself made Empress of India. Prior to that era the royal family had hired the jewels which were then set in the crowns.

Once a year the crown jewels are taken off display in order that they may be cleaned properly by Garrard the jewellers.

The Royal Menagerie

London has had displays of exotic animals since the C13th. The original zoo was the royal menagerie kept in the Tower of London. Exotic animals were one of the standard coins of diplomatic exchange in the late medieval period.

In 1830 the royal menagerie from Windsor was transferred to the care of the Zoological Society of London, as was the royal menagerie from the Tower in 1834.

The Tower's Ravens

After the Great Fire of 1666, ravens took to roosting in the Tower of London. King Charles II was asked to order their removal. However, his soothsayer said that such would lead to the end of royalty in England. (The soothsayer would not have found house sparrows quite as adept at engendering atmosphere.) Since then, six ravens have been kept in the Tower by a ravenmaster. The birds are let out every morning and called in every evening. Some have lived for several decades.

Despite their often brazen behaviour, ravens appear at heart to be bashful creatures. The Tower sends its birds to mate at a zoo in Colwyn Bay, North Wales.

Direction

Leave the Tower and ascend to Tower Hill.

All Hallows

On the left is All Hallows Church, which survived the Great Fire of 1666.

Tower Hill

From 1388 on Tower Hill was a site for the public execution of eminent public people. The first person to be executed here was Sir Simon de Burley (1336-1388). He had been the tutor of King Richard II (1367-1400). (It was not an instance of the pupil avenging himself on the teacher. Rather, de Burley's enemies had accused him of having led his charge to form a corrupt court.)

In 1747, at the execution of the Jacobite 12th Lord Lovat (1667-1747), a public stand collapsed killing several people. A stone in the pavement in the Trinity Square Gardens to the north of Tower Hill marks the site. Lovat's was the last public execution to be carried out at Tower Hill. (Lovat was the last person in England to be executed by beheading with an axe.)

Tower Hill has since been used for public gatherings, speeches and performances.

`Tubby' Clayton

The amenities of Tower Hill were created largely through the efforts of the Rev. Philip `Tubby' Clayton (1885-1972), the creator of the Toc H organisation, and through the generosity of the businessman and philanthropist Lord Wakefield of Hythe (1859-1941). Clayton set up the Tower Hill Improvement Trust in 1926.

Roman Remains

In April 1995 it was announced that the remains of a Roman building, 50 metres by 100 metres, dating from the 380s, had been discovered on Tower Hill. Archaeologists believe that it may have been London's first cathedral and that, if so, it was probably built by Magnus Maximus (d.388). Maximus used Britain as a power base from which he briefly ruled the western Roman world.

Trinity House

To the north of Tower Hill is Trinity Square. To the right (east) of the monumental No. 10 Trinity Square (the former headquarters of the Port of London Authority) is Trinity House, the home of the Corporation of Trinity House. The

Corporation's principal activities are to ensure safe navigation in the waters around the British Isles and to assist in the relief of poor seamen.

The Brotherhood of the Most Glorious & Undivided Trinity received its first royal charter from King Henry VIII (1491-1547) in 1514. The organisation was then based in Deptford in south-east London.

Trinity House's jurisdiction was extended beyond the Port of London in 1566, when Parliament authorised it to establish sea marks to indicate stretches of coast and to levy dues from shipping to pay for the maintenance of those buoys. In 1593 its income was firmly underwritten when it was given the rights on the Thames to ballastage, beaconage and buoyage.

In 1604 King James I (1566-1625) granted a new charter which gave Trinity House a monopoly on granting pilotage licences for the Thames.

In 1609 the Corporation built its first lighthouse at Lowestoft.

In 1660 King Charles II (1630-1685) granted the Corporation a new charter. However, he still continued to grant patents to erect lighthouses to private individuals.

After the Restoration of the monarchy in 1660, Trinity House moved its headquarters to Water Lane, Lower Thames Street, in the City of London. However, it retained its association with Deptford until 1852; the Corporation would meet each year there on Trinity Monday.

In 1676 the diarist Samuel Pepys (1633-1703) was elected the Corporation's Master. Pepys drafted the charter which King James II (1633-1701) granted in 1685, and which is still largely in operation.

The Corporation established its first light vessel at the Nore in 1732.

Control of all English lighthouses and navigation marks was granted to the Corporation in 1836, a loan was provided by the government to enable it to buy the privately-owned lighthouses.

In 1894 the right of ballastage was transferred from Trinity House to the Thames Conservancy.

In 1988 responsibility for district pilotage was transferred from Trinity House to local harbour authorities.

(The Nobel Prize-winning economist Professor Ronald Coase's 1990 book `The Firm, The Market and The Law' contains a paper in which Coase uses the example of Trinity House, a private corporation fulfilling public duties, to examine issues of economic doctrine.)

Direction

Walk by the perimeter of the Tower of London, keeping it to your right.

Cross Tower Bridge...if you can. If you can't, wait until you can. Cross on the right (west) side.

Tower Bridge

The idea of a bridge to provide some relief for London Bridge was mooted in 1876. The design was the work of both the City architect Horace Jones (1819-1887) and the engineer John Wolfe Barry (1836-1918). Work started on the bridge in 1886 and was finished in 1894.

At the time of its construction Tower Bridge was widely disliked, there being an opinion that it was out of character with its surroundings; the bridge's towers had been intended to blend in with the Tower of London. The bridge is probably now more of an icon of London in the popular mind than is the Tower.

Between the bridge's two towers is a walkway. This was closed many years ago because of the tendency of undesirable elements to gather there.

The bridge's road sections can be raised to allow vessels to pass underneath. On some days the bridge will be opened and closed several times. Tower Bridge's original hydraulic machinery was replaced by an electrified system in 1976.

The Pool of London

The Pool of London was the heart of London's dock life until the walled docks began to be developed in the early C19th.

The Upper Pool extends from London Bridge to Cherry Garden Pier and the Lower Pool from Cherry Garden Pier to Limekiln Creek.

Direction

After going through the bridge's southern arch descend the steps and turn so that you are walking westwards along the river's south bank (the Tower of London will be on the opposite shore).

The Silver Jubilee Walkway

The path which runs along this section of the river's south bank is part of the Silver Jubilee Walkway. The Walkway is a twelve-mile-long route through central London. It was started in 1977 to commemorate Queen Elizabeth's first twenty-five years on the throne. The final section - between Tower Bridge and Blackfriars Bridge on the south side of the Thames was opened in November 1994.

The Kuwait Investment Office - The K.I.O.

The empty land on the left is owned by the Kuwait Investment Office. Before the Iraqi invasion of Kuwait in August 1990, the Office was an important financial player in the City of London.

In 1974 the Kuwait Investment Office bought the St.Martins Property Corporation. St.Martins is one of the City's biggest landlords. The company owns the as yet only partially developed London Bridge City site on the Thames's south bank.

In 1987 the British government sold its remaining 31% stake in the oil multinational British Petroleum. The sale flopped, enabling the Kuwait Investment Office to acquire a 21.7% stake in the company. After pressure was brought to bear by the British government, the Office reduced the size of its stake. At the start of 1996 the Office owned 5.95% of BP.

Mud, Mud, Glorious Mud

On the right, if the tide is out, the river's mudbanks should be exposed.

The Society of Mudlarks & Antiquarians

The Society of Mudlarks & Antiquarians is a group which carries on its activities within guidelines set by the Port of London Authority. The Society's members search the Thames's foreshore, between the Houses of Parliament and Thames Pier, looking for artefacts which have been dropped there through the centuries. Any items that are discovered have to be offered to the Museum of

London for a period of display before being sold. Among the items which members of the Society are unlikely to find are genuine Billys and Charleys.

Billys & Charleys

In the middle of C19th Billy and Charley were two people who eeked out a living by scouring the Thames's banks for artefacts which they sold on to dealers. In 1857 it struck them that it would be more efficient - and profitable - if they manufactured the antiquities rather than searching for them. This they did, claiming that their sudden steady flow of items was being generated by the excavation of a new dock at Shadwell. The following year their fraud was unmasked by the archaeologist Henry Syer Cuming.

Billys and Charleys are still traded but openly so, being valued as curiosity items.

Fish

In the late 1950s it was reported that the only fish to be found in the tidal Thames below Richmond was the eel. Subsequently, following the introduction of legislation, the state of the river steadily improved. In 1974 the first salmon since 1833 was caught from the river. In July 1993 a 17 lb. salmon was caught at Teddington Weir.

The non-tidal river above Teddington maintained a fish population in the C19th and early C20th. This was carefully fostered by the Thames Angling Preservation Society.

Seals

In September 1995 a grey seal was netted in the Thames at Petersham, which is on London's western edge.

Tower Subway

Across the river, to the left (west) of the Tower of London is the Tower Subway (1869), which was constructed by P.W.Barlow (1809-1885). The Subway comes up on the south side of the Thames in Vine Lane. It was closed in 1896.

Tunnels

Tunnels are a feature of the river to the east of Tower Bridge. It was necessary not to block off maritime access to the Pool of London and the upriver docks such St.Katharine's.

H.M.S.Belfast

Moored on the south side of the Thames, at Symon's Wharf, is the H.M.S.Belfast, a former Royal Navy cruiser. The Belfast was built in 1939 and taken out of service in 1963. In 1971 the Imperial War Museum opened her as a museum.

The Custom House

The classical building on the the north side of the river, opposite the Belfast's bow, is the Custom House (1817).

Customs duties have been levied in London since at least the 970s. There has been a Custom House in Lower Thames Street on or near the Custom House site since 1275. The present building was opened in 1817. Representatives from each ship in the Port of London had to go there to pay the due duties on their vessels' cargoes.

Billingsgate Market

The building to the left (west) of the Custom House is the former Billingsgate Market (1877).

The fish trade moved from Queenhithe Dock to Billingsgate Market in Lower Thames Street during the reign of King Edward III (1312-1377).

The modern fish market was established by Act of Parliament in 1699. The quay was used for landing a range of goods other than fish, notably coal. However, fish came to predominate as London's population gradually moved out of the City of London.

The market's porters were renowned for their traditional hard, flat hats. These enabled them to balance weights of over 100 lbs. upon their heads. The porters' other claim to fame was their colourful language ('colourful' that is if your can appreciate a range of blue hues).

In January 1982 Billingsgate fish market moved eastwards to a 13-acre site in West India Dock on the Isle of Dogs.

Hay's Wharf

The Hay family first acquired a brewery around Tooley Street in 1651. They moved their business activity from brewing into warehousing and transport.

Direction

After passing The Horniman pub, turn left and walk through the covered Hay's Galleria. Turn right when you reach Tooley Street.

(The Hornimans were tea traders. One member of the family founded an anthropological museum in south-east London, while another introduced repertory theatre into England.)

The London Dungeon

On the left, at Nos. 28-34 Tooley Street, in the arches under London Bridge Station, is the tourist attraction The London Dungeon.

Direction

At the end of Tooley Street (Duke Street Hill to be pedantic) turn right and walk out onto London Bridge.

London Bridge

Before the embankments were built the river was both broader and shallower and therefore it could be forded at certain points - London Bridge was one of these. (Other sites included Chelsea, Fulham and Brentford.)

The Romans availed themselves of the ford just east of the present London Bridge to construct the first London Bridge. Their wooden construction was kept in a state of repair until the late C12th when it was replaced by a stone bridge.

The moving force in the building of the stone bridge was Peter de Colechurch (d.1205), a priest. The bridge's 30-year-long construction and subsequent maintenance was overseen by the Fraternity of the Brethren of London Bridge, a church-based organisation. In 1282 the Fraternity received a royal warrant.

A permanent, resident community developed on the bridge. (The only bridge on which people still live in Britain is Pulteney Bridge in Bath.)

For many years there was a custom of displaying the heads of executed traitors on London Bridge. The heads were heavily salted to discourage birds from devouring them. In 1661 the custom came to an end. (From 1684 to 1746 the heads of traitors were displayed at Temple Bar, the westernmost entrance to the City.)

The stone from the 1762 demolition of Moorgate, one of the City's gates, was used to mitigate the effect that the tide was having on London Bridge.

The C13th bridge was built on a series of small arches. During winter the water often froze upriver of the bridge. If the ice then proved thick enough for people to stand on then a frost fair was sometimes held on the river. The last Frost Fair took place in the winter of 1813-4. The 1830s rebuilding of the bridge by Sir John Rennie (1794-1874) sped the Thames's flow and so made it harder for the river to freeze over. (Three of the old bridge's alcoves were preserved. One is now in Guy's Hospital, while the other two are to be found at the eastern end of Victoria Park in east London.)

The C19th bridge was replaced by a new one in 1972. The Rennie bridge was sold, dismantled and re-erected at the Arizona resort of Lake Hava City. (According to an urban myth, the American purchasers assumed that they were buying Tower Bridge and did not appreciate their error until it was too late for them to retract.)

Bridge House Estate Fund

The Bridge House Estate Fund is one of the large financial resources which the Corporation of the City of London controls. The income it generates is intended to pay for the maintenance of the City-owned bridges (Blackfriars, London, Southwark, and Tower).

The Fund's origins can be traced back to start of the C13th when it was established by King John (c1167-1216) (`Bad' King John, the younger brother of King Richard the Lionheart (1157-1199)). The Bridge House Estate was amassed during the Middle Ages through bequeathment. In the C13th King Edward I (1239-1307) allowed the rent of the market which subsequently became the Stocks Market to be assigned to London Bridge's maintenance.

The Bridge House Estates Committee of the Corporation was founded in 1592. It is the senior Corporation committee. The Committee's chairman is the Chief Commoner, the leader of the Common Council.

In April 1995 the Common Council agreed that the Bridge House Estate Fund's surplus income could provide income for a Trust which will make grants to organisations and charitable bodies in greater London which have worthy objectives.

London Bridge Waterworks

In 1581 Pieter Morice erected a waterwheel on London Bridge, the wheel was powered by the rush of water through the Bridge's narrow arches. Sufficient power was derived to pump water drawn from the river as far as Cornhill. (The London Bridge Waterworks' rebuilding was not incorporated into Sir John Rennie's plan.)

Direction

Turn around and walk past Tooley Street (a.k.a. Duke Street Hill) and walk towards the railway arch directly south of the bridge.

Southwark Cathedral

On the right is Southwark Cathedral, which until 1897 was the Church of St.Saviour. The diocese of Southwark's first bishop was enthroned in 1905. As a church it was a fine Gothic building in its own right, dating from the early C13th.

Direction

Walk through the railway archway and down into Borough High Street.

London Bridge Station

On the left is London Bridge Station, which in 1837 was the first railway terminus to open in London. The London-Greenwich railway was built along a four-mile viaduct built on top of 878 brick-built arches. The first section of the railway opened in 1836 and ran between Spa Road in Bermondsey and Deptford. Much of its initial traffic came from Londoners curious to experience railway travel.

London Bridge Station was initially a fairly ramshackle affair. Serious money was only invested in station building once the venture looked as though it was going to be a success. The station's development necessitated the removal of St.Thomas's Hospital from its original site. (The hospital did not find a permanent home until the development of the Albert Embankment (1871).)

The first regular long-distance commuter service started in September 1844. It ran between Brighton and London.

Direction

Turn left into St.Thomas Street.

The Old Operating Theatre

On the left, at No. 9a St.Thomas Street, is the Old Operating Theatre, Museum & Herb Garret, an early C19th operating theatre.

Originally, the Old Operating Theatre was part of St.Thomas's Hospital. After St.Thomas's move away from Southwark the Theatre was used as a place to store herbs, it then fell into disuse and was forgotten about for many years, thereby ensuring its survival.

The Theatre was rediscovered in 1956, after having been sealed for almost a century.

Guy's Hospital

On the right, further along St.Thomas Street, is Guy's Hospital. Most of the modern hospital is now housed in the towerblock to the old hospital's east.

Thomas Guy M.P. (1644-1724) had a bookshop on the corner of Lombard Street and Cornhill. He made a £500 000 fortune from printing and selling Bibles and from timely speculation in South Sea Company. In 1707 he built and furnished three wards of St.Thomas's Hospital. St.Thomas's Hospital lay on the north side of St.Thomas Street. In 1721 he founded Guy's Hospital on land on the south side of the street.

Guy's was London's first purpose-built hospital. Previously, hospitals had usually evolved from the buildings of earlier religious establishments.

Guy's medical school was established in 1769.

In 1818 the first transfusion using human blood was carried out in the hospital.

Direction
Retrace your way back to Borough High Street. Turn left into Borough High Street.

The George Inn
On the left is The George Inn, the best surviving (if incomplete) example of a coaching inn. Southwark's coaching inns were doomed with the 1837 opening of London Bridge Station.

London Coaching Inns
London's coaching inns played an important role in the social and economic life of the city and its environs during the C17th, C18th and early C19th. They acted as a mixture of hotel and embarkation point for travellers from other parts of Britain. Often the inns had a strong association with a particular part of the country. By arriving or departing at the inn businessmen and gentry who came to London knew that they had a good chance of travelling with people they knew or knew of. While those people who originated from a region, but who, through work or official service, had to live in London, would often spend some of their leisure time frequenting the public rooms of their `local' inn to hear news of home or eat regional delicacies.

Trust Houses
The advent of the railway age meant that many of Britain's provincial coaching inns declined. The managers of some of these inns sought to boost their takings through liquor sales, which led to an increase in public drunkenness. In 1904, to address these twin problems, the 4th Earl Grey (1851-1917) set up Trust Houses to buy and improve inns and to put them under the management of people who would promote the properties as hotels and restaurants and downplay their aspect as bars. The first Trust House opened in Hertfordshire in 1904 and proved a great success. In each county, the local aristocracy were foremost among those who subscribed . capital to set up a new venture. The chain was so successful that it ended up acquiring many of London's most prestigious hotels.

In 1970 Trust House merged with Forte Holdings the catering and hotels company to form Trusthouse Forte, which subsequently renamed itself Forte. Forte is now owned by Granada.

Talbot Yard
On the left is Talbot Yard, an alley which stands on the site of the Tabard Inn, which was where the pilgrims of Geoffrey Chaucer's (c1340-1400) `Canterbury Tales' were supposed to have set out from on their pilgrimage to Canterbury.

The poems of Chaucer mark the literary birth of the English language (not that one would think it from reading his work). His writings were indicative of how the language of the court (from 1066 onwards Norman French) and the demotic language (Anglo-Saxon) had merged to become one.

Direction

Turn around and walk back up Borough High Street for 40 metres. Cross the Borough High Street and then Southwark Street. Go into Stoney Street, to the right of the Southwark Market Tavern, a pub.

Borough Market

On the right is Borough Market, which now functions as a wholesale fruit and vegetable market. The Market is reputed to be the oldest municipal fruit and vegetable market in London, the successor of one which was held on London Bridge in the C13th. It was established on its present site in 1756.

Direction

Continue along Stoney Street, which curves to the right. Pass under the railway arch and carry on until you reach Clink Street. Upon reaching Clink Street turn left.

The Clink

From the early C12th to the early C17th, the Bishops of Winchester had their London palace on Bankside. Its grounds were possessed of ecclesiastical privilege. To raise money for the episcopal coffers, the bishops' stewards allowed various entertainments to be set up within the palace's grounds to avail themselves of its privilege and thus avoid the restrictions laid down by the City of London and Surrey magistrates.

The last Bishop of Winchester to live at Bankside was Lancelot Andrewes (1555-1626).

After the Restoration of the monarchy in 1660 the property was restored to the bishopric but by then it had become so dilapidated that it was leased out to building speculators.

Winchester Geese

Among the Bankside entertainments were brothels. In the C16th Southwark prostitutes were known as `Winchester geese'; the brothels being regulated by the bishop's ordinances.

The Clink Prison

The Clink Prison was the prison of Winchester Palace. Originally, it was built for holding those who veered from religious orthodoxy but it came to act primarily as a penitentiary for those whose behaviour transgressed the smooth operation of Bankside as a pleasure ground. The prison was burnt down during the Gordon Riots of 1780.

`In clink' is a phrase for someone being in gaol or in disgrace.

Direction

Continue along Clink Street. Pass under the railway arch and turn right.

The rest of the walk will be along the Thames's south bank.

Cannon Street Station

On the right, on the north side of the Thames, are the towers of the original Cannon Street Station, which opened in 1866. The decorative turrets remained overlooking the river after the station itself was relocated further inland during the 1960s.

The Financial Times

Just before Southwark Bridge on the left is the building of the Financial Times, the distinctive pink financial newspaper.

The 1950-72 editorship of Sir Gordon Newton was perceived as something of golden era for the Financial Times. Newton's style was to hire those who looked as though they might be the best and then let them write about what they thought was important.

Sir Samuel Brittan

The newspaper's best known economic columnist is Sir Samuel Brittan. Brittan studied economics at Cambridge University, where he was an orthodox Keynesian. (Keynesians believe that the state should actively involve itself in the economy.) On leaving university, he established himself as a financial journalist. In the 1970s he converted to monetarism and, with Peter Jay, was responsible for the idea's introduction into Britain. (Monetarists believe that the economy should be left to do whatever it does.) Subsequently, Brittan has been seeking to wed monetarism to certain aspects of Keynesian thought.

Direction

Pass under Southwark Bridge.

Southwark Bridge

The original cast-iron bridge was built for the Southwark Bridge Company, a private concern, in 1819. In 1868 the City Corporation bought the bridge.

The Globe

On the left is The Globe Theatre, which opened to the public in May 1997.

The Shakespeare Globe Museum

The Shakespeare Globe Musuem of Elizabethan Theatre History is in Bear Gardens, Southwark.

Cardinal Wharf

On the left is Cardinal Wharf. Sir Christopher Wren (1632-1723) is supposed to have lived at No. 49 Cardinal Wharf during the construction of St.Paul's Cathedral.

Bankside

The Sir Giles Gilbert Scott (1880-1960) designed Bankside power station was completed in 1963. It was decommissioned in 1981.

In April 1994 the Tate Gallery unveiled its intention of acquiring the power station from its owner the generating company Nuclear Electric. Bankside has twice the capacity for showing art as The Tate, it will be the largest modern art gallery in the world.

The Gallery is scheduled to open in 2000.

The Millenium Bridge
In December 1996 it was announced that a pedestrian bridge would be built which will link St.Paul's Cathedral to the new Tate Gallery at Bankside. The bridge's designer is Sir Norman Foster.

The City of London School for Boys
The five-storey redbrick building, with the City of London's red cross on a white background at either end and a white entry, is the City of London School for Boys.

John Carpenter (c1370-c1441) was the town clerk of the City of London. Carpenter left lands and rents to the Corporation of the City to provide for the education of boys.

The City of London School for Boys was founded in Milk Street in 1837 as a successor to Carpenter's foundation. In 1883 the School moved from Milk Street to the Victoria Embankment. In 1986 it moved to its present building in Queen Victoria Street.

Direction
Pass under Blackfriars Railway Bridge.

Express Newspapers
Just before Blackfriars Bridge, on the left, is the Express Newspapers building.

Sir Cyril Pearson (1866-1921) launched the middle market The Daily Express newspaper in 1900.

Max Aitken (later Lord Beaverbrook) (1879-1964) made his fortune in his native Canada. In 1910 he arrived in Britain. The following year he started putting money into the Daily Express. In 1916 he acquired control of the newspaper in order to prevent its closure. Two years later The Sunday Express was launched.

Beaverbrook viewed his newspapers as a medium through which to convey his political views and with which to entertain himself. Although Express editorials tended to be right-wing, the papers employed numerous left-wing writers and politicians, as it was these people who were able to provide the most enlivening copy.

In 1977 the company was bought by the conglomerate Trafalgar House. In November 1978 the company launched the mass market The Daily Star newspaper. In part, this was done to utilise spare printing capacity.

Trafalgar House floated off Express Newspapers in a company called Fleet Holdings. By October 1985 Fleet Holdings was owned by United News & Media.

The dominant figure within United News & Media is the financier Lord Hollick, a supporter of the Labour Party.

Blackfriars Bridge
Pass under Blackfriars Bridge (1869).

The first Blackfriars Bridge was opened in 1769. The bridge was officially called the William Pitt Bridge. However, it soon became known as Blackfriars Bridge.

Roberto Calvi

In July 1982 the corpse of the Italian financier Roberto Calvi of Banco Ambrosiano notoriety was found hanging from an arch of Blackfriars Bridge.

In 1987 Francesco Di Carlo, a British resident, was sentenced to 25-years for his part in a Mafia heroin importing racket. In June 1996 it was revealed that Di Carlo had confessed to the murder of Calvi.

Unilever House

On the north side of the Thames to the left (west) of Blackfriars is Unilever House (1931), the headquarters of Unilever the Anglo-Dutch multinational.

The Lever family were originally wholesale grocers. Their business was adversely affected by the 1880s depression. William Hesketh Lever (later Lord Leverhulme) (1851-1925) decided to become a soap manufacturer, soap being a product the sales of which were unaffected by economic cycles.

In 1884 Lever Brothers opened a soap factory in Warrington in Cheshire. In 1889 the firm opened one on The Wirral. This had purpose-built housing for its workers. It became Port Sunlight.

Lever Brothers sought to vertically integrate its operations right from milling vegetable oil seeds through to selling its products to retailers. This led the company into the food business; during the First World War the government asked the company to use its expertise with oils and fats to produce margarine.

After the First World War the Lever Brothers-controlled Joseph Crossfield Ltd. acquired the English rights to Persil the soap powder brand; in France the rights were owned by the Societe Marseilleise de la Marque Persil; throughout the rest of the world the brand rights belong to Henkel of Germany the company which created the brand.

Following the war, Lever Brothers found that its food processing activities had turned it into a rival in the margarine business of two Dutch companies Jurgens and Van Den Berghs. In 1929 the three companies merged to form Unilever.

De Keyser's Royal Hotel

Unilever House occupies what was formerly the site of De Keyser's Royal Hotel (1874).

Sir Polydore De Keyser (1832-1898) was a Belgian who came to London to work as a waiter and ended up serving as Lord Mayor of the City of London. He opened his hotel in September 1874. It closed after the First World War.

Sion College

The grey building to the left of Unilever House is a former home of the City of London School for Boys. The red brick building to the left of the former school is Sion College.

Sion College was founded in 1624 by Thomas White (c1550-1624), who was the vicar of St.Dunstan in the West. The College exists for the benefit of the Anglican clergy of London and its neighbourhood.

Under the Copyright Act of 1710 Sion College was able to claim a copy of every book printed in London.

Doggett's Coat & Badge Race

On the south side of Blackfriars Bridge is Doggett's Coat & Badge pub, which takes its name from the Doggett's Coat & Badge Race. The Race is over a century older than the Oxford & Cambridge Boat Race.

The Doggett's Coat & Badge Race was established by Thomas Doggett (d.1721), a successful actor-manager. As a manager Doggett was dependent upon the court's good grace for his licence to run a theatre. In 1714 the Hanoverian dynasty arrived on the English throne. It made good business sense for Doggett, quite besides any sincere feelings he may have had, to flatter them. He did this by establishing an annual race for the Thames watermen (the taxis of the day). The race's prizes, the Coat & Badge, bore on them a white horse, the heraldic symbol of the Hanoverians.

The first Doggett's Coat & Badge Race was rowed in August 1716. The original course ran from London Bridge to Chelsea, a distance of 4.5 miles.

Old Swan House, at No. 17 Chelsea Embankment, marks what was, until the river's embankmentation, the site of The Old Swan Inn, which was the original finishing post for the Race.

The Race is still run in late July each year. It is organised by the Fishmongers' Company, a City guild.

Sea Containers House

To the left is Sea Containers House. The building was constructed as a hotel but found its use as a corporate headquarters.

Sea Containers is a diverse transportation company, which grew out of one of the first businesses to embrace the use of containers for the movement of goods internationally. Sea Containers owns the Orient Express.

The Oxo Tower

To the left, several floors up, is the Oxo Tower (1930).

The Oxo Tower Wharf building was originally an Edwardian-built Post Office power station. The Art Deco-style Oxo Tower was added subsequently as a means of circumventing the advertising restrictions of the London County Council which were in force at the time. (Oxo is a brand of beef cube, which can be turned into a drink.)

In September 1996 Harvey Nichols the department store retailer opened a restaurant on the roof of the building.

Inner Temple Garden

To the right, across the Thames, is the Inner Temple Garden. The Inner Temple is to the right and the Middle Temple to the left.

Coin Street

To the left is Coin Street.

From 1970 to 1984 the 13-acre Coin Street site was the subject of a running planning battle between commercial developers and their opponents. In 1984 the latter won and the Greater London Council sold the site to Coin Street Community Developers.

The shops and restaurants are known as Gabriel Wharf.

London Weekend Television

On the left, in the building with the tower, is London Weekend Television the commercial television broadcaster, which holds the weekend I.T.V. franchise for London, which runs from Friday evening to Sunday night.

The company developed a reputation as something of a television hothouse. If someone could thrive in L.W.T. they could thrive anywhere in British television. This may have been the result of the company having to go up against the B.B.C. on Friday and Saturday nights. Former L.W.T. employees include John Birt the Director-General of the B.B.C., Greg Dyke the head of Pearson's television interests, Michael Grade the former head of C4, and Sir Christopher Bland the Chairman of the B.B.C. Board of Governors.

L.W.T.'s `Six O'Clock Show' went out early on a Friday evening. The programme was created by its editor Greg Dyke. Among the show's presenters and researchers were a number of individuals who went on to become influential in British television.

In the late 1980s it became apparent that the next round of I.T.V. franchises were going to be awarded by auction. At the time, L.W.T. was one of the strongest of I.T.V. companies. Christopher Bland appreciated that in the run-up to the award of the franchises there was a serious danger of the company's managers being poached by other bidders and thereby undermining L.W.T.. Therefore, Bland decided to lock-in 40 senior managers by giving them a financial incentive to stay with the company. The 40 purchased 15% of the company's stock under an agreement whereby a multiplier would come into operation if the company's stock price reached a certain value, which it did. Bland earned £11m from his options. In September 1993 it was reported that L.W.T.'s senior managers had between them reaped £17m profit as a result of a `golden handcuffs' deal.

One of the side-effects of the L.W.T. golden handcuffs episode was the partial financing of the politician Tony Blair's successful campaign for the leadership of the Labour Party. The linkman was Blair's adviser Peter Mandelson M.P., who is a former L.W.T. producer. Mandelson persuaded Greg Dyke and a number of other former L.W.T. managers to make donations to Blair's war chest. (Bland is a member of the Conservative Party.)

In February 1994 L.W.T. was taken over by Granada a conglomerate which owns the I.T.V. franchise for north-west England.

In March 1996 Bland succeeded Marmaduke Hussey as chairman of the B.B.C..

Cilla Black

Cilla Black is probably Britain's highest-paid television performer. She was the cloakroom attendant of The Cavern Club in Liverpool. Brian Epstein, The Beatles' manager, managed her recording career, which included the 1964 number one hit `Anyone Who Had a Heart'.

In 1984 Black started presenting L.W.T.-made early Saturday evening audience-grabbing shows such as `Surprise, Surprise' and `Blind Date'. She is at the core of `Blind Date's' success on British television. Culturally, a man would be unacceptable as host, and a young, unmarried woman host would be unable to flirt with male contestants.

IBM

On the left is the London office of IBM the American computer company. IBM built itself up by manufacturing `washing machines from hell' and which brought itself to its knees by not taking the developments of the personal computer and networking seriously. On every desk visible from the walkway there seems to be a computer, perhaps the sign of a lesson well learned.

The North Shore

On the north bank to the right of Waterloo Bridge are Somerset House, King's College, and the Howard Hotel.

The Royal National Theatre

On the left is the Royal National Theatre (1976).

The idea of a National Theatre was first put forward in 1848. The scheme was not pursued seriously until 1904 when H. Granville Barker (1877-1946) prepared a National Theatre Scheme and Estimate; appeals raised enough funds to purchase a site in Cromwell Gardens in 1930. However, the Second World War intervened.

In 1951 the foundation stone was laid. In 1963 the National Theatre Company was set up under leadership of the actor Sir Laurence Olivier (1907-1989) and took over the Old Vic as a temporary home. In 1969 construction of the Sir Denys Lasdun designed building finally started.

In 1973 the director Peter Hall succeeded Laurence Olivier as the head of the National.

The National Theatre's South Bank complex was opened in 1976.

The Royal National Theatre has developed a close relationship with the West End. A number of plays and musicals, such as `Les Miserables' and Jonathan Harvey's `Babies', have started out as National Theatre productions and then transferred to the commercial stage.

In March 1996 it was announced that the director Trevor Nunn would succeed Richard Eyre as the Director of the National Theatre in October 1997.

Sir Denys Lasdun

Lord Cottesloe (1900-1994) was chairman of the South Bank Theatre Board which supervised the building's construction. He gave the architect Sir Denys Lasdun free rein.

The National Theatre building is one of those instances where the British show both their aesthetic blindness and their capacity to act like sheep. Ever since the building's character became evident it has been derided. If there is an edifice on the South Bank which deserves opprobrium it is the Hayward Gallery (1964), a building designed by members of the London County Council's Architects Department.

Waterloo Bridge

The first Waterloo Bridge opened in 1817. Originally, it was intended that the bridge should be known as the Strand Bridge. However, an Act of Parliament was passed changing its name to Waterloo Bridge.

The original Waterloo Bridge was used to build part of the foundations of Heathrow Airport. The present bridge dates from 1942.

Georgi Markov

That speech radio is a powerful medium was illustrated by the Bulgarian regime's September 1978 assassination of Georgei Markov, an exiled Bulgarian playwright and B.B.C. World Service broadcaster. Markov was killed by the rather elaborate means of a ricin pellet being shot into his leg from a pistol made to look like an umbrella, while he was waiting for a bus near Waterloo Bridge. Four days later he died.

The National Film Theatre

To the left, loitering under Waterloo Bridge, is the National Film Theatre.

The British Film Institute opened the Telekinema cinema as part of the South Bank celebration of the Festival of Britain. Initially, the cinema's principal purpose was to act as a showcase for the latest technical developments in cinema. It proved so popular with the public that it kept on operating after the Festival had finished. In 1958 it was moved to the site underneath the bridge and its name was changed to the National Film Theatre.

The South Bank Centre

To the left is the South Bank Centre arts complex.

The Festival of Britain

The idea of a centenary celebration of the Great Exhibition of 1851 was first floated by John Gloag in a letter to The Times newspaper. Sir Gerald Barry (1898-1968), a manager at the News Chronicle newspaper, capitalised on the basic concept with an open letter addressed to the Labour politician Sir Stafford Cripps (1889-1952) the then President of the Board of Trade, which called for the event to have a cultural and trade character. In 1948 Barry was appointed both the Festival's director-general and the chairman of the committee which oversaw its arrangements.

The Festival took place in 1951 on formerly derelict ground in the area between Waterloo Bridge and Westminster Bridge.

The Mystery of the Skylon

The Labour government organised Festival was applauded as a great success. One of the features of the festival site that made a particular impact was the 296 feet tall Skylon, which was designed by the architects Sir Philip Powell and Hildago Moya (1920-1994). When the Festival closed the Skylon, despite its size, disappeared. What happened to it has long been a mystery. One theory is that members of the incoming Conservative administration sought to raze every trace of the Festival that they could.

The South Bank

The South Bank Centre arts complex started with the Festival of Britain in 1951. Through the course of the 1950s, 1960s and 1970s a series of arts buildings sprung up around the Royal Festival Hall (1951) on the former festival site: the National Film Theatre (1958), the Queen Elizabeth Hall (1967) concert hall, the Purcell Room (1967), the Hayward Gallery (1968), and the Royal National Theatre (1976).

The South Bank was essentially the creation of Labour Party politicians active in London's city government, the likes of Herbert Morrison (1888-1965) and Sir Isaac Hayward (1884-1976). They worked in concert with - although not always harmoniously with - Jennie Lee (1904-1988) the Labour Arts Minister. (Morrison was the grandfather of Peter Mandelson.)

In 1986, following the abolition of the Greater London Council, the South Bank Board was set up to take over and manage the G.L.C.'s South Bank assets. The Board is an Arts Council-appointed quango (quasi-autonomous, non-governmental organisation). The South Bank Board is the largest single beneficiary of Arts Council subsidy.

Cleopatra's Needle

To the right, on the north bank, with Victoria Embankment Gardens behind it, is Cleopatra's Needle, which was sculpted c1500 BC and which originally stood in Alexandria. Cleoptra would have known the obelisk but to her the events recorded on it would have been ancient history. The Needle was given to the British in 1819 by Mohammed Ali, the Viceroy of Egypt. It did not come to London until 1878. The obelisk was brought over largely through the efforts of the dermatologist Sir Erasmus Wilson (1809-1884). The Needle arrived after a dramatic voyage. It was towed from Egypt on a raft. In the Bay of Biscay a storm blew up and the crew of the ship which was pulling the Needle's raft, cut it loose for fear that it would sink and drag their vessel down after it. When the storm abated the Needle's raft was found to be still floating nearby. It was erected on the Victoria Embankment in 1878. (Its sister stands in Central Park, New York City.)

Charing Cross Station

To the right, on the north bank, devouring Charing Cross Railway Bridge is Terry Farrell's Charing Cross Station.

The Shell Centre

To the left is the Shell Centre.

The Anglo-Dutch oil multinational Royal Dutch Shell Group has two headquarters, one is in The Hague in The Netherlands and the other is in London. The London one, that of Shell Transport & Trading, is located in the Shell Centre.

In 1833 Marcus Samuel (1799-1872) opened a shop near the Tower of London which sold shells and other decorative curios. From this start, the Samuel family built up an Oriental import/export business. One of the commodities in which the business came to deal was kerosene oil.

The first delivery of oil to Britain by tanker was made by a Russian vessel in 1884. The vessel was chartered by Frederick Lane (1857-1926).

In 1885 Marcus Samuel (later 1st Viscount Bearsted) (1853-1927) was a member of a syndicate which shipped oil from the Far East. In 1890 he was approached by Lane, who acted as the representative of the French branch of the Rothschild family. Lane proposed an alliance of Samuel's business connections in the Far East with the Rothschilds' money. The formula worked and a substantial oil business mushroomed. The company sought to find petroleum sources in the Far East and struck oil in Borneo. In October 1897 the Shell Transport & Trading Company was formed to separate the Samuels' oil interests from their other trading activities. It was Lane who in 1902 orchestrated the formation of Shell Transport, a marketing alliance between Shell and Henri Deterding's Royal Dutch company.

Samuel never developed any thorough technical understanding of the oil business, and preferred to operate a small C19th-style, family-filled office. He used his new wealth to advance his social ambitions, buying a country house and serving as Lord Mayor of London in 1902. Lane became close to Deterding. Lane played a part in allowing Deterding to promote his own interests, so that when Royal Dutch merged with Shell in 1906, it was the Dutch company which emerged with a 60% stake of the new Royal Dutch Shell Group.

In 1982 the Samuel family's representation on Shell board ended when Peter Samuel (later 4th Viscount Bearsted) (1911-1996) stepped down from it.

Jubilee Gardens

To the left is Jubilee Gardens, which opened in 1977 and was named in honour of the Queen Elizabeth II's Silver Jubilee (twenty-five years on the throne). During the early 1980s the Gardens became a popular gathering place thanks to a number of G.L.C. sponsored events.

There is still a sign on the site which reads `G.L.C. Jubilee Gardens'.

The Ministry of Defence Building

To the right, the north bank is dominated by the Ministry of Defence Building.

County Hall

On the left is County Hall (1912-63).

The London County Council

Upon its creation in 1889 the London County Council (L.C.C.) inherited the Metropolitan Board of Works's Spring Gardens offices. In 1905 the Council resolved to acquire new premises. The County Hall site was acquired, it having been previously something of an eyesore, being packed with small factories and wharves.

In 1912 County Hall became the seat of the London County Council. In 1922 the building was officially opened although construction work on it was to continue until 1963.

Labour Dominance

In 1934 the Labour Party won outright control of the L.C.C. for the first time. Herbert Morrison (1888-1965) was able to use London as a base from which to turn himself into a figure of national importance.

During the years 1934-9 nearly 85 000 new houses were built. This had political overtones because council tenants were more likely to vote for Labour than for the Conservatives.

The Greater London Council

In 1965 the Greater London Council (G.L.C.) replaced the London County Council. County Hall became the headquarters of the new London-wide local government. De facto London - the contiguous urban sections of Essex, Kent, and Surrey, and the whole of the county of Middlesex - became de jure London. (The City of London was unaffected by these changes.)

The G.L.C. members were elected for seats which had the same boundaries as London's Parliamentary seats. Outer

The Boroughs and Central Government

The advent of the G.L.C. was to lead to Labour losing the monopoly on the city government which it had enjoyed since the 1930s. However, the Party did continue to have periods of controlling the Council.

Within the G.L.C. there soon came to exist a degree of tension between the new, outer boroughs and the old, L.C.C. ones. The flow of money tended to give the impression of the suburbs subsidising the inner city. The G.L.C. had varying relations with the 32 boroughs. This stemmed in part from the G.L.C.'s vision being city-oriented rather than locally-focussed but it also arose from the fact that at any given point whichever party controlled the G.L.C. the other party would control many of the city's boroughs. The keenest battles tended to be between the G.L.C., when it was Labour-controlled, and the outlying Conservative boroughs.

Road planning has become an important pawn in the relationship between central government and local government. One of the reasons for the creation of the G.L.C. was that Whitehall felt the L.C.C. (which had been made up of the inner boroughs) lacked the unitary scale to allow for effective road planning. It was easier for Whitehall to deal with one council than with twenty.

Unfortunately, the G.L.C. committed the greatest sin that any local government body can commit - in the eyes of central government that is - by going native and promoting the anti-road, pro-housing views of the people it represented.

The local government politicians were often out of step in their attitudes with the mandarins of Whitehall. The mandarins were able to remove a number of the G.L.C.'s functions which were passed on to less obstreperous bodies.

In May 1981 the G.L.C. again fell under Labour control. Under the leadership of Ken Livingstone the G.L.C. proved highly adept at baiting the central government. (County Hall faces the Palace of Westminster across the Thames.)

By the mid-1980s the city had become highly politicised. The Labour-controlled G.L.C. enjoyed considerably more popularity with the populace than did the Conservative national government.

The Conservatives' allies in the national press seized upon every opportunity to distort the minutiae of the first rumblings of political correctness to portray the G.L.C. and its allied inner city boroughs as being concerned only with nursing the interests of the minority groups which had helped create the Council's Labour majority.

In April 1986 the Conservative government abolished the G.L.C..

The Complexities of London Politics

Irish Catholics have been an influential force in the Labour Party during London in the C20th. Much of their influence was based upon individuals in office within the dockyard unions. The cultural and historical pulls could produce politicians who seem to hold somewhat paradoxical views; John Brannigan (1911-1994), who represented Poplar from 1949 through to 1983, was both a monarchist and a supporter of the Territorial Army, yet he was able to welcome the I.R.A. associated politician Gerry Adams to County Hall in 1983 and had no reservations about the G.L.C.'s anti-nuclear policy.

The Thames As A County Border

The Thames was once a county border.

Modern greater London essentially covers the whole of Middlesex and parts of three other counties - north-eastern Surrey, north-western Kent, and south-western Essex.

Kent and Surrey lie south of the Thames and Middlesex and Essex to the north. Middlesex and Essex are divided from one another by River Lea.

The greatest ramification of the old counties in modern London life is probably cricket and that is by no means a `greatest' ramification which is `great'.

(North Woolwich was part of Kent despite being on the north side of the Thames and not being contiguous to the rest of the county.)

Middlesex

The first reference to Middlesex dates from the early C8th. `Middlesex' translates as `the land of the Middle Saxons'.

The County of London was formed under the new Local Government Act of 1888. The new county included much of Middlesex.

Middlesex disappeared in 1965 when the G.L.C. was created.

The South Bank Lion

Supervising Westminster Bridge is the South Bank Lion, a statue which was made of Coade stone in 1837. Originally, the Lion stood in front of the Lion Brewery, which was demolished in 1950. The Lion then moved to Waterloo Station from whence it came in 1966.

Coade Stone

The Coade family came up with the formula for their `stone' in the mid-C18th. The recipe for it has been lost. The mixture, which was fired in a kiln, is thought to have contained stone dust and ground glass. It has exceptional resistance to weathering when compared to other artificial stones.

St.Thomas's Hospital

On the south side of Westminster Bridge is St.Thomas's Hospital.

St.Thomas's is descended from a Southwark hospital which was established by Augustinian monks there in 1173 and dedicated to St.Thomas a Becket (c1118-1170).

At the Dissolution of the Monasteries (1535-40) St.Thomas's was closed. In 1551 the hospital was re-opened but was re-dedicated to St.Thomas the Apostle (King Henry VIII (1491-1547) had decanonised Thomas a Becket for having opposed the authority of King Henry II (1133-1189)).

St.Thomas's original home was demolished to make way for the building of the London Bridge Station. (Its early C18th chapel survived and is now the Chapter House of Southwark Cathedral.) In 1868 the hospital moved to Lambeth Palace Road, the site being part of the Albert Embankment (1871) development.

The Lambeth Palace Road hospital was made up of seven pavilions. The plan was devised by Florence Nightingale. The pavilions were demolished after being damaged during the Second World War.

Florence Nightingale

Florence Nightingale (1820-1910) was from a wealthy Derbyshire landowning family. For someone from her privileged background to enter nursing, which was held in low regard in the mid-C19th, was extraordinary.

Nightingale's work during the Crimean War of 1854-6, for which she is best remembered, took up only a couple of years of a very active life. In 1856 she returned to Britain a national hero. She used her fame to raise £45 000 to establish the Nightingale Training School for Nursing, the first modern nurses' training school, at St.Thomas's Hospital. The School opened in 1861, marking the arrival of nursing as a respectable profession in Britain.

Nightingale's other achievements included overhauling medical care in India, turning hospital building into a science, and playing a leading part in raising funds for the newly founded National Society for Aid to the Sick & Wounded in War (which became the British Red Cross Society).

The Florence Nightingale Museum is a museum of the history of nursing. The Museum opened in St.Thomas's Hospital in 1989.

To Finish

Cross over Westminster Bridge and then descend into Westminster underground station, which is on the District and Circle Lines.

To Continue

Cross over Westminster Bridge and then descend into Westminster underground station, which is on the District and Circle Lines. Take the westbound Circle Line service to High Street Kensington.